Three Yiddish Plays by Women

YIDDISH VOICES

Series Editors

Alyssa Quint, Tablet Magazine and Yeshiva University, USA
Elissa Bemporad, Queens College and CUNY Graduate Center, USA

Yiddish Voices is an exciting new series of translated works that connects today's readers with Yiddish literature, in its full range of authors, genres, and subject matter. Published in partnership with the YIVO Institute for Jewish Research, each volume presents a rich and engaging literary work in English translation with a well-matched historian's introduction, one that is both erudite and readable. Expertly curated by Alyssa Quint and Elissa Bemporad, the series is organized to showcase first-time translations of enduring Yiddish texts—memoirs, novels, and plays—from which arise topics and themes that have powerful resonance today.

Editorial Advisory Board

David Samuels, Tablet Magazine, USA
Jeffrey Shandler, Rutgers University, USA
Stefanie Halpern, Director of the Archives, YIVO, USA
Barbara Kirshenblatt-Gimlet, Polin Museum, Poland
Francois Guesnet, University College London, UK
Joel Berkowitz, University Wisconsin, USA
Miriam Trinh, Hebrew University, Israel
Naomi Seidman, University of Toronto, Canada
Anita Norich, University Of Michigan, USA

Upcoming Titles

The Memoirs of the Mother of Yiddish Theater: Esther-Rokhl Kaminska's "Thorns and Flowers," Mikhl Yashinsky
Mississippi (1935) By Leyb Malakh: A Yiddish Play about the Scottsboro Boys, Alyssa Quint

Three Yiddish Plays by Women

Female Jewish Perspectives, 1880–1920

BY MARIA LERNER, PAULA PRILUTSKI, AND LENA BROWN

EDITED BY ALYSSA QUINT

TRANSLATED BY ELYA PIAZZA, ALLEN LEWIS RICKMAN, AND MIRO MNIEWSKI

BLOOMSBURY ACADEMIC
LONDON • NEW YORK • OXFORD • NEW DELHI • SYDNEY

BLOOMSBURY ACADEMIC
Bloomsbury Publishing Plc
50 Bedford Square, London, WC1B 3DP, UK
1385 Broadway, New York, NY 10018, USA
29 Earlsfort Terrace, Dublin 2, Ireland

BLOOMSBURY, BLOOMSBURY ACADEMIC and the Diana logo are
trademarks of Bloomsbury Publishing Plc

First published in Great Britain 2023

Cover image: *Warszawa, 1930s. Malke Hamerow poses for a portrait
with Chaim Sznejer, a member of the Vilna Troupe, and others.* © YIVO
Institutue. *Piece of white paper tear* © Piman Khrutmuang /Adobe
Stock. Marriage Record © New York City Municipal Archives
Department of Records and Information Services.

A catalogue record for this book is available from the British Library.

A catalog record for this book is available from the Library of Congress.

ISBN: HB: 978-1-3503-2102-1
       PB: 978-1-3503-2101-4
   ePDF: 978-1-3503-2103-8
  eBook: 978-1-3503-2104-5

Typeset by Integra Software Services Pvt. Ltd.
Printed and bound in Great Britain

To find out more about our authors and books visit www.bloomsbury.com
and sign up for our newsletters.

CONTENTS

CONTRIBUTORS

Miro Mniewski (translator of *Sonia Itelson or A Child ... A Child ...*) grew up hearing Litvish and Galician Yiddish from her mother and father respectively. In addition to being a Yiddish translator, Mniewski is a poet, teacher, and Zen practitioner. They identify as nonbinary and live and work in upstate New York. Their translations can be read at jacobmorgenstern.com, ingeveb.org, yiddishbookcenter.org, http://museum.yivo.org/translations/Dr-Ow-It-Hurts.pdf, and various other print and online publications.

Elya (Zissel) Piazza (translator of *The Chained Wife*) is a PhD candidate at UC Berkeley in Near Eastern Studies with Designated Emphases in Gender and Women's Studies and Jewish Studies. Elya is also a rabbinical student at the Reconstructionist Rabbinical College. They are a Yiddish translator and a former fellow at the National Yiddish Book Center's Translation Fellowship. They are currently working on their doctoral dissertation, which explores how queer readings of the Talmud reveal subversive impulses and discursive strategies that came to influence many later generations of Jewish thought. Elya is passionate about community building through teaching and learning, song, ritual, and care. They are especially called to expanding access to Jewish language and culture to community members who have historically been excluded from the tradition and animating Jewish tradition in the struggle for greater social, economic, and environmental justice. They teach Yiddish language and Talmud classes and completed a Pedagogy fellowship at SVARA: A Traditionally Radical Yeshiva. Elya loves hiking, boxing, and cuddling their dogs, Ketzele and Porcini.

Alyssa Quint (editor of volume and introduction) is an associate editor at *Tablet Magazine* and teaches at Yeshiva University. With Elissa Bemporad, she is the co-editor of Bloomsbury's "Yiddish Voices" series. Quint is the author of *The Rise of the Modern Yiddish Theater* (2019), a finalist of the Jordan Schnitzer Award and The National Jewish Book Award, and is the co-editor of *Women on the Yiddish Stage* (Legenda 2023) and *Arguing the Modern Jewish* Canon (Harvard 2013). She has published numerous articles on various aspects of Jewish cultural history.

Allen Lewis Rickman (translator of *One of Those*) is a director, writer, translator, and actor, with extensive credits in both English and Yiddish. He has directed Off-Broadway, Off-Off Broadway, and in regional theater; directing work in Yiddish includes the Drama Desk-nominated Yiddish *Pirates of Penzance* and the critically acclaimed off-Broadway *Tevye Served Raw*. He is an internationally produced playwright whose work has been presented in five languages. His co-written farce *Off the Hook* was produced across Europe, his music-hall musical *The Small Empire* was presented regionally at Centenary Stage, and his revue *The Essence: A Yiddish Theatre Dim Sum* has toured widely. Among his published works are *The Essence* (*Yiddishkeit*), and his farce *Off the Hook* (co-written with Karl Tiedemann) (*L'Avant Scene Theatre*). Other translations from the Yiddish include the melodrama *Money, Love, and Shame!* (Target Margin), Leon Kobrin's *Breach of Promise* (YIVO), and translations for Kino/Lorber's Yiddish cinema box. As an actor he has appeared on Broadway, Off-Broadway, and on film and television. He is best known for his recurring role on *Boardwalk Empire* and for his performance in the Yiddish prologue to the Coen brothers' Oscar-nominated *A Serious Man*, for which he also translated the dialogue.

PREFACE

Judith Rosenbaum

I have not had the privilege of hearing the words of the three plays featured in this volume delivered dramatically from the stage; nevertheless, their urgency carries from the page and across more than a century with clarity, historical truth, and resonance.

Much of my previous exploration of Yiddish theater has come through the Jewish Women's Archive's (JWA) many resources devoted to the subject. More than just a cultural pastime, Yiddish theater served as a center of community, experimentation, and adaptation. It provided a leisure activity for workers, a meeting place for immigrants, an agent of acculturation, and a stage on which to process and poke fun at modernity's challenges. JWA's articles on the development of Yiddish theater in both European and American contexts, as well as its profiles of female legends (such as Molly Picon, Pepi Litmann, Rokhl Holzer, Sara Adler, Celia Adler, Bessie Thomashefsky, Bertha Kalich, Bella Bellarina, Rose Shoshana, and Ida Kaminska), illustrate the theater's critical place in modern Jewish culture and the significant role of women in shaping it.

That most of those articles address women as performers, not creators, reflects their prominent representation in the Yiddish theater as actors more than as playwrights. As performers, they did powerful cultural work: animating the words of others; taking up space with brio, drama, pathos, and humor; and becoming icons of a new Jewish womanhood. The smaller number of (known) female writers, however, had a different opportunity: to bring women's perspectives and experiences to the page and, ultimately, to voice.

These three fascinating and little-known plays illustrate why women's contributions to Yiddish theater as writers were so essential. In these plays, women tell stories about women. They address intimate relations within the context of larger social structures: marriage and divorce, prostitution, motherhood, and abortion—topics that were hotly debated at the time and remain contested in the twenty-first century. In giving voice and nuance to these debates, they both engage with and offer alternatives to public discourse about Jewish communal norms and values of the time, conveying ambivalence and an undercurrent of resistance through melodramatic but recognizable renderings of women's lives.

Each play depicts Jewish women navigating tradition and law, family expectations and the pull of independence, impulses of rebellion and shame, and the power and limitations of agency. A longing for bodily autonomy and self-determination weaves through all three plays, as one would expect from a time when abortion was a fact of most Jewish women's lives, and likely their most accessible form of birth control. So does a thread of despair that this longing could ever be fulfilled; each play ends, after all, with the death of the female protagonist. That two of the deaths result from acts of suicide suggests that women of the time could only hope to some day have broader opportunities for expressions of women's agency. Reading these plays more than 100 years after they were written serves as a warning not to take any hard-won agency for granted.

The women writing these plays depict one of modernity's great challenges: envisioning possibilities that are not (yet) within reach. Sonia Itelson, the eponymous character of Lena Brown's previously unpublished and never staged play, expresses this yearning when she wonders, "Will my greatest desire for happiness give me happiness? ... Yes, everything is fine but my heart longs and gnaws for what I'm missing" (p. 211). Some of the male characters, too, are sensitive to the predicaments of Jewish women. Adolf, the romantic lead of Maria Lerner's *The Chained Wife* (*Di agune*), exclaims, "So many Jewish daughters are paralyzed—they see a beautiful world before their eyes, oh how it draws them in. They want to move but they are chained!" (p. 73). The protagonists in these plays bring to life the particular pain of women who recognize that the world could be different but whose attempts to create a freer reality for themselves are thwarted at every turn.

Encountering the vibrant, but ill-fated, women featured in these plays, I am left wondering: what does it mean for the characters to die but for their words to live on, thanks to the dedicated work of performers, scholars, and translators? When Maria Lerner's and Paula Prilutski's plays were staged, their doomed female characters were resurrected at each performance, thus enacting a kind of resilience. Though Brown's play was never performed, its unlikely preservation among her son's family papers represents both the frightening near-loss and the ultimate survival of a woman's voice, bolder and more insistent on the page than perhaps it was in life.

Brown's play ends with Fanny and Sonia's brother attributing the deaths of his two sisters to "crimes against nature"—that is, their ambivalence about motherhood and vain attempts to control their reproduction. This final judgment, however, is challenged by the survival and continued relevance of these three plays, which—taken together—illuminate and normalize the pervasiveness of these concerns in Jewish women's lives, both then and now.

Despite these plays' tragic tone, I hear in them a vigorous demand that we listen attentively to Jewish women's voices and expand the canon of Yiddish theater to include the women who overcame obstacles to contribute in ways other than at center stage. I also look forward to inviting these playwrights and characters into conversation with Jewish women writers who took on similar themes in other times and places. What might Grace Paley's Faith have had to say to Lena Brown's Fanny about the necessity of abortion? What would Paula Prilutski and Israeli poet Yona Wallach have discussed about sex and power? In my work at the Jewish Women's Archive, I take pleasure in imagining these conversations rising among the digital files of the women and stories we document, and I take pride in the scholarly explorations and analysis that access to these stories makes possible. It's an open invitation, not bound by our archive. Read these plays, listen carefully, join your voice, and spark new conversations and creative imaginings.

ACKNOWLEDGMENTS

This volume was prepared for press with the diligent editorial assistance of Pamela Brenner, Rebecca Turner, and Emma Waxlax. Many thanks to them for the care and dedication they showed this project. Thanks to the cast of a fabulous zoom reading of *The Chained Wife*: Rebecca Turner, Eden Augustine, Shannon Constantine, Shlomo Enkin Lewis, Zara Fox, Shelby Haber, Aitana Juristo Andrade, Kennedy Oliver, Sarah Schipper, and Zoë Schipper. Thank you to the Brown family, especially Jeffrey and Johanna, for giving us access to the manuscript of Lena Brown's play *Sonia Itelson or A Child ... A Child ...* and for supplying us with the information on Lena. A debt of gratitude is owed to the YIVO Institute, which supported Rickman's translation of Paula Prilutski's *One of Those* and hosted a reading of it in 2019. Thanks to YIVO, as well, for the images of Prilutski and a scan of the Yiddish version of *The Chained Wife*, which is now accessible on the web. Thanks to the amazing Chana Pollack for efforts in tracking down documents relating to Lena Brown's life in America. Thank you to the very wonderful Miryem-Khaye Seigel for encouraging Miro to submit the play to this volume and for eagled-eye editorial work on the Brown and Lerner plays. Thanks, as well, to Nan Bases, Elissa Bemporad, and Daniel Steinman.

Elya Piazza: The translation of *The Chained Wife* was made possible by the generous support of the Yiddish Book Center's Translation Fellowship. I would like to thank my cohort of Translation Fellowship peers and workshop leaders who read and provided feedback on earlier scene drafts; editors Alyssa Quint and Amanda Miryem-Khaye Seigel for their time, edits, and encouragement; and my many brilliant teachers of Yiddish language and culture over the years, including community members who have worked hard to share the legacy of Yiddish-speaking feminists, radicals, and queers past and present.

An Opened Drawer:
An Introduction

Alyssa Quint

In a significant sense, the modern Yiddish theater was born no sooner or later than when women were integrated on the Yiddish-language stage. The first such integrated performances were produced and directed by the father of the modern Yiddish theater, Avrom Goldfaden (1840–1908), first in Romania and then in Odessa from 1876 to 1883. Yiddish-language performance culture (in the form of synagogue choirs, wedding jesters, Purim players, and cabaret, et al.) constituted an important part of Jewish life before Goldfaden. Before Goldfaden's pioneering actresses, however, there is no evidence that women figured in these performances, public or private, secular, or religious. Goldfaden insisted on the form of the operetta that he passionately observed in European opera halls, and he insisted on Yiddish, the vernacular of East European Jewry.[1] For this, he knew he needed to create the Jewish actress.

The valued presence of women on the Yiddish stage spawned—not just more female performers but women theater managers, set designers, directors, and, yes, playwrights. The three plays included in this volume—Maria Lerner's *The Chained Wife* (*Di agune*, 1880), Paula Prilutski's *One of Those* (*Eyne fun yene*, 1912) and Lena Brown's *Sonia Itelson Or A*

Child ... A Child ... (*Sonia Itelson oder A kind ... A kind,* c. 1920)[2]—lock into a Yiddish theatrical world of considerably robust participation by women cultural producers.[3] The plays, however, also force us to confront the fact that, in the arena of playwriting—in contrast to that of performance—women fell short of accomplishing the great heights achieved by their male counterparts. In other words, these plays are—and were, even in their day—rare artifacts: they are not the tip of an iceberg of women's writing that has been thus far unjustly neglected, but rarities, all the more valuable for their uncommonness.

Indeed, the experiences of women playwrights resemble more closely those of women novelists. Especially over the past five years, scholars have uncovered an array of novels by women that had been neglected by previous curators of the modern Yiddish literary canon.[4] Recent work on women in the Yiddish theater has turned up a similar trove of work. In an important first glance at the landscape of women playwrights, Rebecca Turner investigates more than two dozen women playwrights that are recorded in the Library of Congress's *Lawrence Marwick Collection of Copyrighted Yiddish Plays.*[5] In both cases—prose and plays—the works that women writers produced underscore the immeasurable value in women telling stories about women. They also confirm that even as women contributed more substantially than the historical record had previously reflected, women generated only a small percentage of what men generated.

The small number of women playwrights is striking as there is no evidence that women playwrights were shut out of the Yiddish theater on an institutional level as potential women writers might have been shut out from the Yiddish-language literary establishment.[6] We know that women held positions of power and management in the theater world in numbers that were far from attainable at Yiddish newspapers, literary unions, and publishing houses. Still, even in the world of the Yiddish theater, so recent scholarship suggests, among women playwrights who did succeed, a good number of them benefited from being married to men in the business. This accords with the women included in this volume: Maria Lerner (1860–1927) was married to the most powerful man in Imperial Russia's booming, if short-lived, Yiddish theater business, Osip Lerner (1847–1907), and Paula's husband Noah Prilutski (1882–1941) was an influential theater critic, among the other positions of cultural and political power he maintained.[7] The discrepancy between what women achieved as performers versus as writers—and the continuity of experience between women playwrights and novelists—might suggest that dimensions of class and education demand more attention to better understand their small number. We might also wonder how pregnancy and motherhood affected a woman's writing career versus her acting career: acting, more than writing, seems to have been more hospitable to motherhood.[8] These questions deserve more attention as they lend more insight into the history of prewar Jewish women whose lives were shaped both by traditional pathways and by forces of modernity. For the barriers with which they were forced to contend, the women who managed to write and see their works published and on the boards deserve particular attention. This volume is a part of a greater effort to make Yiddish theater available to English readers. It is also intended to contribute to our understanding of women on the Yiddish stage, our knowledge of the modern Yiddish theater and to the reconstruction of East European Jewish women's creative lives, more generally.

The Chained Wife

The earliest play in the volume is Maria Lerner's *The Chained Wife* (*Di agune*). First staged in 1880 in the Russian Empire, it is named for the halakhic or Jewish legal category that describes a woman who is separated from her husband but is unable to obtain a Jewish writ of divorce from him and so remains barred from remarriage under Judaism's adultery laws; literally, she is "chained" or "anchored" to an unwanted marriage.[9] The play was one of only a small number of Yiddish works, mainly operettas, mounted on stages (in Odessa and throughout cities in the southern provinces) during the first days of the modern Yiddish theater, a brief period that lasted from, roughly, 1879 to 1883.[10] A tragic drama set in Odessa, *The Chained Wife* purports to critique its society's values—particularly its tolerance of what it presents as a religious archaism—but the play works most effectively in promoting the values of what it projects as the conservative bourgeois Russian-Jewish family.[11]

Maria Lerner's (1860–1927) career as a Yiddish writer and playwright was an unlikely one: a product both of her rarefied education and of her husband's cultural tastes as well as his standing in late-nineteenth-century Odessa's flourishing cultural world.[12] She was born Miriam Rabinovitsh in Berdychiv, Ukraine, to a prominent family. After finishing her schooling in Kishinev, she was married to Osip (Yoysef-Yude) Lerner (1849–1909), and the couple settled in Odessa, where Osip Lerner wrote as a journalist and cultural critic for the Russian press. The Yiddish theater biographer Zalmen Zylbercweig reports that the Lerners struggled financially as well as in their marriage, which was later reported by their son to have been an unhappy one. Remarkably, the Lerners converted to Christianity and converted their three children.[13] While it is unclear when their conversion took place, their attraction to Christianity is evident in Osip's Yiddish plays, but not in Maria's.

Osip's successful career as a journalist and his fondness for Yiddish are somehow intertwined with Maria's budding career as a playwright, although we will never know the nuances of this relationship. Osip's appreciation for Yiddish—a language much maligned at the time by his fellow Russian-Jewish reformers—is evidenced in a homage he published to the Yiddish writer Yisroel Aksenfeld.[14] The Lerners learned together of the growing popularity of Yiddish theater in places like Iasi, Romania, where thousands of Russian troupes were stationed during the Russo-Turkish War (1876–7). Most of the performances were staged under the tutelage of the aforementioned Russian-Jewish intellectual Avrom Goldfaden: they benefited from Russian-Jewish spectators and the freedom to perform publicly in Yiddish—something that was forbidden within the borders of the Russian Empire.

For a time beginning in 1878, however, Goldfaden prevailed on Russian officials to permit the performance of Yiddish theater, and other acculturated Russian-Jewish writers like the Lerners began participating first as playwrights and then as impresarios. When, in 1881, Goldfaden fell out with the manager of Odessa's Mariinsky Theater, Osip secured his lucrative contract with the theater to produce its twice-weekly Yiddish-language performances.[15] Still in its infancy at this time and until this point, Goldfaden had jealously guarded his contract with the Mariinsky, Odessa's largest opera venue. When he left, he took his popular operettas with him. To fill the content void, Osip worked on his own translations and adaptations for the Yiddish stage (like his Yiddish translation of *The Jewess*) and cast around for works by other Yiddish playwrights, including *The Chained Wife* by Maria. The number of times it was staged and the fact that it was published— many works staged during this period were never published— suggest it found substantial success. *The Chained Wife* is the earliest known Yiddish play by a woman playwright and the first of its kind to be staged. Maria's play advances a portrait of Rosa, a dutiful daughter and wife, who suffers all manner of indignities to avoid bringing embarrassment to her family's name; throughout, she is a picture of honor.

Beyond its animating plot, *The Chained Wife* takes place in an unnamed town where the successful Jewish merchant Mr. Grossman and his wife Chayele live with their daughter Rosa. Chayele and Adolf, Grossman's loyal bookkeeper, share an unspoken love for each other, but Grossman urges his daughter to marry Mr. Neumann, a seemingly sophisticated Jewish broker from Moscow with whom he has recently begun to do business. He also pressures Adolf to put distance between

himself and Rosa. Out of respect for Mr. Grossman, both
Rosa and Adolf comply. After the marriage, the Grossmans
discover Neumann to be a gambler and a scoundrel who has
cheated Rosa's father in business and who abandons Rosa
without giving her a writ of divorce. With time, Adolf tracks
Neumann down and, through a trusted broker, Yisroel, secures
the divorce, and marries Rosa. They have two daughters
together, Amalia and Adele. Nineteen years later—soon before
the eldest daughter is to be married—Neumann returns to the
Grossmans to embarrass and blackmail Rosa, threatening to
expose the fact that her marriage to Adolf is invalid as he had
never properly signed the *get,* or Jewish divorce document. The
possibility that her daughters with Adolf might be considered
mamzerim "bastards"—fruit of extramarital relations—haunts
Rosa and threatens to undermine Adele's upcoming marriage
as Jewish law forbids marriage to someone with the status of a
mamzer. By the end, the stress of the situation depletes Rosa so
that she collapses and dies in the play's final scene.

The Chained Wife is informed by norms embraced and
propagated by a cadre of conservative Russian-Jewish social
reformers or *maskilim* in the name of the Jewish Enlightenment
movement or Haskalah. Their journalism, novels, and plays
penned in Hebrew, Yiddish, and Russian reflect an optimism
that followed from the progressive policies of Alexander II
during the Era of the Great Reforms (1855–81). The *maskilim*
looked forward to the day when the Czar deemed the Jews
deserving of emancipation. To prod Jews in this direction—
of becoming more engaged Russian citizens—they drew
appealing Europeanized Jewish characters, comfortable in
both Russian and Jewish society.[16] In *The Chained Wife*, for
instance, the Grossman family modeled the behavior and
manners of a bourgeois Jewish family that remains Jewish but
dresses and lives according to the cultural norms of their non-
Jewish neighbors in Odessa.

Like much of the literature of the Haskala, *The Chained
Wife* also offered audiences a model of romantic love outside
the bounds of traditional matchmaking, in what the scholar

Naomi Seidman describes as a "sentimental revolution."[17] Seidman explains:

> While some modernizers of the Eastern European Haskalah, particularly those influenced by Russian radicalism in the 1860s and 1870s, championed free love, more moderate or conservative Jewish social reformers were compelled to resolve, contain, or circumvent the explosive powers of sexual desire, even if what they considered an unsuitable match was different from those an older generation might have ruled out.[18]

Thus, in *The Chained Wife*, Grossman's choice of husband for his daughter is proved mistaken, and the love that blooms organically between Rosa and Adolf proves to be the legitimate romance even as it is still considerably "contained" within the structures of the patriarchal family. The couple's love is different from the versions of free love explored by the playwrights of the other two plays in this volume. Here, for instance, Rosa and Adolf's love is still consistent with the ideal of the doting wife who remains in the domestic sphere, who enjoys the tasks of homemaking and child-rearing, and—however much wiser she is than the men in her life—remains a compliant and docile daughter and wife. Her wishes are never depicted as out of sync with the wishes of her father and her rightful husband.

Lerner wove the plot of *The Chained Wife* from two existing tropes of the Haskala, the first one being the city of Odessa, the city in which Adolf's assistant is swindled by Neumann. At the time, Odessa was a relatively new city located in the Pale of Settlement with a port on the Black Sea that made it into a booming center of commerce. According to the historian Steven Zipperstein, Odessa was also the center of modern Jewish cultural life: the cradle of Zionism, the wellspring of both modern Yiddish and Hebrew literatures. It was also the incubator of the modern Yiddish theater. The translator and critic Hillel Halkin explains the more modern sensibility of the city's Jewish population:

Odessan Jewry remained less traditional and less subject to rabbinical influence than other Eastern European Jewish communities. Warsaw's wealth of neighborhood synagogues, yeshivas, and Hasidic courts were not duplicated by Odessa; though it had its share of observant Jews, it had more than its share of laxer ones and observance, too, took on more liberal forms in it.[19]

Of Odessa's approximately 350,000 residents in 1880, Jews comprised 6 percent of the population and enjoyed a sense of enfranchisement.[20] They were, for instance, permitted to participate in municipal affairs, and a relatively large number of them enjoyed wealth from vigorous business activity. This socioeconomic landscape is the backdrop of *The Chained Wife*.

But even more significant to the play than the historical reality of the city is the *trope* of Odessa as it grew in the Jewish imagination: one of a city that breeds a kind of social chaos that is exploited by crooks like the play's villain Neumann. This idea is reflected in such Yiddish phrases as *lebn vi got in Odes* (living like God in Odessa), and *zibn mayl arum Odes brent dos gehenem* (the fires of hell burn for seven miles around Odessa). Jewish literature of this era depicts Jewish men and women arriving from tight-knit shtetls to take advantage of Odessa's big-city anonymity and experiment with different mores—mores as benign as shaving one's beard (a symbol of one's religious observance), and as malignant as Neumann's duplicitous behavior. His name tips the audience off: Neumann meaning, literally, "new man," dupes the Grossman family into thinking he is a businessman of sophistication, but he is someone with no knowable roots and background—no family—and thus no one to vouch for his integrity. In an Enlightenment drama, this type of pretender is a most dangerous villain and animates a cautionary tale about the dangers of Odessa and big cities, more generally.

The second trope in the play, the chained wife, provides the play's main conflict and tension, but it, too, works off the energy of the *cultural idea* of the *agune*, or chained wife, just as much as its historical reality. According to the scholarship on the topic, we cannot know how many Russian-Jewish women were affected by the *agune* category, but most who were seemed to have been shtetl-bound and poor, rather than women of established middle-class families.[21] In *Jewish Marriage and Divorce in Imperial Russia*, Freeze explains that "malicious desertion" where the man simply vanished without divorcing was one cause of the *agune* problem; stories of this kind were not uncommon in the Jewish press of this era.[22] In these cases, husbands left home, ostensibly on business, and never returned, deliberately leaving their wives anchored out of revenge or resentment. Desertion "became more pronounced after the Great Reforms, when mobility became considerably easier."[23] Most *agunes* reflected in the rabbinic literature were a result of the second and greater cause of the *agune* problem: immigration that separated women from their husbands by great distances and for long periods. Under such circumstances—just as under circumstances of war—the death of a husband might go unreported and leave a wife still at home, for instance, without certainty or proof of her widowhood. *Agunes* were not allowed to remarry and any children fathered by a man besides the original husband were considered *mamzerim* or "bastards" by Jewish law, and thus only permitted to marry other *mamzerim*. Rabbis sought ways to release women from the *agune* status and also found ways to declare children of such circumstances to be other than *mamzerim* for the purpose of integrating them into society and saving them from unnecessary shame.[24] In the play, of course, no matter the sympathetic attitude of the rabbi, he cannot soften the blow of the law; and in the service of suspense—more so than any accurate depiction of any widespread phenomenon—this is just how Maria Lerner prefers it.

Lerner might have been inspired to write about an anchored wife by the Hebrew poet and maskil Y. L. Gordon (1830–92) and his satiric epic "*Kotzo shel yud*" (The tip of the letter yud),[25] a poem that singlehandedly transformed the *agune* into a literary trope. The poem depicts a woman who is left a chained wife because of the stroke of a *yud*—the tenth letter of the Hebrew alphabet—that is not completed on a writ of divorce, leaving the woman unable to marry the man she loves. The poem created great controversy and discussion in the pages of the Russian-Jewish and Hebrew press—not least because of how farfetched it struck many of the readers.

What was the attraction of an implausible *agune* scenario, first for Gordon and then for Lerner? The historian Michael Stanislawski explains that Gordon had his logic for choosing it:

> In "The Tip of the Yud" Gordon strove not to depict a typical, or even likely, scene in Russian-Jewish life, but to satirize the treatment of women in traditional Jewish society in order to kill three birds with one stone: to write a great poem, to demonstrate once more what he took to be the ignorance and obscurantism of the Russian rabbis, and, for the first time in verse, to argue for the emancipation of women.[26]

With her version of a chained wife, Lerner might have sought to reference Gordon's poem and remind her audience of his championing of women's rights.[27] There is, for instance, a nod to women's equality with men in the play: Adolf and Rosa read books together—an activity that also indicates their budding romance—and when Neumann expresses his attraction to Rosa, Grossman responds, "We just need to ask my daughter. She has free will, after all." In the play's final scene, Adolf reacts to the ruling rabbi with a lament for Jewish women, "How much longer will we be so indifferent as we look on as our Jewish daughters fall like sacrifices to this awful law?" For such moments as this, the translator of this play Elya Piazza believes that "this script offers a dramatic but nevertheless crucial and revelatory snapshot of the lived personal consequences of legislation governing personal autonomy." This is true of the Yiddish original as well as Piazza's excellent English translation of this dense and challenging text.

But twenty-first-century readers of this play will also see that just as much as she is a strong and independent-minded woman, Rosa is an obedient daughter and decides her own fate only insofar as it does not conflict with what she thinks her father might dictate. In a sense, the choice on the part of Gordon and Lerner to focus on very remote circumstances of the *agune* allowed them and their audiences to avoid the more knotty and relevant issues that beset women of their age—issues, for instance, having to do with motherhood and reproductive health-as they might conflict with the bourgeois aspirations of the rising Jewish middle class.

For Lerner, however, a play about a chained wife was first and foremost a vehicle to write melodrama and explore the use of elevated emotional expression. The play struck at least one theater-goer as excessive in its language: in a review of an 1889 production of the play, the historian Simon Dubnow deemed *The Chained Wife* clichéd both in content and in form: "With predictable tropes such as swindlers, murderers and an innocent victim," the play is "full of sentimental and ornamental language."[28] Readers should keep in mind, however, that this play was one of the first Yiddish plays to be staged that was not a music-driven operetta and was likely part of Lerner's husband's effort to introduce high-minded or literary content to the Yiddish stage.[29] The play offered the Yiddish stage one of the first examples of what the theater scholar Alex Eric Hernandez calls "prosaic suffering," a modality that tested the performance of a range of "ordinary feelings." Hernandez continues:

> Unlike the "heroick suffering" of classical, pathetic, or otherwise "high" tragic forms prevalent at the earlier part of the century, prosaic suffering performed its grief with troubling immediacy and a raw intensity, in ways that were personal and familiar, absorptive rather than theatrical.[30]

As she rises to meet the challenge of her shameful chained status, Rosa gave Lerner the opportunity to model emotions on the

Yiddish stage in a way that was new to its audiences. In this respect, the character of Rosa is evocative of Goldfaden's most important female character Shulamis: both women are prepared to suffer for the bad choices made by the men in their lives, and both are practically without human flaw. Rosa says to her beloved Adolf[31]:

> I don't allow myself to be terrified by the thought that I might be left here an abandoned wife. Our love simply *must* be realized through an honest, decent life together. This situation is the last thing standing between us. If you think about it that way, it's almost a relief. Believe me, Adolf, one fleeting moment of your love is worth more to me than anything in the world. I simply don't know what else a person could possibly need.

The immediacy of emotion in this scene is tempered neither by historical pageantry nor by music as is the case in *Shulamis*. The actors speak their lines (instead of singing them as they do in Goldfaden's operettas) and they live in a milieu that the audience knows well. In other words, the play presents the audience with characters that look like them and display their emotion in relatable manner and language. Thus, the characters perform emotions of longing, love, contempt, and suffering in a contemporary Jewish and Yiddish-speaking context—something that was virtually unprecedented for its time. In this sense, *The Chained Wife* pioneered the staging of sentiment and emotion on the Yiddish stage, an important precedent for the two later plays included in this volume.

One of Those

The second play in the volume, Paula Prilutski's (1876–194?) *One of Those (Eyne fun yene)* premiered thirty years later in 1912 in Warsaw under the direction of the legendary Yiddish actor-director Esther Rokhl Kaminska (1870–1925). Until the First World War, the centers of Yiddish theater in the

United States and South America were becoming more robust than those heavily restricted by Russian Imperial rule where staging good Yiddish-language performances ranged from extremely difficult to utterly doomed. Still, with persistence and savvy, Polish-Jewish pioneers of Yiddish theater like Kaminska and playwright and director Marek Arnshteyn (1879–1943) mustered not just Yiddish theater but an elevated Yiddish theater with artistic aspiration. They did so in a kind of dialogue with one of the Yiddish theater's earliest critics, Noah Prilutski, who wrote about the Yiddish theater for newspapers like *Der veg* (The Way) and *Der tog* (The Day).[32] While scholars of Yiddish culture know well the name "Noah Prilutski," few would know the name of his wife, Paula.

Paula Prilutski was born to a wealthy Warsaw family and received an education befitting these conditions, including Polish gymnasium and courses at the city's elite musical conservatory. Married to a Jewish dentist named Adam Rosentol at the age of seventeen, Prilutski held a salon in their home, where she hosted famous Polish artists. During these years, Prilutski also wrote in Polish. After her divorce from Rosentol, Paula married Noyekh and, under his influence, began writing in Yiddish. Several of her works were published and found acclaim on the stage, but none more than her drama *One of Those*, which was staged under the direction of Kaminska in 1912.

One of Those hearkens back to the far better-known *God of Vengeance* (1906) by Sholem Asch (1880–1957) in its storyline about a prostitute, and to Jacob Gordin's (1895–1984) *Sappho* in its reference to a strong woman grappling with the ethical and social dilemma of bearing a child out of wedlock. At the center of Prilutski's play is the young woman Judith, whose father has driven her away from home after her mother dies, and he remarries happily. Still devastated over the loss of her mother, and resentful of her stepmother who forcefully establishes herself in the family, Judith tries and fails to pit her father against his new wife. In Act II, once she has left the house for St. Petersburg, Judith turns to prostitution to support herself. As in Asch and Gordin's earlier dramas, Prilutski's *One of Those* explores a woman's awakening to her emotional and financial subservience to the men in her life.[33]

Judith's life as a prostitute is not romanticized but; it is presented as a viable way for a woman in difficult social and financial circumstances to maintain a kind of independence. According to the play, the most difficult aspect of prostitution for Judith is its social stigma. When she returns to her home and tries to reintegrate into her community, she understands that, to do so, she must lie about her past. Eager to have Judith back, her father and stepmother do not ask Judith about how she survived during the seven intervening years since they last saw her. Do they suspect she was a prostitute but prefer not to address it for fear of learning something they cannot bear to know? The play leaves this question unanswered.

These feelings take time to coalesce, but it is not long before Judith realizes she cannot continue to lie about her time away. When her family attempts to arrange her marriage to someone who does not know of her past, she forces her father to confront the hardship she endured and the shame of it. The tense scene unfolds in the presence of the family of her groom. "You're forcing me to— to tie my soul to someone who maybe deserves to be with an honorable person ..." And then Judith goes further as she connects the dots in the moment. She likens the arranged marriage to prostitution: "And you're forcing my body to be the property of someone who might be a stranger to me my whole life. Isn't that also 'selling yourself'?" Judith's experience outside her community allows her insight into it, but it also alienates her from it. She leaves Warsaw again and returns to St. Petersburg.

In St. Petersburg, Judith tries to reform her fellow prostitutes by creating an all-women cooperative where they live communally, but it is not long before the women feel like prisoners of its structured days and hard work. They miss the creature comforts that they could afford as prostitutes. A letter from their former pimp Yitskhok-Leyb Charb luring them back to their old lives reveals the ugliness of prostitution; there will be "no more rough stuff" he assures them. But the letter also reveals the appealing family structures that prostitution gave them, much less the financial comforts: "I kiss your rosy cheeks … Are they still rosy? From me, your bridegroom, Yitskhok-Leyb Charb." The letter and the women's excited response to hearing it unveil the potent familial bond that formed between pimp and the prostitutes. According to recent scholarship on Jewish prostitution, pimps often held themselves out as protective husbands to their prostitutes. Here and elsewhere, *One of Those* veers away from clichéd narratives of the sex-trafficking world in which women were its victims and pimps were predators.[34] The play is also pessimistic about the prospects of prostitutes returning to the fold of the Jewish community.

In the play's final scene, the audience does not know what runs through Judith's head when she convenes the women and asks them to talk about their families and how they became prostitutes. One explains that she blames herself more than anything: "To point is just to point, but to actually go … When you see where that road leads, (to herself) you have to turn yourself." One woman named Franke complains that even after their move to Judith's cooperative, members of society continue to see them as the prostitutes they used to be:

> What do you think, because we don't do anything wrong here, people look at us differently than they used to? The Society saved us, they threw us a bone. Fine, who are we now? They're just as horrified by us as they were before. That Society isn't interested in us, what we went through, what we're going through … They took away our words. We don't have the right to speak. The same people that allowed our bodies to roll around in trash, now they're doing us a favor, they're feeding us. Well, I don't have any gratitude for them, none at all. Just a curse.

Allen Lewis Rickman's translation transports us to early-twentieth-century St. Petersburg while it remains resonant and relatable. "One of those," the title of the play, might refer to the indelible mark of shame they bear in the eyes of their community. No matter what they do to improve their standing, they will always be "one of those."

This indelible mark of shame leads Judith to commit the horrible act that marks the play's finale: her murder/suicide of the members of the collective. As the young women prepare for bed, Judith plays the role of a mother-figure, coaxing them toward a peaceful sleep, turning off the bedside lamps, and sealing the shutters on the windows. "I want you to have all the shutters closed tonight," she commands the young women. When the women are in bed, eyes closed, she opens the gas and gets into bed herself. It is a disturbing scene, one that suggests the lack of alternatives for women who cannot abide the pathways informed by a patriarchal society; Judith has failed to create a functioning all-women community, a last chance according to her own values. On the other hand, we must question how much the play advocates for women's free will, if it urges, as Judith does, death over prostitution, something that the women would choose were they not deprived of the chance to awaken the next day. Judith's final gesture demands women reject prostitution and insinuates they also reject motherhood and marriage.

Sonia Itelson or A Child ... A Child ...

Lena Brown's Yiddish play *Sonia Itelson or A Child ... A Child ...*, presents us with a third tragedy, this one set in the second decade of the twentieth century in Jewish immigrant New York. Educated, cultured, and newly middle-class, 28-year-old Sonia and her sister Fanny continually struggle through their child-bearing years with the expectation that middle-class women like themselves bear children and be homemakers. Sonia is sharp-witted and intellectually alive to the dilemmas that lie before her—until her love for a man, Leo Edit, forces her to reset her priorities and let go of her aspirations to lead a life of free love. She marries and puts her ideas about life to the side, as if in a drawer.

The play manuscript itself was discovered in a drawer in 2010 by Jeffrey Brown, the grandson of the playwright Lena Brown. He came across it when going through the effects of his father who, about fifty years earlier, had saved a few items from his mother's effects, this play among them. The play had never been staged or published. There is no evidence that anyone read it but for the author herself. Jeffrey could recall hearing little about his grandmother, who had died before he was born. What he knows with certainty is that she lived on President Street in Brooklyn and had one son, Jeffrey's father, David. But for this play in a drawer, there is no evidence that anyone knew Lena to be a writer or someone who internalized some of the more radical ideas of her day.

While they don't use the word "abortion," the characters speak about the subject with a measure of casualness and with the shared knowledge that reproductive choice is a vital key to their personal freedom. Perhaps precisely because she was writing for the drawer, Brown writes with a satisfying frankness about abortion as she touches on such issues as aging and adoption, and the effect of men's desires on women's own conflicting and conflicted desires. Each thematic thread unspools with subtlety in Brown's original Yiddish, which Miro Mniewski translates with great sleight of hand.

Fanny's inexplicable depression in the play's first scenes is the foreboding backdrop to Sonia's gradual emotional unraveling over the course of the play. Fanny gave birth months earlier to twins, one of whom died soon after delivery. But she is not grief-stricken over the baby's death, and she spends little time with the surviving twin, who is cared for by a wet nurse. Sonia believes that her sister is depressed because at the age of twenty-two she is too young to have a family.[35] The seven intervening years between Acts I and II confirm this hypothesis, as Fanny will rely on multiple illegal abortions to avoid having more children. They might even suggest that she should not have had children at all. She says to Sonia, "I could never get used to being tied down again, going around with a carriage. Oh, it's so good to be free now."

We are introduced to Sonia through the gaze of Fanny's husband, Simon Rabinov, who wonders aloud to her why she can't spend more time dolling herself up for the theater. "You're just like your sister, she takes five minutes to get ready, ... That's why you two never look like ladies." Fanny is not intimidated: "We want to look like people, not like ladies." Simon responds with impatience: "That's enough. If you continue, I'll start to think Sonia was doing the talking. [...] As it is you're not far from turning into the little lady philosopher that she is."

When Sonia comes onto the scene, she delivers on the wit and intelligence that Rabinov promises. And, later in the act, Leo Edit, a man eight years her junior, declares his love for Sonia and his admiration for her independence of mind and spirit. Even as the play makes clear Sonia's instinct is not to get married, this reader could not help but root for them to fall in love and marry—as indeed they do.

The constraints that hem in these women have a Chekhovian invisibility: their middle-class lives liberate them from the back-breaking factory work that was more typical of early-twentieth-century immigrant life, but impose expectations that not even the fierce and spirited Sonia has the wherewithal to resist. Act II, seven years later, reveals Sonia and Leo's relationship to be strained. Sonia is weighed down by the need to provide Leo with a child, even though she had never wanted to have children of her own and has learned from a recent doctor's visit that she cannot have children. She contemplates a dangerous operation that might help her to conceive. This is yet another scenario in which Brown forces us to wonder about repercussions of women making choices about their own bodies, even when it means putting themselves in danger.

Sonia Itelson reads like a blend of an art play and the more commercially driven Yiddish theater.[36] The characters do not mention their Judaism, and most of them share an openness to feminism that didn't get much play in the more culturally conservative space of the early-twentieth-century American Yiddish stage. There is no intergenerational drama; no nagging *kleyn-shtetldike* parents. Instead, there is quick banter between well-rounded characters, as when Sonia and Dave discuss the possibility of marriage to Leo:

> **Dave** You sound like someone who's head over heels, my sister.
> *Lowers his voice.*
> And what's your plan for making him happy—free love?
>
> **Sonia** Leave that to me.
>
> **Dave** Don't get mad at me for pressing you about this. You know how much you two sisters mean to me.
>
> **Sonia** And you are precious to me, but I would never mix into your private life.
>
> **Dave** I am a man.
>
> **Sonia** Ha, ha. You just said we were equal!

Brown explores the divide between the characters' lip-service and their decisions, and then moves on to philosophical ideas. About bringing children into the world, Sonia laments to her husband, Leo, "Oh—there are enough already. If only they were well-loved and properly raised and cared for. So many of them wouldn't die then! The less born the better." Leo replies impatiently, arguing that her well-thought-out Malthusian theories do not hold a candle to the power of human instinct to reproduce. He continues:

> I'm not in a position to philosophize. I'm at a loss as to what to call this foolish idea you've cooked up in your head Sonia. Let's say it is justifiable to devote oneself to those

who are already here rather than bringing more into the world. What do we do with our instinct then? What do we do with our urge to bring children into the world? Does it satisfy either you or me that there are already so many? We don't have any! To have them there is no other choice but to bring them.

To Leo's self-indulgence, Sonia responds, "I could answer you plenty on this but I'm not in the mood." Moments like these demonstrate Brown's sure hand in drawing characters and letting them speak—and, here, showing their rhetorical and emotional limits when debating with loved ones, showing them shut down.

While we know little about Lena Brown's artistic life and influences, the ideas Leo accuses Sonia of "cooking up" are evocative of those of Emma Goldman (1869–1940) and Margaret Sanger (1879–1966), who were both roughly Brown's contemporaries.[37] In 1920s New York, Brown might have bought a Yiddish-language copy of Goldman's book *Marriage and Free Love* for six cents. Sanger believed birth control (she coined the term) and "voluntary motherhood" to be essential to a woman's self-determination. And, in keeping with Sonia's ideas, Sanger believed the ability of women to control the number of children they have would limit war, famine, and oppression more so than diplomatic efforts by self-important male political leaders.

Sonia Itelson bridges a divide between vocal birth control activists of this era and those who practiced birth control and family limitation as private individuals. The historian Melissa Klapper explains that well before the birth control movement coalesced, Jewish women in America averaged fewer children than other ethnic groups, a discrepancy that suggests Jews were early adopters of contraception, including abortion.[38] This trend was true of Jews in European cities and also in Palestine. The historian Lilach Rosenberg-Friedman explains that historical evidence suggests the prevalence of abortion in the Yishuv, even as Zionist leaders encouraged Jewish women to have more babies and increase its Jewish population.[39] The birth control movement in the United States, with its disproportionate numbers of Jewish activists, was, in part, a response to a landscape in which illegal abortion was already a widespread form of birth control among Jews.[40]

We can't be sure exactly when Brown wrote her play, but the activism it reflects and represents precedes the mostly strictly prohibitive stance again abortion that would come to characterize the Orthodox halakhic establishment by the 1930s.[41] Jewish community leaders and influential newspaper editors who might have been even more vocal in support of abortion were restrained—but not by Jewish leaders or law. In the 1920s and 1930s, more than anything, federal obscenity statutes kept activists in check. Obscenity, for instance, was the charge for which Goldman and Sanger were jailed after speaking publicly about birth control or distributing leaflets about reproductive rights. Still, there are early examples of progressive rabbis endorsing birth control publicly during these early years of the movement, arguing for the safety and privacy of the mother and the economic health of the family.[42] Before the Orthodox establishment dug in its heels against abortion, historical evidence suggests that even women who considered themselves pious sought illegal abortions; observance of Jewish law was mostly regulated according to public practice.

Also in the backdrop of *Sonia Itelson* is the popular and propagandistic play on the Yiddish stage from this era that unequivocally championed the legalization of abortion the left-wing German play called *Cyankali*, which débuted in Berlin in 1929 and was translated for the Yiddish stage in 1931.[43] We can hardly be sure that Brown knew of the play before she wrote her own. In it, Hete, an impoverished factory worker has lost her job and goes to a backstreet doctor for an abortion. He sells her cyanide and advises her to swallow five small drops of it to end her pregnancy, but she poisons herself accidentally and dies. With *Cyankali*, the playwright, the German-Jewish doctor and committed Communist Friedrich Wolf, argued the hypocrisy of banning abortions as society's rich always found a way of securing safe albeit illegal abortions, while the poor were forced to take their lives into their hands. With it, Wolf succeeded in making a potent piece of propaganda that became a sensation throughout Europe. As Fanny dies from an abortion in Act III, Brown suggests that the ban on abortion does not endanger only the underclass; birth control is an issue for women of all classes.

Throughout the first four acts, Brown thoughtfully pulls several thematic strands into tension with each other, but she is less patient with her play's denouement. In Act III, Sonia has lost her confidence and stays at home complaining she has nothing to do. Leo's sympathy for her has drained away and the reader shares in his frustration with Sonia. Even her loving brother, Dave, delivers some tough love to Sonia toward the play's end: "You've got to change Sonia, change. Display some mobility; be more flexible, it will change how you look." After Dave leaves her alone, Sonia asks aloud of herself: "Change how I look?" And, as she looks in the mirror, she continues, "The wrinkles will not smooth themselves out. They only keep my depression captive." In the end, Sonia swallows a bottle of carbolic acid and kills herself.

Any Yiddish theatergoer worth her salt would pick up on Brown's clues that this is where *Sonia Itelson* was heading. In Act I, Brown references the Yiddish play *Elisha Ben Abuya* by Jacob Gordin about the rabbi-heretic who figures prominently in the Talmud. It played often after its début in New York City in 1908. A kind of heretic to the immigrant dream of American success, Sonia is, indeed, a modern-day Elisha Ben Abuya. Even more revealing is Sonia's reference to Carmen, whose song she sings gaily to her baby niece and Leo in the first act with an invisible tambourine in hand. *Carmen* was immensely popular with Jewish immigrant audiences who took it in droves at the Metropolitan Opera, and who read and attended Yiddish translations of the opera.[44] Carmen insists on free love, refuses to commit to her beloved José, and, in the end, dies at his hand. Sonia follows a different trajectory but is equally doomed.

Finally, Brown's *Sonia Itelson* resonates most closely with another Yiddish play on reproductive rights written by the New York-based playwright Harry Kalmanovitz: *Geburts control oder Rassen Zelbstmord* (Birth Control or Race Suicide), which hit the New York Yiddish stage for a short run in July of 1916.[45] According to Melissa Klapper's reading of it, some of the play's characters make a good case for birth control—"We poor workers must not make more slaves for the wealthy," one cries but the voice of the play ultimately condemns abortion as against both nature and the will of God. *Sonia Itelson* comes at the issue of voluntary motherhood from a middle-class and more secular perspective; still, it too invokes the idea of man's "natural instinct" to procreate through the character of Leo. Although we do not know him to speak along these lines throughout the play, Dave pronounces accordingly with the final words of the play: "Both my sisters have been punished with death because of crimes against nature." Certainly, Dave's words go furthest in undoing the play as one advocating for abortion access, but they also feel false in relation to all that Brown's characters have contemplated and explored until this point. In their wake, we long for what is lost, for Sonia's thoughtfulness and nuance.

Piazza, Rickman, and Mniewski deserve credit not just for the intelligence they brought to bear on translating these pieces but also for the thoughtfulness they put into recovering artifacts of history in a way that resonates with new audiences today. Their engagement with these texts has given them and their authors either a renewed currency or a currency they never had. Each of these playwrights—each in their own slightly different time and place—had a keen sense of their marginal status that they translated into words. In all three plays, the female protagonists—each one of them alter egos to the educated middle-class playwrights who created them— die in the final scene, two by their own hands. Their body and experiences have told them one thing and the worlds to which they want to belong tell them something else. Their deaths register, at once, as a form of surrender and protest, like a provocative play written in a notebook and put away in a drawer that is slammed shut. I am grateful to Piazza, Mniewski, and Rickman for opening the drawer.

Notes

1   French and Italian opera and theater were regular and important parts of the diet of theater-goers in the Russian Empire, where almost all theater was regulated by the Czar throughout the nineteenth century. Women participated in French theater as performers in the provinces as early as the 1540s (and by 1620 in city theaters) and as playwrights as early as 1650. See Perry Gethner and Melinda J. Gough, "The Advent of Women Players and Playwrights in Early Modern France," *Renaissance Drama*. Vol. 44, No. 2 (Fall 2016), 217–32.

2   Maria Lerner, *Di agune: a drama in fir akten un zeks bilder* (Varshe: yidishe bine, 1908); Paula Prilutski, *Eyne fun yene: a drama in fir akten fun Paula Prilutski (Paula R.)* (Varshe: Nayer farlag, 1914); and Brown, Lena, *Sonya Itelson; oder, a kind, a kind* ms. From the personal collection of Jeffrey Brown. The latter was never published and the date of its composition is unknown.

3   See Alyssa Quint and Miryem-Khaye Seigal eds., *Women on the Yiddish Stage* (Oxford: Legenda, 2023) and an accompanying series of primary sources on Yiddish theater published on the Digital Yiddish Theater Project site beginning in 2022, https://web.uwm.edu/yiddish-stage/women-on-the-yiddish-stage-primary-sources.

4   Some recent translations of these works to English include Miriam Karpilove, *Diary of a Lonely Girl, or the Battle against Free Love*. Translated by Jessica Kirzane (Syracuse: Syracuse University Press, 2019); Chana Blankshteyn, *Fear and Other Stories*. Translated by Anita Norich (Detroit: Wayne State University Press, 2022).

5   Rebecca Turner, "Forgotten *Froyen*: An Analysis of Women Yiddish Playwrights and Their Works from 1877–1938" Honours Bachelor's Master's Thesis McGill University, 2022, 7. Turner also digs up half-discovered women who Zylbercweig

records as writing under the name of their husbands, like Fryda Friedman, the true librettist of Joseph Rumshinsky's operetta *The Golden Bride (The Golden Kale)*. See also "Plotting Yiddish Drama" page in online Digital Yiddish Theatre Project's https://web.uwm.edu/yiddish-stage/plotting-yiddish-drama for additional plays written by women.

6   I found evidence of this among documents and letters (e.g., from writers' unions) that are now included in the Yiddish Language and Literature Collection (RG 3) at the YIVO. See, as well, Anita Norich's introduction to *Fear and Other Stories*.

7   Kalmen Weiser, *Jewish People, Yiddish Nation: Noah Prylucki and the Folkists in Poland* (Toronto: University of Toronto Press, 2011).

8   In part, we may attribute the gap to educational background. Consider the song-writing career of Molly Picon, the radio shows written and then performed by Miriam Kressyn, or the plays translated and then directed by the Polish-Jewish actress Ida Kaminska. All three women benefited from their middle-class upbringings and the benefits of rigorous educations. Actors—especially Yiddish actors—relied, instead, on vocal and acting talents. Ida Kaminska's mother Ester Rokhl Kaminska is a case in point: she grew up the daughter of a poor shtetl-bound cantor. Orphaned at a young age, she had little formal schooling and sought out factory work in the city before falling into acting, chiefly because of her beautiful voice. After many years of honing her singing and acting skills—all self-taught—she emerged as the most celebrated Yiddish actress and the "Mother of the Yiddish theater" by the time of her death in 1926. Talent and necessity pushed her to excel, not education. Educated women—potential writers and playwrights—might marry men of their class who could support them and without the need to work—and with domestic and childcare responsibilities—writing might have fallen by the wayside. In any case, the scarcity of women playwrights demands further attention. But this class gap applies equally to both men and women.

9   Haim Sperber, "Agunot, 1851–1914: An Introduction," *Annales de démographie historique, 2018*, No. 2 (136), *Familles juives: Europe Méditerranée*, XIXe–XXe siècles (2018), 107–36.

10 For a history of the first period and crystallization of modern Yiddish theater including the rise of the Yiddish actress, see my book, *The Rise of the Modern Yiddish Theater* (Bloomington: Indiana University Press, 2019).

11 For discussion of the genre of the bourgeois tragedy, see Alex Eric Hernandez, "Prosaic Suffering," *Representations*. No. 138 (Spring 2017), 118–41.

12 On Maria Lerner among other Yiddish women writers who had been neglected until recently, see Nurit Orchen, *Holding Their Own: Early Modern Yiddish Women's Fiction* (Jerusalem: Magnes UP, 2021).

13 Biographical information from Zalmen Zylbercweig and Jacob Mestel, *Leksikon fun yidishn teater*, vol. 2, 6 vols. (New York: Elisheva, 1931), 1162–70. For more on Osip Lerner's Christianity, see Quint, Ibid.

14 For more on the career of Osip Lerner, see Alyssa Quint, *The Rise of the Modern Yiddish Theater* (Bloomington: Indiana University Press, 2019), 122–5.

15 Ibid., 122–5.

16 For more on the Yiddish Enlightenment drama, see my article "The Currency of Yiddish: Ettinger's Serkele and the Reinvention of Shylock," *Prooftexts* 24 (2004): 99–115.

In it, I refer to a body of plays that were written throughout the nineteenth century before their writers could expect them to be performed publicly or even published. Often in hand-copied versions, these plays exerted a strong influence on the first writers of the Yiddish stage, including Goldfaden and the Lerners. Osip Lerner tried staging a production of Ettinger's *Serkele*, which is the focus of my study.

17 Naomi Seidman, *The Marriage Plot (Stanford Studies in Jewish History and Culture)* (Palo Alto: Stanford University Press, 2016), 33–4 *Kindle Edition*. This sentimental revolution was not novel to all segment of Russian Jewry as evidenced by the notion of love in popular culture etc. As Seidman explains: "Traditional forms and new romantic models coexisted for many decades, with parents and children strategically mobilizing multiple ideologies and conventions for maximum erotic, social, and economic gain."

18 Ibid., 33. Stanford University Press. Kindle Edition.

19 Hillel Halkin, *Vladimir Jabotinsky: A Life* (New Haven: Yale University Press, 2014), 5.

20 Steven J. Zipperstein, *The Jews of Odessa: A Cultural History, 1794–1881* (Stanford: Stanford University Press, 1986), 7.

21 See ChaeRan Freeze, *Jewish Marriage and Divorce in Imperial Russia* (Hanover: Brandeis University Press, 2002); Bluma Goldstein, *Enforced Marginality: Jewish Narratives on Abandoned Wives* (Berkeley: University California Press, 2007). See also the scholarship of Haim Sperber, including "The Agunot Phenomenon from 1851–1914: An Introduction" M.S. https://www.academia.edu/20040452/The_AGUNOT_Phenomenon_FROM_1851_TO_1914_AN_INTRODUCTION.

22 Freeze, Jewish Marriage and Divorce, 232.

23 Ibid., 234.

24 I am grateful to Joshua Karlip for sharing his expertise on the historical experience of halakhot pertaining to *agunes* and *mamzerim* in nineteenth- and twentieth-century Russia.

25 Michael Stanislawski, *For Whom Do I Toil: Yehudah Leib Gordon and the Crisis of Russian Jewry* (1888).

26 Ibid., 127.

27 The first lines of the poem read:

> Jewish woman, who knows your life?
> You come in the darkness and never see the light,
> Your woes and your joys, your hopes, and desires,
> Are born within you and die unfulfilled.
> Daughters of other peoples and tribes,
> Enjoy some pleasure and comfort in this life
> But the fate of the Jewess is eternal servitude. Ibid., 125.

28 See Elya Zissel Piazza's note for their discussion of the play.

29 Quint, *The Rise of the Modern Yiddish Theater*, 122.

30 Hernandez, "Prosaic Suffering," 120. For more on the performance of emotion on the stage see Jonathan M Hess, *Deborah and Her Sisters: How One Nineteenth-Century Melodrama and a Host of Celebrated Actresses Put Judaism on the World Stage* (Philadelphia, PA: University of Pennsylvania Press, 2018).

31 For more on Goldfaden's operetta *Shulamis* see Quint, *The Rise of the Modern Yiddish Theater*, 163–173.

32 For more on Paula's husband Noyekh, see Kalman Weiser, *Jewish people, Yiddish nation: Noah Prylucki and the Folkists in Poland*. (Toronto: University of Toronto Press, 2011). For their tragic end during the Second World War, see Mendel Balberyszski, *Stronger than Iron: The Destruction of Vilna Jewry 1941–1945m An Eyewitness Account* (Jerusalem: Gefen Publishing House, 2010).

33 For historical accounts and analysis of young Jewish women leaving traditional homes, see Rachel Manekin's important study, *The Rebellion of the Daughters: Jewish Women Runaways in Habsburg Galicia* (Princeton: Princeton University Press, 2020).

34 For a nuanced historical treatment of Jewish prostitution, especially as it intersected with emigration, see Mir Yarfitz, "Marriage as Ruse or Migration Route: Jewish Women's Mobility and Sex Trafficking to Argentina, 1890s–1930s," *Women in Judaism: A Multidisciplinary Journal*. Vol. 17, No. 1 (2020): also, Rachel G. Fuchs, *Gender and Poverty in Nineteenth-Century Europe* (Cambridge: Cambridge University Press, 2005). While societies of Jewish reformers arose to combat Jewish prostitution, and portrayed its women as victims, the reality of it was far more complex, with social, class, and gender dimensions. Still, clichéd narratives had great currency on the Yiddish stage. See for instance, Stefanie Halpern, "Crossing Over: From the Yiddish Rialto to the American Stage" Ph.D. thesis JTS (2017), for a discussion of plays that depict Jewish prostitutes who, we discover, are, in fact, just pretending to be prostitutes in order to live in St. Petersburg or Kiev, where they want to attend school. The premise behind such plays is that Jewish women are too pure to work as prostitutes.

35 For another depiction of postpartum depression in Yiddish literature, see Yenta Serdatsky's "Cribside: A Dramatization of Life in Politics" Translated by Jessica Kirzane, *Pakn Treger* (Summer 2022). Accessed online, https://www. yiddishbookcenter.org/language-literature-culture/pakn-treger/2022-pakn-treger-digital-translation-issue/cribside. Other sources relevant to Jewish women and reproductive health in 1920s New York include Kate Simon's *Bronx Primitive: Portraits in a Childhood* (Philadelphia: 1982), Rose Pastor Stokes's plays *The Woman Who Wouldn't* (NY: 1916).

36 I am grateful to the anonymous reviewer of an earlier draft of this essay for this insight and many others I included in the text.

37 On Sanger and Goldman as crusaders of reproductive rights, see Melissa R. Klapper, *Ballots, Babies, and Banners of Peace: American Jewish Women's Activism, 1890–1940* (NYU: London: NYU Press, 2013).

38 Ibid., Klapper's *Ballots, Babies, and Banners of Peace: American Jewish Women's Activism, 1890–1940*.

39 Lilach Rosenberg-Friedman, "Abortion in the Yishuv during the British Mandate Period: A Case Study of the Place of the Individual in a Nationalistic Society," *Jewish History*. Vol. 29 (2015), 331–59.

40 Ibid., *Ballots, Babies, and Banners of Peace: American Jewish Women's Activism, 1890–1940*.

41 For two contrasting perspectives on the literature on the halakhic or Orthodox approach to abortion, see Aharon Lichtenstein, "Abortion: a Halakhic Perspective," *Tradition: A Journal of Orthodox Thought*. Vol. 25, No. 4 (Summer 1991), 3–12 and Ronit Irshai, *Fertility and Jewish Law: Feminist Perspectives* (Brandeis University Press: 2012).

42 See Melissa Klapper, "The Drama of 1916: The American Jewish Community, Birth Control, and Two Yiddish Plays," *The Journal of the Gilded Age and Progressive Era*. Vol. 12, No. 4 (October 2013), 502–34.

43 See documents relating to the 1931 Yiddish staging of *Cyankali* in Poland at https://ataleoftwomuseums.yivo.org/exhibits/show/a-day-at-the-museum/polandyiddishtheater/translations. Visited on September 7, 2022.

44 See Daniela Smolov Levy, "Grand Opera for Yiddish Speakers in Early Twentieth-Century America! Who Knew ?!" at https://web.uwm.edu/yiddish-stage/grand-opera-for-yiddish-speakers-in-early-twentieth-century-america-who-knew. Visited on September 8, 2022.

45 Ibid., "The Drama of 1916: The American Jewish Community, Birth Control, and Two Yiddish Plays."

Translator's Note by Elya Zissel Piazza

The Chained Wife offers a glimpse into the mind of an early Ashkenazi feminist who took to the Yiddish stage in order to tackle one of the oldest struggles faced by Jewish women within a cultural context shaped by Jewish marriage law—that of the *agune*. The term describes the position of a woman who is abandoned by her husband without a proper divorce, and is therefore, in literal translation, "chained" to an unwanted marriage. By giving voice to this struggle experienced by too many Jewish women throughout history, Lerner sheds light on a broader tension which continues to echo in Yiddish-speaking spaces today between cultural forces which continue to promote adherence to a conservative and oppressive expression of tradition and those that find in this tradition the language and tools of resistance, revolution, empowerment and subversion. That tension is one I have struggled with personally in different iterations in my work and life as a queer and trans Yiddishist and one of the reasons that I felt an affinity and sense of rootedness in this story.

Since the writing of this play, the process of family-building has oscillated between being a family affair, a personal affair, and a sociopolitical affair as we have seen in the recent overturning of *Roe v. Wade*. This script offers a dramatic but nevertheless crucial and revelatory snapshot into the lived personal consequences of legislation governing personal autonomy.

This translation has gone through many iterations in which I experimented with privileging different values. In any given scene I weighed the importance of maintaining Yiddish syntax to mark the text as a translation from another language and another time and attempt to transport the reader/audience, alongside the demands of readability and equivalence of chosen terms. Perhaps the major challenge of translating this piece is the archaic and often stilted language in the original, which, when rendered literally in English can read as an awkward and failed attempt at proper Victorian English (a language I have no fluency in as a queer millennial) with only occasional Yiddishisms. In much of the play, the manner of speech stands in contrast to modern English associations with the language (however reductive or misguided they may be) as intimate, relatable, or even crass. This style discourages futile attempts to familiarize the reader with an elusive "essence" of Yiddish through untranslated terms and *bubbie-zayde* syntax. Ultimately, I opted most often to privilege a balance between accuracy and readability, a necessary choice particularly for the genre where the text is meant to be read and acted aloud rather than primarily studied as an historical text.

Toward the same end, I took some liberties with differentiating speech patterns in the different characters to try to mark them as more distinct in the text. The script, which seldom employs character descriptors or stage directions and includes occasional confusing or inconsistent dialogue, suggests the intention to bring the play to life less on the page and more in the rehearsal studio/stage. I have sought to produce a text that cues a new generation of actors amply enough to bring this play to the stage once more.

The Chained Wife

A drama in four acts and six curtains.

By Maria Lerner

Translated by Elya Zissel Piazza

Characters:

GROSSMAN: A rich merchant.

CHAYELE: Grossman's wife.

ROSA: Grossman and Chayele's daughter.

ADOLF: Grossman's bookkeeper.

NEUMANN: A swindler.

AMELIA, JULIA: Neumann's friends.

YISROEL: A broker and Neumann's friend.

ROSEMAN and BRANCH: Swindlers.

AMALIA, ADELE: Adolf and Rosa's daughters.

ROSENCRANTZ

HIS WIFE

RABBI

SERVANTS, GUESTS

Between the third and fourth acts, nineteen years pass.

ACT I

First Curtain.

Scene 1

(A nicely furnished room at Grossman's house)

(GROSSMAN and CHAYELE)

Grossman   I just hope it's not too late. But I've been saying for a while now that we ought to pay a little more attention to Rosa.

Chayele   Believe me, Avram, Rosa doesn't see Adolf as her equal …

Grossman   Well actually, you've got it all wrong. She sees him as much more than her equal! In truth, he's quite a remarkable young man. But our Rosa spends far too much time with him. She wanders around with him too much, reads with him too much … it all simply isn't fitting! From the way that she speaks of him, I suspect he's already made an enormous impression on her. It shouldn't have come to this! You know all too well how busy I am and I simply haven't the time to constantly watch how Rosa spends her time. But you! You should've paid more attention!

Chayele   Avram, do you really think—God forbid—that I've been neglectful?

Grossman   Oh, you're too sensitive. I'm just saying that we ought to create a little bit of distance between Adolf and Rosa. To be quite honest, I feel so proud when I think of our Rosa: how smart she is, how mature, how her gentle heart knows only what is good and pure. Surely no one would say that Adolf isn't deserving of respect or high regard, God forbid, but if we're being practical, it makes sense for us to find such a fine young man among *our* peers who would be all the more suitable both for her and for us. In the meantime, please, don't say a word to Rosa about our conversation. It must look like the friendship between Rosa and Adolf is simply coming to an end on its own. This is a very delicate matter, and we mustn't interfere openly.

Chayele   So, how exactly do you suppose it'll happen, that their relationship will suddenly end all by itself? To tell you the truth, you've filled me with doubt. Maybe it's true that our Rosa *does* think too highly of Adolf?

Grossman   I know all too well that she thinks too highly of him, but let *me* work this out. I'm sending Adolf away to Kiev today. I'll tell him that it's just for a short time, but I plan to leave him there indefinitely. I need to have a full-time accountant there anyway.

Chayele   Oh ... Don't you think he'll write to Rosa?

Grossman   Of course he will! Surely, there will be letters, but I know Adolf's good heart all too well ... I'll go with him to the station, and I'll explain to him that he should see to it that their friendship ends. He might not be able to understand entirely what I'm asking of him right then and there, but with a little distance, he will easily be able to grant this wish of mine.

Chayele   Well, that sounds reasonable! Everything you're saying is smart; we should surely do as you say ... But, if she thinks as highly of him as you're saying she does, that might be something else entirely. Are you sure that you'll really be able to tear Adolf away from *Rosa's* heart?

Grossman   Well, what do you think?! It surely won't be easy! It'll require some effort, and we need to be careful how we go about this. We're a bit late to the game, but I reckon I can still get what I want ... But let's put this aside for now. There's something else I wanted to discuss with you that's also important … I've been meaning to ask you: what kind of impression has our new acquaintance Neumann made on you? How do you like him?

Chayele   What do you mean? Why are you asking me all of a sudden whether I like him? Your question is quite odd to me.

Grossman   I simply want to know how he looks in your eyes. Sometimes women have better judgment than we men do. A woman is like a guest who comes for a while and sees for a mile.

Chayele   I don't understand the reason why you're asking me this, but I'll answer you. Honestly, it's hard for me to even have an opinion about someone I barely know, but he seems to be a pretty good merchant.

Grossman   I already know that he's a fine merchant; that's obvious. He manages sizable businesses, and he's quite exacting. Just today I gave him a promissory note to the tune of 3000 rubles. I came to him at one o'clock, and he wondered why I arrived a whole hour late. In Moscow, he says, you get to the office as promptly as they do abroad. When you are scheduled to pay at one, you're already there ready with the money at twelve. You see, Chayele, it's hard to come by people who conduct business so methodically around here. Here, people are so conditioned to taking not only two or three hours but even several days to do things. Usually it doesn't matter, but sometimes it really becomes quite a serious inconvenience. I quite like his promptness. Oh, a man like that—at his age already so settled and punctual, running his businesses so well—he has a good future!
So what do you think, Chayele, for our Rosale? Seems it wouldn't be such a bad lot?

Chayele   So that's why you're asking me what I think of him? I had no idea why you found him so interesting.

Grossman (*smiling*)   So, now that I've told you, do you know?

Chayele   Know what?

Grossman   Oh, don't get smart now. Do you like him or not?

Chayele   What can I say? I barely know him. He seems like a fine guy. But we need to be careful. We should consult … So, what—did he bring this up with you himself? Did he send someone? Or did this just occur to you on your own?

Grossman   You see, Chayele, you're a mother and you barely take notice of how people talk about your own child, how they speak to your child. It's obvious you haven't even noticed that Neumann is completely charmed by our Rosale. He's simply in love with her! I am sure that as soon as tomorrow morning he will raise the matter with me directly; he's already let on several times.

Chayele   Don't rush! We need to ask around about him a little bit.

Grossman   I already inquired about him around several offices. There was one fellow saying only good things of him: how rich he is; you should see how he lives—like a prince!

Chayele   If so, if he's really such a fine man, you're right in wanting to distance Rosa from Adolf.

Grossman   Well, that needs to be done in any case.

Servant   Mr. Neumann!

Grossman   Invite him in.

Chayele   Well, I don't want to disturb you.

Grossman   Come back in here with Rosa. I want *you* to invite him to have breakfast with us.

Chayele   Yes, alright, Avram. We'll return shortly. (*Exits.*)

Scene 2

(GROSSMAN and NEUMANN)

Neumann   Good morning, Mr. Grossman.

Grossman (*approaching him*)   How are you? How have you been? All too well, I hope.

Neumann   Thank you, thank you! How are you finding things?

Grossman   Fine, thank God—sit, sit! (*Pulls an armchair toward Neumann.*)

Neumann   How's the fine young lady? And your wife?

Grossman   They're healthy, thank God!

Neumann   Well then, will we have the honor of seeing them?

Grossman   Certainly, they'll come in shortly.

Neumann   It pleases me very much to see them. Especially the young little Rose. Your daughter, I have to tell you, is indeed a rose among thorns in our town.

Grossman   Yes, we taught our daughter well, to the extent that it was possible.

Neumann   And aside from that, nature also endowed her with beautiful gifts. You know, Mr. Grossman, I am not entirely indifferent to your daughter.

Grossman (*smiling*)   Yes, I've noticed that.

Neumann   Well, since you yourself have noticed, allow me to open up to you. I like your daughter very much. Even more so—I love the young Rosale. Oh, if I could only hope to consider such an angel my own …

Grossman   See, from my side, I for one have no opposition to it. We just need to ask my daughter. She has free will, after all.

Neumann   In that case, I'm thrilled. I would go to great lengths to earn her friendship and love ... In the meantime, thank you so much (*shaking his hand*) for your good opinion of me and the invaluable hope that you've given me from your side ... And now, to business! We can move forward with the business matter that we discussed yesterday. But first, I just have to talk it over with General Skritsky—surely you've heard the name?

Grossman   Yes, Skritsky—I've heard of him.

Neumann   You see, Mr. Grossman, it all depends on him. With only a snap of his fingers, we can get the permits and business will be ours for the taking—and I certainly don't need to persuade you of what we could earn in such a business. You know well already what kind of success we could find for ourselves.

Grossman   What do you think? Do we need a lot of capital?

Neumann   I still don't know how much money we'll need to have upfront. I haven't yet finished the estimates. Most importantly, I want you to think everything over carefully—perhaps it's not worth your while?

Grossman   Well, I reckon you're already quite familiar with licensing ...

Neumann   Sure. I have quite enough experience in business. But my rule is consistent. All opportunities should be carefully considered to be sure that your partner in business is confident about his investment. More than anything, I don't like to persuade people into doing a deal. Even when I'm completely confident, I hold myself back from coaxing. I want you to think hard about this business and see whether it's worth it for the capital and effort it would require of you … I don't want you to get nervous if it takes a little while for the business to become fruitful.

Grossman   What are you talking about, Mr. Neumann? You think you're dealing with an amateur? I understand all too well who's talking to me and exactly what he's saying.

Neumann   I'll go right away to General Skritsky and by tomorrow morning we'll know where we stand.

Grossman   Good, very well … I have the money ready.

Scene 3

(Enter CHAYELE and ROSA)

Chayele   Are we disturbing you?

Neumann (*approaching them*)   Ah, Madame. How could you disturb us? And the fine young lady (*reaching out a hand to Rosa*): Good day! How are you, Madame?

Chayele   Well, thank God, thank you!

Neumann   And the young lady?

Rosa   As usual, mercí.

Neumann   You must be quite bored, fine Miss? We have no distractions here in this town. (*To Chayele.*) Were it not for your house, fine Madame, there would simply be no place to go! If I didn't have the good fortune of coming here to your house, where I spend my free time—always with great pleasure—I wouldn't remain here a single day longer! I would have to leave someone else to look over my businesses. And you, Miss, I reckon you'd rather be traveling the world.

Rosa   Oh, it's not so unpleasant to me. I love it here.

Neumann   Of course. Because you grew up here. But you haven't yet been to Europe in the big, beautiful cities ... if you traveled through Europe just once, you would see how everything is changing. An entirely different life! Happy and calm! People much different from us here.

Rosa   People can be happy or unhappy any place. It just depends on how you define happiness. For some, happiness means having big houses, lots of money, and being able to show off to the world everything you can buy with your money. But for others, happiness means living peacefully in one's nest, as they say, with those whom you love and treasure. Some people are delighted by the sparks they make fly before the eyes of others; they find happiness in that alone. Others, though, don't actually feel so happy among the big marble columns, among the expensive pictures that adorn the house, where so many tears are often shed, where residents often greet each other with a smile across their lips and with hate in their hearts. Simply having so much, Mr. Neumann, does not make the place they live a happy one. Only the people with whom they live can give happiness. Often—almost always, in fact—the people from smaller places are happier because they don't have such big eyes and are satisfied with very little. It's not the place that glorifies the person but rather the person who glorifies the place!

Grossman   That's right, my dear girl. But how good is it when both the place and the society together can satisfy the person?

Neumann   These few words of yours, lovely lady, prove just how pure and innocent your heart is. Oh, happy years of beautiful youth! May you always see the world through such eyes. Then you would surely be the happiest of all! But I have to tell you, with time, you'll no longer believe the same things you believe now. You'll understand that the poor man isn't necessarily honest and decent, nor does a rich man's wealth take away from his decency.

Rosa But very seldom, Mr. Neumann, is the man who has never experienced any hardship, who has never lived through a bad hour, able to understand that there is suffering in the world, that tears are shed not for foolish pride. Oh, the one who knows no hardship doesn't feel the suffering of others. He doesn't love his neighbor. He doesn't forgive others, and doesn't consider anyone else. As long as everything is good for him, what else is there to say? How can someone feel when he has never encountered even one spark of human love, in whose mind no questions arise, who thinks that the way that *he* lives is the way that it ought to be for everyone, without understanding that not everyone can be in such a position. In the blink of an eye, someone can wake up and suddenly see that there are other feelings, other ways of being. Then, he can no longer sleep peacefully in large palaces; he is unable to rest, even in Europe, where people live so happily, according to you.

Grossman Oh, my darling. Everywhere, there is always both fair and unfair, happy and unhappy. You're still all too young; you know all too little about life.

Chayele Please, let's have breakfast. Please, Mr. Neumann, give us the honor of joining us.

Neumann Thank you, lovely Madame. Unfortunately, I must turn down the pleasure of eating together with you. I must leave soon. I made a commitment at exactly twelve o'clock and, unfortunately, I'm already five minutes late. (*Looking at the clock.*) One has to be punctual. (*Shakes hands with everyone.*)

Chayele In that case, agree that you'll come join us for supper.

Neumann At what time?

Chayele Around five o'clock.

Neumann   With pleasure. I'll be free by then.

Grossman   We will surely not have to wait: You're so punctual, after all!

Neumann   Yes, yes, yes ... *Adieu*! (*Reaching out his hand to* CHAYELE, ROSA, GROSSMAN) Tomorrow at twelve I'll be back here again, or, better: tomorrow you come to me and we will thoroughly think through the business matters. Let's speak no further about business today. I'll come to you for supper, to eat and spend a few good hours.

Grossman   Right, very well ...

Neumann   Yes, everything has its time. Again, *adieu*!

(GROSSMAN *and* CHAYELE *escort* NEUMANN *out.*)

Scene 4

Rosa (*alone*)   Oh, what could this mean? It's already been two days since I've seen Adolf ... What could possibly be keeping him so busy? ... Hmph! That Neumann ... there's something about him I just don't like. I couldn't even tell you what. Surely it's on account of the fact that I have a feeling my father's friendship with him is much greater than with other merchants ... Sure, it's possible that if it weren't for Adolf, I wouldn't have anything against Neumann. Yes, it's on Adolf's account that I feel this antipathy towards Neumann, because who knows? Perhaps my father fancies him for a future son-in-law ... I don't understand. Why does my father praise him so much at every opportunity? He is so charmed by his abilities. "Neumann is a smart man, a businessman, a very capable man." That and the like is all he says, and when he talks about Neumann, he always talks too about Adolf. I'm convinced he means to insinuate something with it: Adolf, he says, will always be a laborer. He is a fine man, he is smart, but he doesn't have the spirit for enterprise, for risk—he will always remain a servant. Surely, he compares Neumann to Adolf because it's so difficult not to linger over Adolf's fine character ... but why do I need to concern myself with this? What does it matter to me who has the spirit of enterprise and risk, after all? What really matters to me is having the spirit of truth. Oh, Adolf, how I love—how I treasure your gentle heart! The richness of your heart is greater than a million others combined. But I won't tell Adolf of my father's dealings with Neumann. I don't want to upset him. He's always so afraid at even the thought of a frank conversation with my parents about my future.

(ADOLF *enters*.)

Scene 5

(ADOLF and ROSA)

Rosa Oh, is it you, my dear friend? ... I've been wondering why I haven't seen you for two whole days. I've been ready to scold you. I started to think that you didn't *want* to see me.

Adolf First of all, my dear, could you at least say "good morning"? (*He outstretches a hand to her.*) Now, allow yourself to notice, Rosa, that you can often be quite hurtful with your words. This isn't the first time I've heard you speak this way. Apparently it's necessary for me to reassert what you are to me every day. You were already ready to chastise me—you don't know how much I've wanted to see you and speak to you, to hear your voice.

Rosa Do you know why I'm speaking to you like this? It's because you don't speak to me like I'm *your* Rosa but like I'm the banker Grossman's daughter. Remember, Adolf, how frequently you take pains to remind me of the distant border that still remains between us. It upsets me, my dear friend! I haven't forgotten what we talked about last time ...

Adolf   You must understand that there's a difference
between my love for you and your love for me. Not to us,
but to other people. And if you want to know the truth, even
in *our* eyes there's a difference. You are facing a struggle—a
struggle for you to renounce everything that you're used to ...
well, and me?

Rosa   Enough of this talk already! I've already heard it a
thousand times. And it causes me nothing but grief! It only
shows me how little you appreciate me ... but please tell me.
Why haven't I seen you for two whole days? You still haven't
told me, even though I'm asking.

Adolf (*ironically*)   Because I didn't want to see you,
according to your view ... I've just been busy trying to settle
the books.

Rosa   What books? Does someone have an outstanding
balance?

Adolf   No, no one has a balance. Your father is sending me
to Kiev on business.

Rosa   For a long time?

Adolf   No, just for a couple of weeks. But that's why I've
had to hand over the books to Milman. You see, Rosa, even
though you say that your issues with me convince you that
I don't love you, actually, apparently I must tell you once
more the same thing you've heard time and time again. I
look at our relationship much differently. I can't hide that
I'm tortured by the thought that perhaps I've sinned against
you by awakening these feelings in you towards me. Oh,
Rosa, it's almost as though I wish you were poor; that way,
I wouldn't have to hide my feelings for you. I would be able
to tell everyone how much I love you, to convince everyone
that neither your stature nor your wealth plays a role; that
you, and you alone, are what's precious to me. Oh, Rosa, I
worship you!

Rosa Adolf! … It's called love! Why do you fear? Why wonder? Why even consider what others will think? Let them think what they will! But *I*—I know, of course, yes, that you don't care about my wealth or status.

Adolf Oh, Rosa! You have to know that I'm afraid of merging your life with mine. You've grown up in riches. For as long as you've lived, you've never known what it means to want for something. It's true, my love. You try to guide your thoughts toward a modest life, but from speech to action is such a long way. Thoughts can't frighten as much as cold reality, Rosa. You don't know what it means to lack, especially not that which you've never wanted for. How often people forget what they are to one another when need lies between them and oppresses their hearts. It's true that bread alone isn't enough to satisfy a person, but when cold reality sets in, and a person begins to wage a daily war for his survival, very seldom does he not forget even what is most holy to him. I must tell you again: I don't want—I cannot bear it—if it seems, even for a moment, that I've taken your carefree life away from you. I don't want your word to force you into something that will later turn out to be a bad fortune for you. I'm afraid this will inevitably enter your thoughts sooner or later …

Rosa Enough, enough! Stop speaking! It's not with words, Adolf, that I'll show you how joyfully I will treasure my life when it is eternally bound to yours. I don't fear for any lack. What kind of lack can there be with you? If you don't want to understand me, my dear friend, perhaps time will reveal to you that I am truly worthy of being yours … (*Pause.*) If love means torture, it would be much better if people never felt such a feeling. How cruel is such a love? It seems to me that to each of love's joys is attached a hundred sorrows. I myself don't know what to think of you, Adolf. You're so proud compared to me.

Adolf I'm proud?

Rosa Yes, yes. You have more pride against me than one could ever need. You're still afraid. If I tell you that I'm ready to renounce everything, as long as it binds me to you, you still won't accept my offering, and that shows me just how proud you are. But you are greatly mistaken if you think that I am totally prepared, solely on your account, to sacrifice the peace of my parents, to renounce everything to which I'm accustomed. You really think that I want to do that *for your sake*? No, I want to do that for my *own* sake, because I can't do otherwise. Our friendship and love is too strong, too holy to me, for me to be able to say that I'm willing to turn away from everything that I'm used to only for *you*. Believe me, Adolf, that I want to do it all for me, because in you I see my joy, my peace. You must understand that ultimately, I don't just love you, I *treasure* you.

Adolf Oh, Rosa, how smart you are.

Rosa But listen to the end of what I'm trying to tell you: There's no guarantee that I will see anything remaining in your words besides pride. If I could, Adolf, you wouldn't even recognize me. Your pride tells you to say that you can free me from my promise. My pride tells me that I will be able to free myself, if I see something in you besides pride.

Adolf If so, you will, shall I say, always, always, love me. But you're a bit mistaken in what you're calling pride. That, Rosa, is reflection. You are simply too dear for me to be able to somehow commit to without first knowing that I will be able to provide you with a life that is free of worry …

Rosa Enough of that, Adolf!

Adolf You're right. I only came here to bid you farewell. Stay well, my dear. Surely you'll write me often. (*He offers her a hand.*)

(Enter GROSSMAN.)

Scene 6

(ROSA, ADOLF, GROSSMAN)

Grossman   Oh, Adolf! I'm glad to run into you here. I wanted to ask you: do you have the invoices from Berman's office with you?

Adolf   Yes, I have them right here.

Grossman   Give them to me. (*Adolf hands over the documents.*) I want to look these over. (*He looks over the documents, making notations.*)

Rosa (*quietly*)   Farewell, my dear friend!

Adolf   *Adieu*, my smart, dear Rosa!

Grossman   Everything looks good. Take care: the train leaves at three o'clock.

Adolf   I'm ready to go.

Grossman   Here's your letter. (*Taking out a letter from his pocket.*) I almost forgot. Give Berman and his family my warmest wishes, and check and let me know how the prices are for sugar. Send a telegram if it's possible to speculate.

Adolf   You'll have a telegram two days from now.

Grossman   Well, you'd better hurry. You only have an hour until the train leaves. Let's get going. I'll accompany you to the train so we can discuss and I'll tell you all you need to know. We'll stop at the notary on the way and I can give you power of attorney.

Adolf   In that case, Rosalia Avramovna, allow me to bid you farewell. Stay well. (*He outstretches a hand.*)

Rosa   Go in good health!

Grossman (*aside*)   Indeed, I am not mistaken. Look how she's all too pale, my poor Rosa. (*Aloud.*) Well, come on.

Adolf   I'd like to bid farewell to Madame Grossman.

Grossman   Well, come in. She's surely in the dining room. (*They leave.*)

Adolf (*by the door*)   Adieu!

Rosa   *Adieu*! (*Quietly.*) Adolf, oh, my dear love, Adolf!

The curtain falls.

Second curtain.

Scene 1

Grossman (*To* SERVANT.)   Did you finish preparing everything?

Servant   Everything. Just as you ordered.

Grossman   Tell the coach to be ready and tell the Madame I'd like her to come here. (SERVANT *leaves.*) Thank God, thank God! Everything's turning out just as I'd hoped! (CHAYELE *enters.*)

Scene 2

Grossman   Well, are you ready? Very well. Where's Rosa?

Chayele   Rosa doesn't want to go.

Grossman   Why doesn't she want to go?

Chayele   Do you really think I know?

Grossman　Well, I'm not surprised. This certainly can't be easy for her, but it will surely pass all too soon. Let her stay home.

Chayele　Yes, maybe it's better if she doesn't come.

Grossman　Well, I was right, Chayele! Do you see how well I've executed my plan? Like a politician, you could say! Adolf is truly quite a fine person. After a few of his letters I could see clearly that my plan was not foolish after all. The letters have had quite an impact on Rosa.

Chayele　And what an impact indeed! Oh, Avram, you really can't imagine how often my heart is torn to shreds looking at Rosa, how sad her face has been, how tears well up in her bright eyes after each of Adolf's letters! She's tried so hard to hide her tears, but I can't help but notice.

Grossman　Well, Chayele, leave it alone. We couldn't have had it any other way. One day she too will understand. We only have her best interest in mind. It's better this way. What, then? Could I go against the ways of the world and marry her into the family of one of my servants, or with the son of a stone mason? You yourself said that Rosa has been a bit more cheerful the last few days.

Chayele　Yes, she's much more cheerful.

Grossman　Well, so?! Deciding to be Neumann's bride has already started to lift her spirits. Everything will work out just fine. Neumann is a fine and enormously capable man. Our Rosa will be happy, and she'll have no regrets. An all too capable man, a businessman—it's a whole new chapter! A head of gold, Chayele! With such a son-in-law—might as well hand over all your business and sit in peace … Sure, it cost me a bit of effort, but my plan has been a success, thank God!

Chayele　You know, Avram, I'm afraid for Rosa's health: you know how weak her nerves are.

Grossman   Well, there's not much we can do about that. Her nerves will get stronger ... Shh! It seems Rosa's coming.

Scene 3

(ROSA, GROSSMAN, CHAYELE)

Rosa   Good morning, Papa!

Grossman (*kissing her head*)   Good morning, sweetheart. So, you aren't coming with us?

Rosa   No, Papa, I'm afraid you'll be going alone.

Grossman   Well, if you say so ... But tell me, Rosa, again: have you decided with certainty to be Neumann's wife? Something's telling me that your whole heart's not in it.

Rosa   No, Papa. It seems that way to you, but it's settled.

Grossman   Believe me, Rosa, this is a good lot for you, and for us it's not bad either. I have to tell you, my dear child, that I can't provide you with the kinds of riches that I once thought, and Neumann is a brave man. It's obvious that he really just wants you for you. He didn't say a word to me about money. Even though six months ago I gave him a cold refusal on your account, he never stopped favoring you. Twice during the week he was away, I received letters in which he would ask about you, about how you're doing. Believe me, my dear, that if I hadn't recognized this as an opportunity for your happiness, I surely would not have striven so strongly for this outcome. But your good fortune is our good fortune. So much happiness filled my and your mother's hearts when we heard that you'd come to this conviction yourself, that you know we only want what's best for you and that you didn't decline ... It'll be the right thing, my child, and when we combine our capital, and work together, it'll be a great fortune for all of us ... Oh, Neumann understands business. It'll be good, Rosa, you'll see!

Rosa   Yes, Papa. I know you want what's best for me. My luck is your luck. Lovely, good, dear Papa, dear Mama!

Grossman   Well, go rest up ...

Chayele (*kissing* ROSA)   Oh, my dear, lovely, good daughter.

Grossman   Good, that's enough. Go rest, daughter. Chayele, we must get going. We talk too much!

Chayele   Rosale, take the key. See to it that everything stays in order, my child.

Grossman   Come, come. We're going to arrive after everyone!

Chayele   I'm coming, I'm coming! See to it, Rosale.

Rosa   Yes, very well. (GROSSMAN *and* CHAYELE *exit*.)

Scene 4

(ROSA alone.)

Rosa   One joy remains for me: that at least I have found a way to put my parents at ease; one consolation: that they don't know of my wounds. Oh, dear father, if you only knew what is happening in your unhappy daughter's heart ... how many tears you would shed alongside her! But what would come of that? It would be even harder for me if I had to see their suffering, their despair! I can barely console myself, as I sacrifice my happiness for the sake of my parents ... So let it be Neumann, let it be whoever—it's all the same! So what?! Love without interest is not holy. But what is holy? Let me at least preserve the love I have for my devoted parents. Oh, how I would have traded my parents' calm for *you*, Adolf. Yes, *before*, I would've been able to, but not now. You didn't earn it. I sacrificed everything for your love—all of my ideals! Oh, if only I were able to console myself, I'd be able to return to the track of my ordinary life. If only I could stop feeling so wronged! Oh, how I've been torn apart, my heart broken, the most holy part of me, shattered and shredded into dust. Yes, I, I alone am guilty for believing in words. Oh, how I'd like to forget him! I don't know what to think of him. Did he ever really seriously consider what he said to me? Perhaps he belongs to the class of people who can say something and really think it one day, and then the next day say the exact opposite and mean it just as much. Yes, perhaps he belongs to the class of people who change their heart's feelings according to how the wind blows. I see clearly now that it wasn't for nothing that I was sometimes afraid. He used to try to convince me with all of his strength that it was possible to free myself from my promise to him. Maybe because he felt within himself that such a thing *was* possible. Well, apparently for him it was possible: he went to a new place, fresh ideas, different people. The mind produces new thoughts. There's no telling what the mind can transmit to the heart. Of course, what does *he* care? *I* can't forget! Should I sacrifice myself for empty platitudes? Who needs such an offering? Finally, from the minute that I decided to become Neumann's wife, I somehow feel so much lighter. Let there at least be some kind of resolution; it doesn't matter what, as long as it's something. I no longer receive Adolf's letters with such fear. I read them now with patience. With patience also I look at every phrase, reading even what is written between the lines—beautiful ideas! And how each letter is colder than the last … so what!? One doesn't have to lose all strength, and especially not pride … I cannot allow my own self-love to be trampled upon. I can still love … but lower myself, never! I remain Neumann's wife! Adolf's heart, Adolf's mind is lost to me. He no longer exists for me. It's only been half a year, but oh, how everything has changed!

Scene 5

(ROSA *is pacing. Resolutely, she crosses to* NEUMANN.)

(GROSSMAN, CHAYELE, NEUMANN)

Neumann   Good day, dear lady. Finally! I've survived the most awful stretch of time.

Rosa   Good day! How are you? Sit! Surely you're tired from the journey.

Neumann (*sitting*)   Thank you.

Grossman   Well, my love, your mother and I will get everything ready for when the guests arrive.

Chayele   Rosale! It seems I must have given you the keys?

Rosa   Yes, here they are! (*She hands them over;* GROSSMAN *and* CHAYELE *leave.*)

Neumann   You said I appear tired from the journey ... I don't take that to be much of a compliment, dear Rosa! I must tell you that not only a short journey such as this but even the greatest sacrifice would not be so difficult for me if only it meant I may be rewarded with your presence. I know you must hate to be spoken to with the ordinary phrases and chatter that are used when I speak with everyone else, but just because the phrases and words are so common, it doesn't necessarily mean that their meaning must be as well.

Rosa   Mr. Neumann, speak with me as you would anyone. I don't know why you would think that you need to speak to me differently than you speak to everyone else. I have to tell you that it very much pleases me simply to be spoken to seriously. Pardon me, Mr. Neumann, I have to tell you that I love very much when a voice speaks to me not from the mind but from the heart. Anyone may speak as they wish, as long as he speaks with integrity.

Neumann   Your last words give me the courage to speak
with you, because indeed, what I want to say to you is
not from my mind but from my heart. You know that our
conditions have arisen somewhat unusually. At this point, we
know quite well what we need to be to one another, but the
reasons that we both have for this we still have yet to frankly
discuss: and you know well that that wasn't my fault. Believe
me, Rosa, I am not looking to sneak myself into the secret
corners of your heart; I also love freedom as you do, but
freedom does not allow me to enter into this as a blind man;
freedom demands that I simply pose the question to you that
consists of these few words: did you, in good conscience, and
with a steady will, decide to be my wife, as your father wrote
to me? I am not asking you about love—the feelings that I
have for you are more than enough to make a joyful bond
between us. I don't want to ask you how sympathetic you are
to me—I don't want to know. I'm allowing myself enough
space to imagine it as I please. I just want to know, I want to
hear from your lips that this is all according to your own will.

Rosa   You're saying that you want me to answer what
you're asking, and to make my declaration from the bottom
of my heart.

Neumann   No, no, Rosa, my love, I guard very much one's
inner feelings and I do not wish to be the boss of anyone's
heart, to know precisely how everything looks within them. I
wouldn't want to touch that temple that is so holy to me. Yes,
Rosa, your heart is sacred to me!

Rosa   It is possible that what I am going to say to you might
extinguish a bit of the fire that you're lighting at the altar of
your temple there.

Neumann   That's why I really don't want to know.

Rosa   If not, then I won't tell you. Stay there at your altar!
As for my part, I only wish that, with time, we will be able to
make a new altar. Mr. Neumann: I've decided to be your wife.

I would like for my heart to become less torn. I'd like for there to be a little place to erect an altar that can bring some joy to one's life. No, my heart is not clear and open for you, but apparently it seems this is what you want!

Neumann   Throw away those discouraging thoughts, my wise Rosa. One takes what one is given in life. (*He kisses her hand.*)

Rosa   You're right! You can't have what's not there!

The curtain falls.

ACT II

Third curtain.

(*A nicely furnished room at* NEUMANN'*s house. A proper table.*)

Scene 1

Rosa (*entering*)   Yet another beautifully set table! Once again we await the guests … Guests! … At least Papa won't arrive tonight of all nights. From his letter it sounded like he needed to come tonight, but surely in that case I would've received a telegram? … Thank God it's not tonight. It's bad enough that he'll find out sooner or later about my misfortune. If I were more superstitious I'd have quite a bit of reproach for a God who would put all this together … I could never have imagined that my own father would make me so unhappy. My poor father! If he only knew what was going on here! He already knows about all the expensive business "permits" that have stolen his wealth, but he has no idea that that is merely a speck compared to the enormous pain that his daughter carries day and night. I should at least be able to hide the disgrace of my depraved lifestyle here in my husband's house. My husband! What dreadful irony! My husband sits entire nights playing cards, people float in and out of the house. From everything pure and good: from honor, from love, even from money, everything reduced to permits. They do business; engage with generals, counts, dukes … Nothing but "necessary business"! Let's just see if my jewelry hasn't yet also run away for the sake of "necessary business"! (*She approaches the table, from which she removes a jewelry box, opens it up, and looks.*) Gone! Surely he took it! (*She paces around the house back and forth.*) Yes, *that's* his business!

Scene 2

(ROSA, NEUMANN)

Neumann What's wrong, Rosa? Why are you pacing around like that? What's the matter with you?

Rosa What's the matter with me? I'm great!

Neumann Tell me, my dear!

Rosa (*glaring at him*) What do you want, sir?

Neumann What do I want? I want you not to call me "sir"!

Rosa And I want you not to call me your dear! What am I to you and what are you to me? True, you didn't want to know what was in my heart before we got married. I took it as a sign that you're a gentleman. Turns out it was just your pathetic depraved nature. You didn't want to know because for you it was more than enough to simply marry Grossman's daughter—who you assumed was richer than she was—but you made a bit of a mistake in the end. And when you decided you'd put enough effort into the masquerade, how fast you threw down your mask! The day after we came here, you were already unrecognizable. Before the wedding, you would never have told me that you spend all your time playing cards, that you make picnics and the like!

Neumann   What is so bad about playing cards? You immerse yourself in a certain society, and when you make a picnic …

Rosa   Sure, it looks like you're just playing cards, but what do you call someone who never does anything else?

Neumann   I have no interest in what you call those people. I have nothing to argue with you about. What is making you speak like this today all of a sudden? You're usually so quiet!

Rosa   It's no longer possible to remain silent. You're always driving me deeper into the abyss. I, Mr. Neumann, will never live as you do. Look at yourself. Do you really believe it is possible for us to live our lives together?

Neumann   Well, why not, Rosale? We can live here or in another city. If you want, we can go to St. Petersburg. If you would just love your husband and muster the desire to understand him we could live happily ever after. I love to live; I love socializing. But you're always hiding, retreating as though you'd like to live the life of our matriarch Mother Rachel. It's not suitable for Neumann's wife. You need to fall in line with your husband.

Rosa   You're being so polite today; there must be some kind of news …

Neumann   Yes, yes, you've noticed, my angel. Today I am feeling lively and I have more love for you than ever before. Today, I have special guests coming, who would very much like to get to know you. I want you to see to it that they are well received …

Rosa   You're quite mistaken. *Your* guests are not *my* guests.

Neumann   What are you talking about? You know very well that I hate being interrupted. Oh, come here, my doll. You'll do this for me, of course. Surely, you love me. All women love Neumann. So what are you, then? You're surely nothing more than a woman. Oh, come here. Beg my pardon for speaking so much foolishness to your husband. (*He starts towards her.*)

Rosa (*taking several steps back*)   I'm already sick to death of all this. Please leave me in peace from your love, your hate, your acquaintances, and your socializing. We are too far away from one another: I consider you a pitiful person. It's a sign that I don't even find it worth asking why you took my jewelry. I already know that you won't give it back.

Neumann   Today, Rosa, you may speak as you wish. I won't be offended. I don't want to spoil the evening. But why do you need your jewelry tonight? Are we going somewhere today? Are we expecting guests?

Rosa   See how you are! You can't, even for one moment, stop showing your true colors. *We* are waiting for guests to arrive *here*; *we* aren't going anywhere. One would think we live a very happy life together that we're never apart even for a minute. I don't know why you talk like this. You know very well that days go by without us seeing one another, where we don't even want to see one another and when we do see one another, even then it's only in spite of you showing *who* you really are while I become more and more convinced of *what* you really are. It's clear you *can't* speak any other way. Your cruelty continues to show itself, even where it is already known too well.

Neumann   Oh, here you are insulting me again! I already told you I don't want to fight today. You know you're in the wrong. Now get ahold of yourself and see to it that you receive General Skritsky's acquaintances nicely. This week all of the permit business will finally come to an end. You'll see, just be polite with the guests.

Rosa Even I could see this permit business came to an end a long time ago. Surely you could as well. You realize, of course, that you've cashed in on these "permits" long enough and there is nothing left to take. You even took my jewelry. You're a practical man. You know when something is coming to an end and where you can make a beginning. So, what? The *treasurer himself* doesn't know the difference between an end and a beginning?! Well, I really must tell you: you know business!

Neumann Oh, how it pains me that you don't even *try* to understand me. Come here, my doll! Do you know how beautiful you are? You must have no idea. Don't be a fool, sweetheart, Rosale; receive our guests kindly. If you want the jewelry, I'll return it to you with the utmost pleasure. It's simply that I knew you would have wanted me to take it if it meant that it would be given to the right person. You already know what for …

Rosa I'm becoming more like you the more I speak to you. It's time I finally understand that there's no use in trying to speak to you like you're a person.

Neumann Well, Rosale, I'm going now. As for you: get ready to greet the guests.

Rosa You can count on it that I will not come out to greet your guests.

Neumann What do you mean? I actually *want* you to be included in our company and you're saying no?! … Do you not know who Neumann is?!

Rosa I've already imagined every possible scenario.

Neumann I am going to tell you one more time: in this house, what I say goes! (*He exits.*)

Scene 3

Rosa (*pacing around the room*)   Oh, this is simply too much to bear!

Servant   Madame: a telegram!

Rosa (*grabbing it and reading*)   From Papa! Quick, get my coat! (*The* SERVANT *leaves and returns with a coat.*) Oh, no, it's already too late (*looking at the clock*). The train already arrived. Why are you only bringing this to me now, so late?

Servant   It was brought straight away.

Rosa   It was late! Run down, and wait by the train. No, I'll go myself. (*She runs head-first and returns with* GROSSMAN.) Papa, dear Papa! (*Kissing him*) It really *is* you!

Scene 4

(ROSA, GROSSMAN)

Grossman   Oh, don't act so surprised! Of course it's me! (*Wiping her tears.*)

Rosa   Yes! You, you: dear, beloved Papa. (*Laughing and crying.*) Take off your overcoat. Come here, I want to take it off for you.

Grossman   Leave it, I'll take it off myself. (*He takes off his overcoat.*)

Rosa   I only just now received your telegram. I wanted to come to meet you at the train station and now look! Here, you've come alone, dear, good Papa! (*Kissing him.*) Oh, how glad I am to see you again ... How's Mama, my dear, beloved mother? Oh, how I'd love to see her ...

Grossman   She wanted so much to come with me, but I didn't want to bring her. It's too much stress for her to travel in winter.

Rosa   Yes, you're right. How could she travel now? Anyway, Papa, what would you like to drink? Tea or coffee?

Grossman   You know I prefer tea … Don't rush. Just wait a moment.

Rosa   No, no … Why wait!? (*Summoning the* SERVANT) Bring in some tea! And something to go with it! (SERVANT *exits.*)

Grossman   Well, my dear daughter, how are you? Come here, I'd like to get a good look at you. You don't look so well. You've lost weight.

Rosa   Oh, it only looks that way …

Grossman   No, it doesn't only look that way … Now, where's your husband?

Rosa   He's not home … he'll return shortly.

Grossman   Well, we'll talk then. I have much to discuss with you. So much. We must remedy this … but later.

Rosa   Yes, of course. We'll speak later. (SERVANT *brings tea and pours it. They both drink.*)

Grossman   You know, Rosale, I'm a little upset with you.

Rosa   Upset?! At me?! What for?!

Grossman   Yes, for your letters! They've been so short. You've written so little about what's going on with you. Your mother and I have been worried sick.

Rosa   You're right. They really were quite short. But what should I have written? … There wasn't anything to write.

Grossman   I understood that. And that's truly what brought me down here. I must know everything! You must not and you need not hide from me, my dear child.

Rosa   Papa, we already agreed to talk later. We will discuss everything then. First, I want you to rest up from your journey, dear, precious Papa! (*Kissing him.*)

Grossman   My dear, lovely child! Calm yourself, sweetheart.

Rosa   Here, come into my room and you can get changed and rest up.

Grossman (*standing up*)   I see that you still haven't eaten lunch. The table is set. You're eating late.

Rosa   Yes, yes. Later. Come, Papa! (*To herself.*) Before he arrives with his guests!

Grossman   Well, sweetheart, show me where to go. (ROSA *and* GROSSMAN *exit arm in arm through the side door.*)

Scene 5

(NEUMANN, JULIA, AMELIA, MINA, GUESTS)

Guest 1   Well, Neumann, you promised a good soirée—let's see.

Julia   Well, it sure won't be anything like St. Petersburg. Do you remember, Neumann?

Amelia   He promised something else as well.

All   What? What?

Amelia   Well, guess!

Julia   Aha! He promised to give us the honor of introducing us to his wife! But something is making it hard for me to believe that it's going to happen: according to what I've heard, she's been somewhat keeping her distance from Neumann.

Guest 1   Maybe he's keeping his distance from her.

Amelia   Neumann, you *did* promise ...

Neumann   Soon, soon! My darling will surely come soon (*Grabbing her by the waist*).

Julia   What are you doing, Neumann! You're unhappy here, watched by such a law-abiding woman. Oh, Neumann! Those law-abiding women cannot bear this! Hahaha!

Neumann   We were married according to the truest and most proper tradition. Under a canopy, with musicians—how do you like that?! (*They all sit around the table. Several start playing cards.*)

Guest 1   Perhaps she's the kind of woman who's worth taking by lawful marriage!

Julia   Well, what else—with how good she is at digging into our daily bread, protecting her husband, one ought to bet she'll give him many children ... Oh, Neumann, yes, in a few years, you'll be raving about domestic joys! You're becoming a true family man!

Neumann   What do you mean, my Julia? You know I was ready to experience those domestic joys with *you*, but you—you're merely a wind fleeting through a field.

Julia   With me you're too late. After all, how would you hope to catch the wind in a field? The wind blows for everyone.

Neumann   Don't think it's such a good thing that the wind blows for everyone.

Julia   If the wind didn't blow for everyone, it certainly wouldn't choose to cool *you* down, would it Neumann? (*She approaches him and takes him by the hand.*)

Neumann   If all women had the kind of fire as you have inside, they would burn the world to ashes—bravo, Julia! With you, no one is disappointed!

Julia   Oh, and you'll be happier with your "Rachel the Matriarch" of a wife? You see, Neumann, I quite like her, for being so tough compared to you. She actually avoids you, so I've heard.

Neumann   Foolishness! It's my house! If I wanted it any other way, she wouldn't avoid me at all!

Amelia (*running to* NEUMANN)   So, Neumann, introduce your wife to us!

Neumann   Soon!

Amelia   You see! (*To* JULIA) They say she's quite beautiful …

Julia   She's not ugly, but she has quite an ordinary face. I've seen her.

Guest 1   As long as she's beautiful, that's good enough. One can accomplish anything if he only has a beautiful wife … especially Neumann! Isn't that right, ladies and gentlemen?

Julia   There are times, however, when even Neumann must forfeit and fail … It's happened before …

Amelia   Never mind that, Neumann can make white from black.

Julia   Once upon a time …

Guest 2   Julia, I'm quite enjoying myself with you today! Neumann's earned a bit of your teasing.

Julia   Oh, and you think you've earned my doing it for your sake?!

Guest 2   It appears so!

Julia   Indeed it's only an appearance. I've been too good to you. That's a mistake—you aren't worth it.

Guest 2   Julia!

Julia   Well, that's me! ... Neumann, enough playing cards already—come here.

Neumann   I am not playing at all. What is it that you want, Madame?

Julia   Oh, how polite Neumann is feeling today: Well—we want the honor of seeing Madame Neumann.

Amelia   Yes, the time has come!

Neumann   Soon! (*He yells.*) Mina!

Mina   What is your order, sir!

Neumann   Go, tell the Madame that the guests have already arrived. Tell her I beg her presence.

Julia   He's begging, you see? Ha ha! He's *begging* her!

Mina   The Madame is not well.

Julia   Do you hear, Neumann? Your wife is ill and you know nothing of it?

Neumann   *Who* is ill? Mina, go tell the Madame we are waiting for her entrance! (MINA *exits.*)

Julia   You'll see, Neumann. You've lost all of your authority. It seems your "Mother Rachel" has turned against you. I've already heard ...

Guest 1   No, not Neumann! He is a master at his craft. She'll come, dear ladies. What do you think—if not, wouldn't it be a shame that we've wasted today's spectacle. Amelia has been longing to make the acquaintance of Madame Neumann. A shame: Louisa is going to the theatre today.

Amelia   Well, you could have gone with Louisa. Who was stopping you?

Guest 1   You stopped me.

Amelia   Well isn't that nice!

Guest 1   Oh, it wasn't you? So what do you call it then when I can't tear myself away from your grip for a single minute? Amelia, bad, cruel Amelia.

Amelia (*kissing his forehead*)   Brat! (MINA *enters.*)

Mina   The Madame cannot come out. She can't leave her papa.

Neumann   What papa?!

All   Papa?! What papa?

Julia   Haha!

Amelia   A papa!

Mina (*angrily*)   Well, yes, the Madame's papa. He's only just recently arrived.

Julia   Neumann, you have a guest, and know nothing of it?

Neumann   To hell with him!

Amelia   Shouldn't she at least have begged our pardon!? Oh, Neumann, give up!

Neumann (*To* MINA)   Go tell the Madame: I *order* her to come in.

Mina   I am sure she won't come. She does not want to leave her papa.

Neumann   No arguing! You go when you are sent—go! (MINA *exits.*)

Julia   A little papa has suddenly appeared! Haha!

Neumann   What kind of a papa? One who shows up on a whim!? *That's* what you call nerve! (*Yelling loudly and angrily.*) Mina!

Mina (*running in*)   Don't yell! The Madame implored you not to yell. Her papa has lain down to sleep.

Julia   Well, if her papa is asleep, surely she can come in to greet us.

Neumann   Well, Mina, did you pass along that which I ordered you?

Mina   Yes.

Neumann   And?

Mina   She cannot come. She isn't well.

Neumann   Why, she ought to have her pride beaten out of her. That would make it easier for her. Go to her *again*. Tell her that I am ordering her to come in. (MINA *exits.*)

Julia   It's a good thing *we* aren't such law-abiding women, lest we would also become ill. Such a scene would make such an impression on our fragile nerves. Just imagine, if I or Amelia would collapse with a scream, God banish the thought! Our cavaliers would be afraid if it were something truly frightful! Oh, isn't it good we aren't such lawful women and that we have such strong nerves?

Neumann   Julia, I can hardly recognize you today.

Julia   You want to recognize me? Come here! (*She kisses him.*)

Neumann   Oh, Julia! (MINA *enters.*)

Mina   Under no circumstances can the Madame come in.

Neumann   She can't come? I think she will come! (*He starts towards the door.*)

Julia   What are you going to do? Come here, Neumann.

Neumann (*tearing himself free*)   Let go of me! What do you care?

Julia   Tell me: what is it you're going to do?

Neumann   Let me go. You yourself wanted this. (*He tears himself free and runs toward the far door.*)

Julia   What is going to happen here? He's gone mad!

Amelia   Nothing is going to happen. He'll come back in with her.

Julia   This has already gone too far, my friends. How could you have allowed this? Such a woman as this?

Amelia   You yourself are becoming a lady with such nerves.

Guest 1 (*tipsy*)   Let her come in. I'd like to see her. (ROSA*'s voice is heard.*)

Rosa (*yelling from the wings*)   What do you want from me?

Neumann   Do you want me to beg you? (*They all stand.*)

Julia   I swear, this has gone too far. (NEUMANN *drags* ROSA *in by the hand, who is pale with fear.*)

Neumann   Here: your presence was requested, Madame. (*He sits her down angrily on an armchair.* ROSA, *terribly afraid, looks around and begins to cry and laugh.*)

Mina   What's wrong, Madame?

Julia (*bringing water*)   Calm down; take a bit of water.

Mina   Leave it; it will pass.

Amelia (*To* GUEST 1)   A whole drama, just like in the theatre. She knows her craft!

Neumann   She's trying to show who she really is—not at Neumann's expense! You didn't want to come when Neumann ordered—well, then! There will be a time when you are searching for him at the far ends of the earth and you won't find him! Well done: you'll need your little divorce but where will your Neumann be?! I'll pay you back for this!

Julia (*looking at* NEUMANN *severely*)   Enough, Neumann!

Neumann   No, it's not enough. Just wait: I'll see to it that you become accustomed to a life of sorrow. Oh, how you'll search high and low for your Neumann!

Amalia   Let her rest; she's exhausted herself, the poor thing.

Neumann   Mother Rachel will search for her Neumann, *she'll* need the divorce, but where—where will he be then? (*He whistles.*) Come, Amelia—only with you can a person truly live in this world. You don't need a divorce—no legal marriage! Live every day like it's your last! And to *you*, Madame, *adieu*!

Amelia   Poor thing, she's weeping. You've made her unhappy. It's undignified.

Neumann   Come, Amelia!

All   Haha! Weeping! What is she weeping for? All her ships have already sunk! (*All exit except ROSA, who stays, weeping and laughing. GROSSMAN runs in, scared. Seeing ROSA, he begins to yell and cry.*)

Grossman   Oh, no! What's happened to you, my dear daughter? Oh, how I've made you so unhappy! …

Curtain falls.

ACT III

Fourth curtain.

The scene is a tavern in Odessa. Many tables with people sitting and drinking. Music is playing. Servers are hurrying between tables with teapots. People enter and exit continually.

Scene 1

(ROSEMAN *and* BRANCH *sitting and drinking at a table.*)

Roseman   A bitter time in this here town ... no work, and that's that. I've already pawned my watch, see? It's so bad, I'm afraid people will need to pawn their own coats as the only way to earn a buck in all of Odessa.

Branch   Nothing like the business we used to have, that's for sure. Say, you remember a year ago when we made a match for that young man from Berdichev? Now, that made us a pretty penny!

Roseman   What match? I don't think I know what you're talking about.

Branch   Oh, that's right. You weren't there. I'll tell you how it all happened. Here's a nice story for you: See, so this young gentleman from Berdichev walks in and he shows up with another man, probably of a similar kind. And they come into the tavern, and he's showing him all the wonders Odessa has to offer: a record player that plays all on its own, the beauty of the parlor and all the other treasures in there. So I start listening in on their conversation, see, and right away I realize that they're just poor little lambs. So, you know, of course I didn't hold back long before I made it my business to become acquainted with the gentlemen, so I started in on the young Polish Jew. I think to myself: *Say, I ought to find out what brought this young man to Odessa.* So, soon as I begin to inquire, I realize that he had quite a nice fortune to his name, see, and his companion there was a matchmaker who brought him to Odessa in hopes of finding him the perfect bride. Well, of course, you know where this story goes: as soon as I hear the word "bride"—in Odessa we have no shortage of brides … So that's when Friedler shows up, see, and it wasn't long before we found a bride and he sure liked her—you know Friedler's wife, don't you? Oh, she's a beautiful one. Who wouldn't like her?

Roseman You suggested Friedler's wife to him? I swear, you all are no fools. Well! So, what happened?! Wow, a great story!

Branch Well, listen here, you see. He liked his bride very much. Gifts were flying like fists in a good fight! First a few earrings, next a broach, until we made sure he had his fill of broaches. Well, after that we sent him on his way! What else could we do—getting married to someone else's wife?! But this year, I'm telling you, it's deadly for business. Terrible business. And the young folks don't even want to be married off. (*He looks over to another table.*) Hey, just a minute. Say, look—who is *that?* Some kind of fresh meat!

Scene 2

(YISROEL, BRANCH, ROSEMAN)

Yisroel (*alone*) Oh, this journey is wearing me out! It's been six months already of running around the world searching for that thief, that charlatan, and I still can't find him. Oh, money! Money—Oh the things one does for just a taste of it. Traveling around looking for some guy! They promised me quite a nice sum if I manage to find him and wrestle out a signature from him on the divorce. But what good does this do for me if I *can't* find him? But what lowlife can't you find here in Odessa!? One more month! And if I don't find

him here, I'm going home. Time to let it be as it may. Such
a pity for that poor, unfortunate woman who can't marry
her true love until she gets a divorce from this criminal …
Almost every day I receive a letter from her and Adolf. They
beg me not to rush home, saying I might find him after all,
that I ought to be questioning this person and that—perhaps
someone has seen him …

Branch (*To* ROSEMAN)   Let me go listen in. He's talking, so
he must be saying something.

Roseman   What do you mean—just go up to a complete
stranger? He'll see right through you and know who you are
and exactly what it is you want, you crook!

Branch   Shh, don't worry about it. I know what I'm doing.
(*He approaches* YISROEL.) Hello there! Where are you from,
sir?

Yisroel   Hello to you! From far away, my friend, very far.
I'm traveling, you see, on such business that I am simply
delighted when someone takes the initiative to approach me.

Branch   Is that so? Yes, well anything can happen in
this world. Say, what do you mean when you say you're
delighted?

Yisroel   Well, sir, I'm searching for a certain man, and I'm
certain that I will find him here in Odessa.

Branch   What kind of a man? Did he steal something? Or
worse—did he cheat you, God forbid?

Yisroel   He's worse than a thief—he deserted his wife. They
sent me out into the world in the hope I can find him and
wrestle a divorce out of him.

Branch   The divorce will be easy. It's finding the bastard
that's the trick. Say, why don't you do me a favor and
describe what this guy looks like. See, I'm the kind of guy
who has a habit of being everywhere at once. I'm a wheat

broker, see, and I've seen the inside of every office, hotel, and coffee shop in Odessa.

Roseman (*To himself*)   All the taverns too!

Branch   From time to time the occasion arises I have reason to visit a tavern as well, such as this one here. It happens, when making a deal with certain types, you go where the business takes you … So, do you recall his appearance? Perhaps some kind of a distinguishing feature?

Yisroel   I'm sure you understand—I myself only met the man once. I'm sure I could identify him, but aside from that there is one giveaway …

Branch (*To himself*)   Oh, one of our guys will fit the bill! (*To* YISROEL) Well, as long as there's some kind of distinguishing feature, that's great. Something that really set him apart; that way, when we find him, we'll know for *certain* that it's him. Perhaps I'll see him somewhere. It could happen, just by chance, I might cross paths with such a man—so, tell me what it is—if I recognize him, I'll come and tell you. (*To himself*) Perhaps I'll need something in exchange, but I just need to wait for the right moment to make my move—let's hear more.

Yisroel   With this, you'll know beyond any doubt! He has a big scar on his right hand, from a fall, but I would know him even without the scar …

Branch (*To himself*)   A scar! Fidler has a scar on his hand, though it's not so big, but surely this guy will believe it is; let's just hear some more about what the guy looks like. (*To* YISROEL) So, what else? What color hair?

Yisroel   Oh, right. He's fair, light hair, even a little reddish …

Branch (*To himself*)   It works! It's a match, as sure as I'm standing here!

Yisroel   Average build—not a big guy, not a small guy—just average.

Branch   Perfect! (*To* YISROEL) Listen to what I'm telling you, my friend—I know someone who has just the kind of appearance you're describing, you see. Perhaps it's him?

Yisroel   You know someone who fits the description? Where! Where is he?

Branch   Don't rush now. It may not be him after all. I can't say for sure.

Yisroel   Oh, you don't know how long I've been searching. I'm wearing myself down to the bone. But aside from me, there's simply a poor wife in need of God's mercy, who's waiting desperately for a divorce. She simply can't bear any more troubles.

Branch   Is that right? Oh, isn't it a shame our poor decent children end up so unlucky!

Yisroel   So you understand the kind of misfortune that has overtaken the poor woman? She lived with him all of two months—but what qualifies truly as *living*? I have to tell you—that Neumann came down to us and gave such a convincing performance that we all thought he was truly a successful man, a sharp man, a businessman. And he played his cards so good that our most successful man, Mr. Avram Grossman, gave him his own daughter, Rosa, still just a child. A little doll still full of joy and God's grace, and now she's left an *agune*—an abandoned wife forever chained to the scoundrel, unless we can find him and make him come to his senses and divorce her! Poor thing. I'm telling you, my heart is torn apart. I have no idea how I can return to them if I don't find him.

Branch (*To himself*)   I think his wallet might also get torn apart. I bet they offered this fool quite a pretty penny. (*To* YISROEL) Don't worry, my friend—I know someone who fits the bill, you see—I can't quite remember his name, but I'll go find him and find out today, and tomorrow or the day after at the latest. I'll come back here to this tavern and if I see you here I'll let you know if he goes by Neumann. It seems … Neumann you said, right?

Yisroel   Yes, yes, Neumann.

Branch   Yes, very well. If his name is Neumann I'll come back and tell you tomorrow.

Yisroel   I beg of you—please come back and tell me, either way and straight away. Perhaps I should come with you?

Branch   No, no. I still have to make my rounds. I'm a very busy guy—but I'll keep you informed.

Yisroel   I must offer you something in exchange for all your troubles.

Branch   Leave it to God's graces—see, I'm not the kind of guy who's interested in such things. I simply see a guy who's struggling, and when I happen to know something about this kind of business, and when it seems to me that I've seen the guy you're looking for, I just want to be helpful, see, out of compassion.

Yisroel   Oh, you can just imagine what kind of reward you'll receive. You'll never do a greater deed as long as you live! I won't leave this spot until you come back to give me an answer. He simply *must* be here. Where else would such a charlatan run off to?

Branch   Well, in the meantime, take care. If the guy's name is Neumann, I'll do you a favor and bring him back here—and if I don't return, you'll know it was the wrong guy.

Yisroel   Go in good health—with God's help. God help us all that we may find him … Yes, even though I only met him once, I'll recognize him.

Branch   What do you mean? Why wouldn't you recognize him?! Goodbye! (*He returns the table where* ROSEMAN *sits.*) Did you hear, Roseman, he's only seen the guy *once*. Did you hear all that?

Roseman   I heard every word—didn't miss a letter. A fine piece of work you've cut out for yourself. But, we must be smart about it.

Branch   See, now we just need to talk Fidler into it.

Roseman   Now that might be a bit of a problem … But say you and I were to work together? We may be able to convince him to do it for a little less …

Branch   What are you talking about? The whole thing depends on Fidler! He has the scar on his hand … He needs to forge the divorce—he'll have to be Neumann. No, this time we have to approach him with a little respect … Truly, we must handle this with integrity, you see … Well, we'll see. In the meantime, you stay here and make sure the dead guy over there doesn't come back to life. Watch from a distance. I'll be back soon. Say, where do you think Fidler might be about now?

Roseman   What is there to think about? Surely Fidler is with Nachman the Ruddy in the cellar. He's probably playing cards with the guys.

Branch   Well, I'm off. Keep your eyes open! (*He leaves.*)

Yisroel   Maybe he really is here. Something in my heart told me he must be here, he must. Well, might as well have a bit of wine. I'm simply exhausted. Oh, I'll bring such wonderful news back home. I wonder where he could be … Based on what the man told me, it simply must be him. Well, can you believe it? Everyone always says that Odessa is a living hell, a merciless place. In the end, there are fellow Jews everywhere. See, that was a stand-up guy. He asked me about everything, wanted to know all the details, not a word about himself. The moment I even mentioned payment he didn't want to hear of it. Apparently there really are decent people in this world. He promised to come back soon. Soon I'll know where I stand. (*He signals for wine and drinks, contemplating everything with wonder as music plays.*)

Roseman (*To himself*)   Look at him sitting and waiting … Ha! That's my boy. I ought not talk to him at all. We have to be careful, so he doesn't suspect anything. My job is simply to sit here and watch the poor fool; the pawn can't move until Branch comes back. Oh, we'll get him alright. The time has finally come. It's been a long enough dry spell since the last time we had such a fine piece of business within reach.

Branch (*running in out of breath*)   Well! It's him! (YISROEL *stands, afraid.*) It's Neumann! Let me tell you what'll happen now: He'll sign off on the divorce but it's going to cost you. As soon as I told him what I need him to do, he said he won't sell his signature for cheap. I told him to come back here with me …

Yisroel   Well?

Branch   He wouldn't come, see. He said: if they want, they can come to me.

Yisroel   Oh really! That little thief!

Branch   And there will have to be enough money!

Yisroel   The money's no problem as long as it really is him.

Branch   Yes, it's him alright. But, in any case, you can't give him as much as he's asking for. Say, I'll help you negotiate.

Yisroel   Oh. I thank God for sending me such a fine man as yourself. (*To himself*) At long last, it seems my journey will come to an end!

Branch   Come on now, let's go! He's waiting not far from here. I think we need to settle this as quickly as possible. Say, how much are you thinking of offering?

Yisroel How should I know what's appropriate?

Branch He mentioned quite a pretty penny to me.

Yisroel About ... how much?

Branch About ... a few thousand ...

Yisroel I have nowhere near that much!

Branch I don't think he'd let you off so easily even with the money. But still, I bet we can get him to shave off a few bucks. Why should we give so much money to such a scoundrel anyway?! It's simply a sin!

Yisroel I beg of you: let's work together. I'll make it worth your while.

Branch Ha! I'm sorry—you're a fool if you think I'm interested in your money or rewards.

Yisroel I beg your pardon, take no offense. I'm begging you. I just mean– why not? Such a favor is no small matter. Offering some kind of reward is only appropriate. But I understand what kind of a person you are: you simply have compassion for your fellow man—even one whom you don't know.

Branch Oh, what's the use of such talk? Come, we'd better go!

Yisroel Yes, let's go! Oh, God help us! May God have mercy on us! (*They leave.*)

Roseman (*following behind*) A pious patsy![1]

Curtain falls.

Fifth Curtain.

The scene is an ordinary living room.

Scene 1

(GROSSMAN, ROSA, and ADOLF)

Grossman   When I said I wanted to go myself, you wouldn't let me.

Adolf   Consider this honestly now—how could you go? You're so sick!

Grossman   Who's sick?! What's sick?! I'm healthy as a giant! I've wanted to go back for some time now—It's you who has been preventing me. (*He coughs.*) Just sit and wait for that fool to send a letter …

Rosa   I don't know why you get yourself so worked up, Papa.

Grossman   What do you mean "worked up"? I'm going crazy, I've waited enough. I'm sitting with my hands tied because of you two. I would travel the entire world, tear up the earth, and move walls if I could. There's nothing I wouldn't do if I could just bring him here myself! … Oh, yes, why I'd bring him, that scoundrel, that murderer!

Rosa   Oh, dear Papa! What has gotten into you so suddenly?

Grossman   What do you mean, "suddenly"? We haven't received even one single letter. That fool.

Adolf   How long has it been since the last letter?

Grossman   Ugh! It's so hard to be me. It's a bitter life I live. None of you knows the real me, and you cannot and need not pardon me.

Rosa   Papa! What nonsense are you speaking about— pardon you?! Of what are you guilty?

Grossman   Oh, *I am* guilty … I have sinned against you, my precious children. My dear, beloved children … Oh, you can't forgive me.

Rosa   Papa! That's just about enough talk about forgiveness.

Grossman   No. I'm not finished. A very heavy burden weighs upon my heart—very heavy, too heavy … (*He cries.*)

Rosa   Papa! Now you're starting to cry again?!

Grossman   Please let me take my leave. Please let me– I'm telling you!

Adolf   Where will you go? After what?

Grossman   I must go—to find *him*. I'll find him hidden underground. I must uncover him! I'll drain his blood as I exact my revenge on him! What did he want from me? He's robbed me rotten, left me beaten to death!

Rosa   Papa—I beg you. Please calm down!

Grossman   How could you ask me to calm down? Should I go to my grave and leave you an abandoned, chained wife?! No, I will not have it! You must let me go!

Rosa (*To* ADOLF)   Again with this nonsense. He's getting himself all worked up again.

Grossman   You can't just hold me here. It won't do any good. No person in this entire world will succeed at stopping me. No, I refuse to die and leave you an abandoned wife … Oh, trapped and paralyzed … imprisoned! (*He cries.*)

Rosa   Father—dear, beloved, beautiful—don't cry!

Grossman (*Hysterical weeping, crying out.*)

Adolf   Here—have some water. (*He hands him water.*)

Rosa You see—he's having another attack. Go, my dear, fetch the doctor.

Adolf What good will a doctor do? Calm down—don't act like this is the first time.

Rosa Come, Papa, you should lie down. (*She leads him out the door.*)

Adolf Oh, poor old man. His conscience never lets up. He's so burdened by the weight of his mistakes! Such great regrets …

Rosa (*returning*) He's lying down. Hopefully he can get some rest … I was afraid he might have another attack like the one the other week …

Adolf The reason he's doing worse than us, Rosa, is because it's on his account that any of this happened at all. It was his own doing. Could you have ever imagined we'd find ourselves in such a situation?

Rosa Why, yes I could, Adolf. I remember how you used to speak to me … You said something like this would happen if we weren't always here for each other. What we wanted so desperately to be between us—it was possible … but Neumann is a rare type of man.

Adolf You didn't want to believe me. It could have been something entirely different if your father hadn't been so fooled by Neumann and so disturbed by the attraction there was between us. We could've been so happy.

Rosa Oh, don't speak that way of my dear father. You see how he's suffering now, how ill he's become over this! The matter grants him no respite!

Adolf The matter couldn't grant anyone any respite!

Rosa You're mistaken, my dear. I myself am quite calm. I don't let myself be terrified by the thought that I might be left here an abandoned wife. Our love simply *must* be realized through an honest, decent life together. This situation is the last thing standing between us. If you think about it that way, it's almost a relief. Believe me, Adolf, one fleeting moment of your love is worth more to me than anything in the world. I simply don't know what else a person could possibly need. I considered you dead to me, and now I have you again!

Adolf   Oh Rosa. Rosa! How could I possibly redeem myself from how I've sinned against you? How could I possibly answer for how little I knew you, my smart, blessed Rosa? But I've already been punished, and it's punishment enough to see you here before my eyes knowing you love me as much as a person can love, and yet you cannot be mine.

Rosa   Why can't I be yours? I am *only* yours. If I cannot be your wife—I'll be your sister! Listen to me, Adolf. When I really think it over, I can see our relationship divided into three parts. You'll see how peaceful, how joyful these phases can make us, especially the last part, if we think about it this way. It's bittersweet: in the first part, I was your beloved Rosa. Oh, how good it is to recall the days; how pleasant it is to remember those precious moments! The second phase is when I was your bride, but not your living bride. No, your adorned and beloved bride lying in her grave. Your dead bride. She was lying in her grave when she went to the canopy with Neumann. But after that, at long last, we can finally enter into the third and final phase—the period of our love—and feel happy and joyous and glad!

Adolf   No, we can feel neither happy nor glad! That man will not keep you chained forever! We will find him and he will no longer stand in our way!

Rosa   Well, when we are freed from him, we will cross that bridge. In the meantime, I must believe with every bone in my body. I must completely immerse myself in the possibility of that third phase of our love. When I am no longer your bride, but your sister ... Oh, how precious, how dear we are to each other. Your sister, Adolf, is your best friend. You will always be able to talk to her about your deceased bride, because she knew her so well. With your sister, you can while away the bittersweet hours, reminiscing about every trait of your dear, beloved bride who is no longer in this world. You are always looking to be in the company of your sister, because she—and she alone—can give you the materials to truly remember what once was, my dear beloved brother! My heart does not ache for your beautiful bride, resting in her grave, but for you, my brother, only for you! How glad will I be in those moments, when I can finally sit with you and ease your suffering, hear you out, empathize with you. And if there comes a time when your sister notices that your pains are beginning to heal, that your worries getting smaller ... Oh, then, Adolf, she will strive to remind you of your deceased bride less and less often. However lovingly she speaks of your dead bride, you sister will hide all of her feelings. She will be happy that her dear brother is finding peace and forgetting what once was. And if there comes a time when your wounds are completely healed, and another woman can take the place of your dead bride, then your sister will no longer exist for you, and it just may be that then you will build a new and joyous life for yourself ... I don't want you, on my account, to deny yourself the greatest joy life has to offer—that of a family life!

Adolf   Rosa, you may be able to make yourself happy through all of these fantasies of yours. There is nothing you cannot find in your gentle heart. But I—I cannot. I can only find joy in reality. Fantasies do not make my situation any easier. I cannot lull myself into denial. I would only feel so good if I knew there were some kind of sacrifice I could offer that would free us once and for all from this law that binds our Jewish daughters. The law that gives no guarantees, no protections for our sisters and daughters, so that their lives should not need to depend upon the evil wills of depraved

men. Yes, Rosa, I feel the harsh reality and I see what it is
that you need to escape through your fantasies ... Oh, what
is it we are chained to, my dear Rosa? To Neumann's will!
You are not the first and you will not be the last to bear the
name of a chained wife. Oh, how many women—young and
fair—are faced with living their whole lives with that mark
of abandonment? How much misfortune is in that name—
waiting for a slim chance, at the mercy of evil men! No good
man leaves behind an imprisoned wife like this! So many
Jewish daughters are paralyzed—they see a beautiful world
before their eyes, oh how it draws them in! They want to
move but they are chained! My dear, I feel their suffering, and
I cannot find peace. I cannot lull myself to sleep while I am
trapped in a cradle of cobwebs. Oh, how strict these laws are.
We must abandon them! Jewish women sacrifice themselves
and live their whole lives lamenting—their parents and
friends suffering with them ... Women, in general, suffer more
than their share among all peoples. There are so many causes
for their suffering, but more than anything it is caused by
women being materially dependent upon men. He who gives
bread—he is a master! Yes, much time will still pass before
a woman is no longer chained to the man any more than the
man is to the woman.

Rosa   There should at least be a limited and specified
amount of time that we must wait for a man who has
abandoned his wife ... but to be entirely with no limit! Oh,
to be an abandoned wife is worse than being punished as a
criminal!

Adolf   There's no time frame—no term! Maybe one day it
will be different. If the rabbis wanted, they could make it so.
There have been some who have written about it. You see—a
man who has been thrown out by a woman can still remarry,
though it never happens. When does a woman throw out
her husband? Where does a woman have such a free world?
Where does a woman get the kind of education that would
allow her to live independently? Yes, seldom does a woman

throw out her husband, but still, an abandoned husband can seek freedom. Avenues for a man's freedom have always existed and still remain now. Because men have always had more rights than women. Even among us Jews, where women have been more valued than among other peoples. Until the ban of Rabbenu Gershom, every man had the right to have multiple wives. The ban forbade having more than one wife and was in effect for a hundred years. But after that, it remained as though it were a law that people had been steadfastly observing for many generations. That's the reason why when a woman throws out her husband, several rabbis or very learned men can free him, because it was just a ban, not a law.

Rosa   So, what? So how do you suppose the rabbis would be able to make it so that women can also be freed from forever being an *agune*, a chained and abandoned wife!? Of course they aren't bound by the ban of Rabbenu Gershom forever; that's why they can permit abandoned men to remarry. But is it not according to Torah that a woman may not have two husbands? Surely that's more than a ban?

Adolf   We do have one possibility: when the groom puts the ring on the bride's finger, as he says: "*hare as mekudeshes li*" "Behold, with this ring you are betrothed to me," he should insert the words that she will be his wife under all circumstances except if he should leave her for more than three years.

Rosa   So why is that not always the way it's done?

Adolf   Do you think that the rabbis resolve all of their questions as quickly as I can discuss them with you? You don't know, Rosa. There are some rabbis who are so attached to every single letter that they can't allow a single reform. It's not that they are doing this out of malice; they're simply so strongly bound to the letter of the law. You and I, my dear Rosale, we won't wait for a reform. If only Yisroel would return with that divorce. That way we could freely discuss these larger questions with a little less suffering.

Rosa It's been a long time since we've received a letter from him. Not since he wrote from Kiev that he was traveling to Odessa and from there back home ... We haven't heard a word from him. I simply don't know what to think.

Adolf I'm sure the reason he hasn't written is because he's expecting to return home soon. But with or without a divorce ... that I don't know.

Rosa However, it turns out—we've worried enough!

Adolf Well, Rosale, I must go. I'll be busy until eight o'clock. Try to relax, Rosa. You said yourself that your own will has the power to calm you down. Don't be too worried, dear. (*He hugs her.*)

Rosa Why do you fret like this? Why do you feel so hopeless about the situation?

Adolf When I see *your* troubles, I forget all about mine. *Adieu*, I'm going. A shame that we must work; I would much prefer to remain here.

Rosa Adolf!

Adolf *Adieu*! (*He approaches the door.* YISROEL *enters.*)

Scene 2

(ROSA, ADOLF, YISROEL, then GROSSMAN)

Yisroel Mazel tov on your divorce! (ROSA *becomes pale;* ADOLF *stands frozen for a moment, overwhelmed.*)

Adolf Now you're mine!

Rosa (*yelling*) Papa! Dear Papa! There's news! (*She runs to the door.*) Mr. Yisroel has returned with a divorce!

Grossman (*running out, he falls upon* ROSA*'s neck*)   Oh, my dear child. My sweetheart. (*He cries.*)

Rosa   Don't cry, Papa! Oh, look how weak you are.

Adolf   Calm down! (*To* ROSA*)* Well, my dear, all issues are eventually resolved, though perhaps only ours for now …

The curtain falls.

ACT IV

Sixth Curtain.

(*The scene is a pretty room at ADOLF's house.*)

Scene 1

(ROSA and ADOLF)

Rosa   Today, my dear, marks exactly eighteen years since we married, and precisely on this day our little Adele is becoming the bride of someone we know well and hold in high regard. Oh, I wouldn't have wanted to make a match for my child with a groom whose parents we didn't know well.

Adolf   What do you think? That our parents used to seek out a match with good lineage for nothing? Usually people carry on many of the qualities from their father's house, especially when it comes to manners … There are, of course, exceptions, when the worst parents produce the best child, or the best parents the worst. There are these kinds of exceptions, but in those cases I can't be completely convinced that the person I'm interested in is really how I want him to be. It is far preferable to me to turn to the parents and their position in order to carefully consider their child, because usually the apple doesn't fall far from the tree.

Rosa But nowadays, Jews have changed what they mean when they talk about "lineage." Good lineage used to mean he descended from a great rabbi, a judge or a great student of Torah, or an honest merchant. Recently, though, lineage means money. Either that or a person with good "lineage" is whoever can dazzle your eyes. No one looks at honesty anymore, but I'm glad that our Adele is going to marry someone we know personally and that we *also* know the house he comes from.

Scene 2

(ROSA, ADOLF, ADELE, and AMALIA)

Adele It's a shame that you didn't go out for a stroll today, Mama. The weather is so beautiful and the air so fresh!

Amalia You're really straining yourself too much, Mama, but I suppose today you can be excused. You really do have enough to do to prepare for lunch.

Adolf Well, once Adele gets married your mother will finally have somewhere to go. She'll *have* to go out; she won't be able to hold herself back for fear of a day without seeing her Adele.

Adele (*smiling*) But *you'll* be able to hold yourself back from coming every day. Is that right, Papa? Did I get that? (*She hugs him.*)

Amalia Come, Adele, let's take a look at your dress. I'll come back soon to help you prepare the table, Mama … Oh yes—we ran into Madame Rosencrantz, Mama. She's going to come to lunch today as well. Come, Adele.

Adolf Well, I must also go: I must hurry in order to be sure I'm free by three o'clock. (*All exit except* ROSA.)

Scene 3

(ROSA, SERVANT)

Servant   Madame—you've received a note!

Rosa (*reading*)   Who brought it?

Servant   A poor man. He said it was on his own behalf.

Rosa   On his own behalf? (*Reading.*) "Allow me just one minute to speak with you, gracious lady. It is regarding a matter that is very important to you." What does this mean? (*To* SERVANT) Go, ask him what he needs. (SERVANT *exits.*) What is this? I can't begin to understand … It's signed "your old acquaintance, but more than an old acquaintance."

Servant   He said that he can't tell me what he needs, and that he must speak to you directly.

Rosa   Well, call him in. (NEUMANN *enters, dressed in ratty clothes, and bows in reverence.*)

Neumann   Good day, precious Madame.

Rosa   Good day! What do you want?

Neumann   I have something to discuss with you.

Rosa   Well, speak! What do you want?

Neumann (*examining the house, considering everything*)   Have your servant leave, and I'll tell you what I need.

Rosa   You may say whatever you like; it doesn't matter.

Neumann   There are some things that you shouldn't speak about in the presence of a servant … That which I wish to discuss with you is not such a trifling matter as it apparently seems to you. (*Pause.*) Do you recall Neumann?

Rosa (*Considering him, terrified. She signals to the servant to leave.* SERVANT *exits.*)   So I remember. Tell me what it is you want.

Neumann   Well, I am in fact Neumann. You don't recognize me, gracious lady? You've barely changed at all. As usual— good circumstances don't age a person much. Your husband suffered through much—surely it's had an effect on him.

Rosa   I don't know for what purpose you have come here or why my husband is of any concern to you, or what it is you have to do here at all.

Neumann   Don't get so upset, precious lady! I will soon clarify for you—you have nothing to get angry about … You should rather be hoping that *I* won't get angry … After twenty years I've finally come to my wife.

Rosa   To your *former* wife.

Neumann   According to law, you are still my wife.

Rosa   According to law, you divorced me. Go back to wherever you came from.

Neumann   I don't know where you got a divorce. I do not know who divorced you there, but it surely wasn't me. I can prove to you that I have never once been in Odessa. I've already asked around about where your divorce was brought from and around what time. I can show you where I was at that time. (*Pause.*) It's a shame, Madame, that you don't speak. I truly mean you no harm.

Rosa   What do you want from me?

Neumann   Oh, I see what kind of a man you take me for, Madame! I don't want to stand in the way of your happy life with your current husband, Madame, much less with your children, may God protect them! I simply want you to imagine yourself in my situation. You must understand, Madame, that as soon as I clarify who I am and that I never divorced you— according to Jewish law, your children will be …

Rosa   Don't you dare speak of my children.

Neumann   Kindly, Madame, I've already told you I wish you no harm.

Rosa   So what do you want?

Neumann   You have to understand, gracious lady, that when my wife is living so happily, and when I must watch from afar as my wife, by my life, has another man—that alone is already quite enough. So, as you are living so happily, you mustn't also forget your husband. You know, of course, that every man is his own worst enemy. It is plain to see that my businesses aren't exactly brilliant. *(He considers himself from head to toe.)* You understand, Madame, you mustn't forget your husband!

Rosa   What is it you are asking from me—money?

Neumann   What do you mean, Madame? If I can't reveal who I am, surely I can't do any business. Surely, you don't want me to say that I am Avram Grossman's son-in-law, your husband? You have children, after all …

Rosa   Yes, my children! *(To herself)* My dear children! *(To NEUMANN)* Even though I don't believe what you are telling me, if there's even a one in a thousand chance that it is true … *(To herself)* My children! Their good name! … It's awful! But I mustn't lose courage … *(To him)* Listen, I see how the misfortune of my younger years are chasing after me even into my old age. I do not believe what you are telling me. I am sure that my divorce contract is a valid one, but when my children are involved, I don't allow myself the time to sit and ponder. I'm begging you! I've already suffered enough misfortune because of you. Please, at least save my children from this suffering. A mother is here begging you, crying tears before you. Have mercy on her children! What good will it do you if they suffer?

Neumann   Madame, who said that I want to make you suffer? You aren't making an effort to understand me; *I've*

put myself in *your* situation, so put yourself in mine! My
finances are now in awful shape. I can't do any business as
I've already told you.

Rosa   What can I give you? (*She goes to the table, opens a
box, and takes out some money, confusedly.*) Here you go. I
beg of you only one thing. I've had enough misfortune. Don't
let any of this get to my husband and children. All of this—
oh, they couldn't bear it!

Neumann   What do you think, Madame? You've dealt with
a person or two in your life; my word is holy. I commend
myself to you, dear Madame.

Rosa   I think if you had a conscience, you wouldn't bring
misfortune to my children. What guilt do they bear?

Neumann   As long as you keep me happy, Madame, I will
continue to keep you happy.

Rosa (*alone*)   Oh, my children. My good Adolf! He mustn't
know! Oh God, please give me the strength to carry this
alone! Oh … may I forget Neumann as a bad dream. (*With
a bitter smile.*) On this day—the day of Adele's engagement!
A nice gift from God! (*Deep in thought.*) It is possible he's
lying. He didn't show any proof that he hadn't signed the
divorce. Maybe I'm terrified for nothing! It could be that he's
only swindled me. But, in case he does have proof? … (*She
bows her head and remains, frozen.*)

Scene 4

(ROSA, AMALIA, then ADELE and ADOLF)

Amalia   The guests have already gathered and you're still
not dressed! (*She looks at her and cries out.*) Mama! What's
wrong with you? (*Yelling*) Adele, Adele, come here! Adele!

Adele　What's happened? Mama, what's wrong with you? Mama, are you ill? Who's there? Come here! (*Servant runs in, followed by* ADOLF.)

Amalia　Mama, what's wrong with you?

Servant (*bringing water*)　Have a little, Madame!

Rosa　Don't worry. It's already passed.

Adolf　You aren't well.

Adele　What came over you so suddenly?

Rosa　Nothing. My head was just spinning a little bit.

Amalia　You got up so early and got no fresh air.

Adolf　Well, how do you feel now?

Rosa　It's passed.

Amalia　Mama, come and get dressed.

Rosa　No, my dear children. I don't want to change.

Scene 5

(ROSA, ADOLF, ROSENKRANTZ, his wife MADAME R.,
the groom, guests)

(ADOLF *approaches them. Everyone greets each other.
The groom hands the bride a bouquet.*)

Rosenkrantz　Good day! What beautiful weather we have today!

Adolf　Yes! Exactly as we'd hoped for today. It seems nature itself is celebrating this joyous occasion with us.

Madame Rosenkrantz　How are you doing Rosale, Adele?

Rosa　Good, thank God.

Madame R.   You aren't looking well, Rosale.

Rosa   My head suddenly started hurting me.

Amalia   Imagine—Mama became ill so suddenly! It's good that I came in when I did. She was all alone in the house. I still haven't shaken the feeling of terror.

Madame R.   I noticed right away that your mother isn't completely herself.

Scene 6

(Same and the RABBI)

Rabbi   Good afternoon! I see I've arrived to you in a good hour: whenever I meet both in-laws together is a precious moment. I'd better have a good contribution for such an esteemed man!

Rosenkrantz   And now we have the rabbi, too! He'll prepare the engagement contract for us now.

Rabbi   Write the engagement contract! You haven't written it yet? We must send for Mr. Avrom, the judge, then. I can no longer see well enough to write.

Adolf   I'll send for him right away.

Rosa   Please, come to the table. The time has arrived! (*All exit. ADELE and the bridegroom, arm in arm. The rabbi stays behind.*)

Adolf   Come, Rabbi. Surely you've already had lunch. Would you have a glass of wine?

Rabbi   With pleasure. I welcome such joyous occasions. May God award us Jews only such joyous occasions. (*Both exit.*)

Scene 7

(NEUMANN *enters, drunk*)

Neumann　No one is here? I heard that there's an engagement happening today. See how I must steal in here, like a thief ... Why should I stay so far away from her? She's still quite a fine little wife. Why does Adolf have more of a right than I do? Honestly, I am prepared to hide who I am, but truly—would it be so bad if she introduced me to everyone as an old acquaintance? Perhaps it could be an opportunity to make a business proposal to her husband. It seems to me that wouldn't be so bad ...

Scene 8

(NEUMANN, SERVANT)

Servant　What do you need? The Madame is busy now. There's a lunch happening.

Neumann　I know. Who is here for your lunch?

Servant　The in-laws with Miss Adele's bridegroom, the rabbi, and other guests.

Neumann (*To himself*)　The rabbi! Soon she'll have to let me in with her company. They're writing the marriage contract now. It's going well! (*To* SERVANT) Go, tell the Madame that the same person from earlier would like to see her.

Servant　They are eating now. I can't interrupt.

Neumann　Go! Go! The Madame won't be angry.

Servant　No, no! I won't approach the Madame now. You may come back tomorrow if you must.

Neumann　Go, go! The Madame will thank you for calling her out. If you don't go, I'll go in myself.

Servant   Well, well! Aren't you a nuisance! I will go tell the Madame, but I know she will not come out.

Neumann   Go, go. But be sure to tell her such that no one else will hear. (SERVANT *exits*.) Now is precisely the time. I only need to step in with one foot, and it will be enough. Have you heard? I am now a stranger in my own wife's home! Where is that written? She thought she could send me away with a mere few rubles—on the contrary! Neumann knows his business well, and as soon as she hears that I'm already on the fourth glass[2] and the deed is nearly done, she'll stop trying to deter me.

Scene 9

(NEUMANN, ROSA)

Rosa (*frightened and angry*)   What else do you want now? It's a joyous occasion here today. Please don't disturb me; I beg you!

Neumann   I didn't come here to disturb you.

Rosa   So, what is it that you came here for? It seems to me that you got what you wanted. I paid you for your silence.

Neumann   Oh, Madame. Who said anything about payment? That is such a trivial matter!

Rosa   So what is it that you want from me now? I cannot stay here long. My guests will notice that I am not there.

Neumann   Only a few words, Madame. You see: I figured that if your *second* husband has the right to be together with you at all times, why then should *I*, your *legal* husband, be with you entirely from afar?

Rosa   What?!

Neumann　It is quite enough that I have to be so accommodating as to see to it, for your sake, that I do not let my true identity be known. Don't forget that it's because of that selfless act that you and your children are protected from shame ... Since I am doing that which is *very* difficult for me, you should at the very least do what I ask of you: I want you to introduce me to your husband and to all of your acquaintances. I've already sacrificed enough in these awful circumstances.

Rosa　(*As* NEUMANN *speaks, she stands up, deep in thought, putting her hands on her head repeatedly*)　Tell me what you want from me!

Neumann　Just one small thing! I simply want to have the opportunity to see my wife *when I want to*. Many years have passed. I'm not the same man I once was. I value a calm life (*with a smile*) and I know now how to value *you* as well. (*He approaches her and tries to take her by the hand.*)

Rosa　(*recoiling*)　Oh, this is too much! I can't hear any more! Oh, you murderer! Apparently what you did to me in my youth wasn't enough for you! You made my father miserable; left me to die a tortured *agune*! And when my fortuitous fate freed me from the chains that you fastened around me, now, after eighteen years, as I am living with the man who is dearest to me in the whole world, you've come to rob away our good fortune, our peace? Oh no, you're mistaken! You won't succeed! I thought that you would come to me for nothing more than money, but that which you're asking from me is simply impossible! You want me to deceive my dear beloved husband, to make *you* his friend, to have my polite children honor you as their guest, and quietly all the while, you'll be reminding me that I'm your wife? No, you won't succeed at that! You think you can fool people forever? No, I tell you! You want to hold me in quiet terror? I'm not afraid! Out! Get out of here, I tell you!

Neumann   Don't scream like that, Madame. Remember that after a scream like that, you'll wish you'd accepted my discreet offer, but it won't help you then. Even I myself won't be able to take it back for you.

Scene 10

(Same and ADOLF)

Adolf   Why did you leave the table so suddenly?

Rosa   Why did I leave? This man had to have a few words with me.

Neumann (*quietly to* ROSA)   Introduce me!

Rosa (*quietly to* ADOLF)   Madame Frankel sent this man with a message from the committee.

Adolf   Ha! Well, let them come back tomorrow. Now really isn't the time.

Neumann (*quietly to* ROSA)   Don't blunder, Madame. You still have time to introduce me before it's too late.

Rosa (*quietly to* NEUMANN)   Go away!

Neumann   Aha! I did my best. (*He runs to the door, opens it, and begins yelling.*) My dear lovely guests, come here! (ADOLF *looks at* ROSA, *taken aback. Everyone runs out, including the* RABBI.)

All   What is it?

Neumann   Who am I, you ask? Allow me to introduce myself, if my own wife refuses. Listen up! After twenty-one years I have returned to *my wife*, thinking that she would greet me gleefully. I would have thought she'd be waiting for me—and in the end I found her with another man and with children!

Adolf (*To* AMALIA *and* ADELE)   Go to your rooms, children. You don't need to be here for this. (*They exit.*) You are Neumann! You have no business here! You divorced Rosa a long time ago!

Neumann (*smiling*)   Don't laugh off what I've told you! *When* was it that I divorced her?

Rabbi   What is this—of course we should laugh it off! I myself signed off on the divorce contract. I myself officiated her wedding to Adolf. Excuse me, but please be on your way now! After nineteen years you come here saying that you regret your divorce? We Jews don't have such laws for that. You cannot take it back because you regret it nineteen years later.

Neumann   It was *you* who really married them? And who are you? Certainly you must be the rabbi?

Rabbi   Yes, I am the local rabbi!

Neumann   Very well—we'll actually save ourselves the trouble of a trip to the rabbi. You can rule in this matter on whether or not she was allowed to remarry, whether this Adolf had the right to be her husband. (*He takes out some documents.*) Sit down, Rabbi, and take a look at these documents, which will show you that twenty years ago I was sent away from Moscow to Siberia. For fourteen years I was in a city from which we were not permitted to leave, and five years ago was the first time I became free to travel to wherever I please. So I ask you, Rabbi: How could I have divorced her nineteen years ago in Odessa if I was sent to Siberia a year earlier? Here you have the letter from the Odessa rabbi with whom the divorce contract was written. Here he himself writes that I proved to him that I was never in Odessa. (ROSA *stands, frozen, and doesn't move.* ADOLF *stands next to her, pale as the walls, and listens to every word that* NEUMANN *speaks.*)

Rabbi   Unfortunately the letter from the Odessa rabbi states exactly what you've said!

Neumann   You see: the letter explains everything. It cost me enough effort to gather these documents. I broke my back for an entire year, quietly trying to find out how they got this divorce and where it came from. Luckily, I was able to find the man from Odessa who swindled the man who had been sent out to obtain the divorce. Take a look. All of the documents are official.

Rabbi   Yes, yes. I see. Oh, dear. Oy vey!

Adolf (*looking at ROSA*)   Rosale, don't lose yourself, my dear. How could this have been? You share no guilt in this! (*To* NEUMANN) I have nothing to say to *you*. I have much to say about the misfortune that you and the rabbis should find, but it won't help.

Neumann   I am asking you, Rabbi, to rule: *who's wife* is she?

Adolf (*To* ROSA)   Why are you silent? Don't give up like this! Why aren't you answering?

Rabbi   Of course. We cannot go against the law. We must uphold our laws. Even when people are very decent, honest. Even when they aren't guilty. Probably God willed it this way. Probably their trial was fated. We must accept God's punishment out of love. His blessed Name wills it this way, just as it was fated for me to trip over this stumbling block. Oy vey. Oh dear!

Neumann   I am asking you, Rabbi, to rule according to the law.

Rabbi   Of course, we must rule according to law. We cannot rule any other way.

Rosa So what will become of my children? What guilt to do they share in this? It simply cannot be that the law must be so strict. Please consider them, Rabbi, our beloved Rabbi! (*She can barely stay on her feet.*)

Adolf This is how our laws are! Who knows how long we will be at the mercy of a letter, which gives so much to one person, and so little to another. That gives something to one person, and robs everything from another! How much longer will we be so indifferent as we look on as our Jewish daughters fall like sacrifices to this awful law? Rule, Rabbi. I know your law! (*The* RABBI *stands.*)

Rabbi According to the law ...

Rosa Oh, don't speak. I know how you want to rule. Oh, my children, my dear children, innocent children! I know you want to rule that my children are ... Oh, don't speak! (*Crying out.*) I know, I know your law! What is it you want to say? My children are to be ... Hush! My children ... my beautiful, kind, dear, good children, won't have the same proper rights as all the others. Are they not as beautiful, as smart, and good as the others? Such that no match can be made with them? You hear, Adolf, what will be for our children? Hahaha! This is how *your* laws are. According to *your* law, there are bastards, but not according to holy nature! She does not discriminate! All are equal to her! My children, hahaha! What will become of my children!? Who dares say it? The rabbis! Hahaha! You'll probably tell me to divorce my dear husband. To part with my beloved children. But who can forbid us from loving each other? Who can tell a father not to be a father? Children not to be their parents' children? I am asking you; why are you silent? You're ashamed? Are you trying to hide? But you have nowhere! Well, you should be ashamed! My children are bastards and this is not my husband?[3] (*She gestures towards* ADOLF, *crying and laughing.*) Oh, quiet. Are you saying something? ... Shh! What are you saying? ... How would you like to rule? What? Oh. I don't know what.

I don't know what! (*She remains standing, frozen. A short pause.*)

Adolf   Rosa, what's wrong with you? Why are you silent? Why aren't you answering? Why are you looking like that? Do you not recognize who is standing before you? Rosa, answer me! Rosa! Dear, beloved Rosa!

All   What is wrong with her?

Adolf   Oh no! What is wrong with my Rosale?! (*He takes her by the hand.*)

All   Send for a doctor! She's lost her senses!

Adolf   No, she's not lost them. Rosa, *my dear wife*, just say one word to me. Look at me! It's me—your husband! They can't take our children from us, my dear Rosa. Come to me; answer your husband. We still haven't lost everything! (*AMALIA and ADELE run in.*)

Amalia and Adele (*crying and yelling*)   Mama! Mama!

Rosa   My children! (*She makes an abrupt movement, falls around AMALIA's neck, and with a deep sigh, dies.*)

The curtain falls.

Notes

1   In Yiddish, "*a yid fun der tsenerene*," lit. A Jew of the women's bible. The insult insinuates a level of foolishness associated with reading the Yiddish text of the *tsenerene* rather than learning the original language Hebrew Bible. Also suggests naïve piety and effeminacy.

2   A reference to the Passover seder in which four glasses of wine are ritually drunk throughout the night. Indicates near completion.

3   According to Jewish law, children who are conceived by a
     forbidden relationship obtain the status of *mamzerim* and are
     subject to a set of legal limitations, including the requirement to
     only marry other individuals with the same second-class status.
     Bastard is a common but merely approximate translation as
     forbidden relationships according to Jewish law is a complex
     category that applies here but does not include the English
     association with "bastard," meaning born out of wedlock.

Translator's Note by Allen Lewis Rickman

It's very important that in your performances you do *not* make a big deal out of the religious references: "Good Shabbos," "Sukkos," reciting the *Havdole*, etc. In this world of the play these things are as normal as breathing.

Paula Prilutski's punctuation, which is recreated here, is intended to recreate a Jewish cadence—the tying of sentences together with a comma, for instance. And the lines ending with ellipses are not cutoffs—the implication is an indefinite ending, a hesitant, rather than a firm, statement. You don't have to be married to them, of course, but don't dismiss them, because the dialogue is very much laid out that way by design. If you have an ear for this it will come quite naturally—the punctuation is just there to help.

(Notice, by the way, that Judith has less of those ellipses than most of the other characters. The author is using that for characterization: it suggests both her bookishness and her firmness of mind.)

The English dialogue is also deliberately structured to recreate the cadences of Yiddish speech; it's how someone who we think of as "very Jewish," especially of prior generations, would tend to talk. Be aware of that, but don't "push the pedal to the floor" with it. The intention is to help the actors *be* people of a different place and time, not for them to give us their *opinions* of people of a different place and time. Don't make them cute and cuddly because they sound Yiddish-y. Yiddish speakers are not automatically, by virtue of speaking the language, funny, harmless, and old. That's bigotry. Avoid it.

And thanks.
– A.L.R.

P.S: I should also mention that certain Yiddishisms—mostly common exclamations—were kept in order to preserve the flavor of the environment. The same goes for the few bits of Russian and Polish: the people of this play lived in a multilingual world, where a different language was spoken in the home than would be used, say, in the marketplace. I kept those in their original languages for that reason; as no important information is conveyed in them, they are far more useful remaining untranslated.

One of Those

A play by
Paula Prilutski

Translated by
Allen Lewis Rickman

Characters in order of appearance

Judith Zaltsman

Maid

Bronke

Reyzl Zaltsman

Reyzl's small son and daughter

Saul Zaltsman

Sheyndl Zaltsman

Pesele

Tatiana Nazarova

Pepa

Bobbi

Officer

Custodian

Matchmaker

Goldman

Groom

Groom's Father

Groom's Mother

1st Sister

2nd Sister

Seamstress

Down Collector

Bandage Nurse

Franke

Embroiderer

1st Melancholic

2nd Melancholic

The action of the play takes place in Poland and Russia, across a span of twelve years, beginning in 1901.

ACT I

(*At the* ZALTSMAN's. *The front parlor of a wealthy house in a small Polish city. It's Shabbos, late afternoon. On the table sit several pairs of candlesticks.* JUDITH *is cleaning the last remnants of lunch from the table. The* MAID *appears in the doorway, ready to go out.*)

Maid (*very hesitant*) Judith? … Maybe I should put off leaving for a bit, so the missus won't complain? She's only happy when she has something to complain about. (*Beat.*) I shouldn't really go at all today. Then you could go out yourself. You haven't been outside in ages! … But what can I do? I want to see my grandchildren, bless them—they're wonderful children. And my son, if he doesn't see me on Shabbos, right away he wonders if I got sick.

Judith Don't worry about it. Go, give my regards to your son.

Maid Sweet girl. When will *you* get married? It breaks my heart, when I look at you. (*Wipes her eyes.*) I'm losing my mind in my old age. Since he married that harpy … He has no idea what's going on with you. He has no idea how poorly you look. It's like he forgot what's right next to him.

Judith He forgot everything. (*To herself.*) It's forgotten … (*Beat; aloud.*) It wasn't long ago, you know, it's like it was yesterday. She was lying there, on the floor there, covered with a black cloth … Like it was yesterday … You remember, Dvoyre? Here (*pointing*) you could see the shadow of her face, down here, from under the cloth. *I'll* never forget. Wherever I go, it follows.

Maid Please, don't talk that way, it's heartbreaking.

Judith I won't say another word. Go, go.

Maid (*running into the entering* BRONKE)   Oh! God himself sent you here, she shouldn't be alone. Be well, Bronke.

Bronke   *Do vidzennya*, Miss Dvoyre.

Maid   God bless you, darling, I hope I get to see you at your wedding.

Bronke   We'll dance the mitzvah-dance with Judith in between us.

Maid   Yes. Good Shabbos! (*Exits.*)

Bronke   You're terrible. I haven't seen you all week. You should be ashamed! What a friend you are! What are you so busy with? You know, my mother didn't want me to come here. She said if you won't come to see me, I shouldn't come to see you.

Judith   Your mother's right. But she doesn't understand how bad it is here … It's like I'm a slave to my stepmother.

Bronke   You take things too seriously. You think you're the last just because you're not the first. You'll survive. (*Beat.*) And how much longer will you live at home? A year? Your father's sure to find you a husband soon, and then, like the Russians say—*do vidzennya*!

Judith   That's easy for you to say. I hope you never go through anything like this. I don't think I can stand it much longer … (*Beat.*) My father remarried almost a year ago. (*Thinking.*) It will be a year. And it never stops. (*Beat.*) Maybe it's my fault, I don't know. (*Despairing.*) We just don't fit together. God knows where it'll lead. She always wants to start fights. I can't. And I don't want to, it's bad for Father. (*Beat.*) I wish he hadn't married such a crude … After he was married to a person like my mother—?

Bronke   You've gotten so high-strung lately. What do you care if she's not educated? Would that really make a difference? Would you ever call another woman your mother?

Judith   You don't understand. With educated people, people with some kind of background, they don't have these arguments.

Bronke   Please, just forget your stepmother and—*do vidzennya*! Come on, let's take a walk, it's beautiful outside.

Judith   I can't go anywhere, my sister is sure to stop by with the children.

Bronke   So she'll wait a little!

Judith   No, I can't leave the house alone.

Bronke   And where is your brilliant stepsister?

Judith   She left too. (*Beat.*) Do you have a good book?

Bronke   I have Ibsen's "*Wild Duck.*" It's a beauty—it's the third time I'm reading it.

Judith   I read it too, more than once. I've read everything by Ibsen ... and that one's nothing next to "Brand". When I read "*Brand*", I felt like I was there ... Like every little breeze touched my skin. I so want to go there and see those places, the places that Ibsen saw, that gave him the ability to create something like that. (*Beat.*) A different kind of wind blows there, I think. It's a different world ... The skies have no clouds, and the sun never goes down ...

Bronke   I never knew you had that kind of imagination. I'm really impressed! "It's a different world, they have different winds ... " But mothers die there too, sweet ... Brand's mother also died. (*Kisses her; chuckles.*) When we both get married, we'll tell our husbands that instead of taking a vacation in Falenica, we should go to Norway! And we'll see it with our own eyes and—*do vidzennya*!

(*Enter* REYZL *with her children, ad-lib greetings.*)

Reyzl   Children, why aren't you greeting your Aunt Judith?

Children   *Dzien dobry*!

Reyzl   Where are they? Asleep?

Judith   Asleep.

Bronke   Reyzl, why don't you take Judith in to live with you? That would be better, definitely. Since they can't get along—

Reyzl   I'd love to have her live with me but, well, unfortunately my place is so small that I don't even have space for the children. (*Beat.*) And it's not like Father can't afford to keep her here. (*Beat.*) She has to realize that mother's not coming back. That's that, period. She has to give in. She's not going to get anywhere by taking those attitudes.

Bronke   I tell her the same thing, but she's so stubborn, it's horrible! She takes things too personally. If she could just get all that out of her head, that would be the best thing. Then—*do vidzennya*! ... But I have to run, we're expecting guests tonight. You know what, Judith? Why don't you come with me? You'll feel better. Come, I'll play you something beautiful. I got some new music—Chopin's Preludes, Liszt's Rhapsody. Come, Reyzl won't mind! (*To Reyzl.*) Let her go with me. She'll at least get some fresh air. She hasn't been outside in weeks. Do you mind?

Reyzl   Fine with me.

Judith   No, Brontshe, it doesn't interest me, not today. I'll come tomorrow.

Bronke   Definitely, you'll come by tomorrow? Remember, I'll be waiting for you! (*Kisses her.*) Bye-bye, children! (*To Judith*) I'll expect you tomorrow. *Do vidzennya*! (*Exits.*)

Reyzl (*annoyed*) I don't know why you have to advertise everything to the whole world. Are things going well, are they not going well, are you getting along with your stepmother, are you not getting along with your stepmother ... As if anyone could do anything for you! If Father found out how you talk about her, he'd explode.

Judith You don't care. Your husband took the dowry, you're happy, so for you she's "Auntie", she could drag Mama out of her grave and you wouldn't care. If she wants to talk Father out of Mama's jewelry, or her other things, fine! She can say whatever pops into her filthy mouth ... She starts listing Mother's shortcomings, how she never kept house, no, she must have been out dancing ... (*Beat.*) I'm telling you, I won't last much longer. If I keep still and listen to this, then I'm complicit. (*Firmly.*) I swear to you on Mother's grave if she says one more word, may God help her ... Nothing will stop me, not Father, nothing!

Reyzl Father will throw you out.

Judith So I'll go wherever my feet take me.

Reyzl Remember you have nobody to go to.

Judith Don't worry, I won't show up at your place. (*Enter* SAUL.)

Saul (*in doorway*) Reyzl!

Reyzl (*runs to him, kisses his hand*) How are you, papa?

Saul And how are my little angels?

Reyzl (*to children*) Say "I'm well, thank God!" (*The children parrot her.*)

Saul Look at those cheeks, it's a pleasure to see them (*pinches one*). Tell me, you little no-goodnik, when will you learn a little Hebrew? You should know it already, you're an old child! (*Laughs.*) You should be studying Torah by now. I've already bought a watch for you!

Reyzl The rabbi says that with God's help he'll start learning Torah on Sukkos.

Saul Well, children, your grandma will be here any minute with Shabbos fruit for you. (*Calling*) Sheyndele! Come in, you have guests!

Sheyndl (*from offstage*) I'll be right there, dear! (*She enters in a silk robe.*) How are you, Reyzele? And how's your husband? Judith, the keys are under my pillow. Would you mind bringing them in? (JUDITH *exits.*)

Reyzl Thanks for asking, we're all fine. How are you, Auntie? (*To children.*) And a kiss for your grandma? (*They kiss her hand*; JUDITH *returns.*)

Sheyndl Give the children something and put something on the table. (*Judith puts dried fruit on a platter and sets it on the table.*) Eat something, Reyzl. Judith, cut up an orange for the children. (*Beat.*) You know, Reyzl, I'm going tonight to an engagement party for my cousin's daughter. She's got a match, please, God, my Pesele should have one like that …

Reyzl Where is Pesele? I haven't seen her.

Sheyndl The troubles I have with that child … She's too refined. If she eats something simple, plain, right away she doesn't feel well. I had them make for today a *tsholent*, it was beautiful, with *kugel*, you lick your fingers—and right away it disagrees with her, she's got heartburn. So she went to take a nap, she'll sleep it off. (*Beat.*) Please God, he should send me a match for her. A girl 17, 18 years old should definitely be married. (*Beat.*) When I was her age I had a child already, and that's why I'm healthy. Look at the color I still have. (*To Saul, cheerful.*) What do you say, Sauly, don't I have nicer coloring than the young girls nowadays?

Saul Oh, sweetie …

Sheyndl You see, Reyzl, the fashion nowadays where the girls wait until their twenties to get married, it just ruins them.

Reyzl Like the Poles say "nobody regrets getting up too early or getting married too soon". Auntie should see to it that Father arranges a match for Judith. That would be the best thing, I think.

Saul That's not going to happen anytime soon, and with her, it's not going to be too easy, either. Not easy at all … She's a precious jewel, she wouldn't accept just anyone. (*Beat. SHEYNDL exits, Saul's eyes following her lovingly. JUDITH sits in a corner with one of REYZL's children on her knee. She presses the child to her and sings to it in Yiddish.*) You know, Reyzl, it's very difficult with her. She gives Sheyndl nothing but trouble. She never has a kind word for her, she sticks her nose in everything, and she has no respect for her at all. (*Beat.*) I should have a year as good as Sheyndl is. She's so easy to get along with. Your mother, rest in peace, it shouldn't be held against her up there, she spoiled her. She let her have her way too much. For your mother, she was the only thing in the world.

Judith Again, Mother! (*Jumps up.*) What do you want from her? You're talking about her too? What did she do to you? How is it her fault if you let just anybody lead you around by the nose?

Saul You hear, Reyzl? She goes on like this for days. I might just come after her, and God help her if I do.

Sheyndl (*entering with PESELE*) Look, Saul, look how pale she is!

Saul Maybe we should talk to a doctor?

Pesele (*capricious*)   I don't need any doctors! I want you to buy me one of those hats, like the one Judith's friend Bronke was wearing.

Sheyndl   Let it be only that, that that's all you need to be well. You'll have whatever kind of hat you want.

Saul   Absolutely, no question.

Pesele   Well, we'll see if you buy it for me. We'll see.

Reyzl (*rising*)   Say goodbye, children, we have to leave, it's getting late. Papa, when are you coming to visit? Come, please, and bring Auntie with you.

Saul   Maybe we can come this week.

Reyzl   Please! Don't be a stranger, please come. (*To Judith*) You need to get smart already, it's time. Nobody's out to hurt you, not father and not dear Auntie either.

Sheyndl   May God do to me any wrong I do to her.

Reyzl   Say goodbye, children! (*They do. She, the children and* JUDITH *exit.*)

Maid (*enters with a lamp*)   Shabbos is over. May you have a good week!

Saul (*pours wine and recites the Havdole*)   "Hiney keyl yeshuosi evtokh veloy efkhod, ki ozi vezimras ..." (*finishes*) A good week, a lucky week ...

Sheyndl   A good week, a lucky week ... Judith!

Judith (*Enters*)   You called.

Sheyndl   Judith, brush off my black tulle dress and father's new satin *kapote* ... Get ready whatever we'll need. And give father a white handkerchief. (*Gently.*) Judith, maybe you could brush my hair out to be more stylish? Please.

Saul   What do you need it for? You're prettier than all those modern girls.

Sheyndl   Thank you. In your eyes, I'm that pretty .... Still, today I want to look fashionable, specially for you.

(JUDITH *starts to brush her hair.*)

Pesele (*whiny*)   Mama, make Judith play cards with me when you leave!

Sheyndl   She'll play cards with you.

Pesele   Oh, yes, sure she will. When you leave, she goes right to her book. I could kill her and she wouldn't move. If she won't play cards with me, I won't stay here. (*About to cry.*) You always go out alone, you never take me!

Sheyndl   Silly, girls don't go to engagement parties! You'll go to your own.

Pesele   Thanks a lot! (*Beat.*)

Sheyndl   You know what I'd like? Let me put on the pearls too. I don't like to wear a lot of jewelry, but, well, you know, at a celebration you have to have *something* to show. Like they say in Polish, "when you're around crows, you have to make crow noises". (*Beat.*) Wearing a lot of jewelry is what the fish ladies in the marketplace do. Anyhow, low-class people. (JUDITH *shivers and drops the brush. Picks it up and continues brushing.*) Get me the jewelry, if you don't mind. (*Beat.*)

(SAUL *exits and* RETURNS *with a box from which he takes earrings, rings, pearls, etc.*)

Pesele (*grabs a ring*)   Mama, you promised to give me this ring! (*Puts it on.*) Look, it fits me perfectly! I'm going to keep it.

Judith   Pesele, that ring is not for you. (*Beat.*) That ring was my mother's first wedding present –

Pesele   Why is *my* mother wearing it?

Judith   My father gave it to her.

Pesele   I'm not giving it back! So help me God! (*Runs out.*)

Sheyndl (*looks at pearls, laughs, shows them to* SAUL)   Oh, gosh, Saul, I hope she'll forgive me up there—but how people talk, you know, they don't even think about what they're saying—(JUDITH *looks on, wild-eyed*) But what they say, well, they're right … (*Beat.*) They say that she—forgive me— that she wasn't very clean, and it's the truth.

Judith (*springs away from her, tossing aside the brush*)   Again!

Sheyndl   Why are you getting so angry? Look for yourself! Look, Saul (*shows him the pearls*), how the band is so grimy. *Feh!* How can you wear it like this?

Saul   It got dusty laying in the box.

Sheyndl   Bless you, the way you defend her.

Judith (*wild-eyed*)   Don't put them on, and don't talk!

Saul (*to Sheyndl*)   That's enough, let's not have her start in with you.

Judith (*gently*)   Father, it was so recent, so recent. You'd say to Mother, "My smart wife, my pretty wife, you could be the wife to a king." You said that just yesterday, Father—it seems to me like it was yesterday—and you've already forgotten. Forgotten your beautiful, brilliant wife, the devoted, beautiful wife, that you once had. Remember? Who was it, back then, who, who stayed at your bedside day and night and wouldn't go away for a minute? She risked her life for you. Maybe, if you'll *remember*, you won't allow just anyone to talk about her like that … Did you forget *everything?* (*Weeps.*)

Saul   That's some lecture. Look, she's crying.

Judith   There is something to cry over here! Go, Father, give it all to your wife, give her everything, but make her stop talking, make her stop! What does she want from my mother? What does she want from me? She didn't know her. Tell her to let my poor mother rest, let her rest in her grave!

Sheyndl   What are you trying to do? Who's talking about her? Just now, when I saw the pearls, I was reminded of what people told me. (*Beat.*) The world's not asleep, people know what goes on. (*Goes to the mirror and holds the pearls to her neck*) She should forgive me, but whose fault is it if she made people talk? (*Laughs.*)

Judith (*jumps at her and yanks away the necklace; it breaks, and pearls fall to the floor*)   There! Now you won't have anything to talk about anymore. You'd have to be worthy to wear my mother's pearls ... Who do you think you are? It's outrageous for you to belittle my mother ... My mother ... You ... May God forgive you for all the sins you've committed against my mother ...

(SHEYNDL *has stood all the while, frozen. She wipes her eyes with a handkerchief.*)

Saul (*tugging nervously at his beard*)   Well, well, so there we are ... You're just lucky it's Saturday night and I don't want to start off the new week like that, or else I'd teach you how to treat people. I'd settle with you good.

Sheyndl   I wish I hadn't lived to come into this house, I wish I'd died before I married you. If I'd have known what was waiting for me here ...

Saul   Please, Sheyndele, don't take her nonsense to heart. She doesn't know what she's saying, she's crazy ...

Sheyndl   So she's crazy, and I have to get the brunt of it? If I'd have known the kind of things that would happen here ... She'll get violent in a minute.

Saul   She wouldn't live to get away with it. I'd finish her.

Judith   If you won't let my mother rest in the ground, you can do whatever you want to me. Anything … I can't listen to it anymore!

Sheyndl (*ironically*)   Well, I guess I'd better leave, then, and just give up all the happiness I have here. (*Exits.*)

Saul (*following*)   Sheyndele, please, get dressed, it's getting late. I'll deal with her. (*Springs at Judith with a raised fist.*) You, you ingrate, I'll tear you apart!

Judith (*moving away from him*)   Please, Father, you're frightening me!

Saul (*screaming*)   I don't care, I'll split your head open—I want you out of my house!

Judith   Chase *her* out, *her*! This all belongs to my mother!

Saul   You should live so long as anything here is your mother's. Everything here is mine! I'll throw you out. I won't give you one cent for a dowry. I gave Reyzele a dowry and made her a wedding—you I don't even want to *know*.

Judith   Mother made Reyzele's wedding. If not, she'd be in the same boat I'm in.

Saul (*frothing mad*)   You're still talking? Wait, I'll deny you your mother's inheritance!

Judith   *She'll* be out of here before that happens.

Saul   You will never live to see that day—you hear me? Stop talking about her!

Judith   She disgusts me, like the worst lowlife from the streets—she has no heart, no pity –

(SAUL *leaps at her and grabs her by the hair. She pushes him away and screams.*)

Judith   You're tearing my hair! Don't touch me! Tear *her* hair, tear *hers*! You never treated me like this—and look, now –

Saul   Now you sicken me. Like a pig.

Judith (*falls into a chair and screams*)   Mama! Mama! Why didn't you take me with you? Who did you leave me with? (*Holds her head in her hands and weeps.*)

CURTAIN

END OF ACT I

ACT II

(*Eight years later. A well-furnished room in an apartment in a large Russian city. A wardrobe sits against one wall; nearby is a writing table; a window opens onto an airshaft.* JUDITH *sits on a sofa in a lace morning robe, her hair down, reading a letter; she is fighting back tears. The maid,* TATIANA, *enters.*)

Tatiana   Miss Pepa is here with the child, madame.

Judith (*annoyed*)   The child … (*wipes her eyes*) Send them in.

(TATIANA *goes off, then leads in* PEPA, *loudly dressed, and* BOBBI.)

Pepa   Go, Bobbi, kiss your mother. (*She pushes the girl to* JUDITH. BOBBI *kisses* JUDITH'S *hand, then is pulled aside by* TATIANA, *who kisses her lovingly.*)

Judith   It looks like you love Bobbi very much.

Tatiana   As if she were my own.

Pepa   Everyone loves her. At our place they're crazy for her. You can't help it. She's so sweet and quiet.

Tatiana Come, pretty doll, let's go to the kitchen. (*Takes* BOBBI's *hand.*) I have some nice toys I set out for you. (*They exit.*)

Judith (*watches them go, then follows after, almost to the door; softly*) How she grows … Like a bread, rising. And I … I thought something would happen to her, but … She lives, grows … and she'll raise herself … And why? For who?

Pepa You know, I don't like to hear that kind of talk. It's your child … What is she guilty of? Such a good child …

Judith Such children should not be born. Can anything good come from there? Anything decent? A child who had fathers, God alone knows what kind of people. Drunks, gamblers, all sorts of criminals. If she inherits even a particle from them, no good can possibly come of it … She'll just be something that nobody wants. (*Pause.*) And I don't love the child. I really don't. It's as though I didn't give birth to it, as though I didn't carry it …

(*Long pause.*)

Pepa Sometimes I just don't understand you at all … What were you crying about before? When I came in, I could see it. I'd thought you'd never cry again. Did something happen between you?

Judith God forbid! He's an amazing person. Since the day he took me out of there, he never once made me unhappy, not once. He loves me. He treasures me. Not once did he remind me that I came from there, not for a second. He's like an angel who spread his wings over me …

Pepa So what do you want? Why aren't you satisfied?

Judith I got a letter today from Warsaw, from an old friend. You remember, the one who used to write me. (*Smiles, ironic.*) She thinks I'm a teacher, that I make a living by giving lectures. She's been married several years already and in every letter she tells me how happy she is with her family. (*Beat.*) Today she wrote that my father lost a lot of money in business, and his wife has long since left him. So ... my father is having a lot of trouble, and he's old, and he's alone.

Pepa What do you care? That old bastard! Wasn't it all his fault, what happened to you? Some father! Good for him!

Judith Don't say that, dear. A father's still a father. And a lot of that was my fault. I shouldn't have left, I should have stayed there and dealt with it. I was a child, I was reckless, I shouldn't have gone out into the world alone ... Maybe it hurts him that I'm not there. Who knows what he's going through, out there all alone ... I wish I could see him, even from a distance ... It's been six years, and I fight with myself almost every day over whether I should go back.

Pepa I remember back when you first came up there. You told me what happened, how you wound up in all that. It was your father, he drove you to it. I got so angry at him. If I'd had him in my hands I'd've torn him to pieces. (*Beat.*) I'm so stupid to remind you about back there. You need to forget it, just toss it aside, like it's some awful dream.

Judith Sweetie, you can't forget that, it won't let you forget ... You can't just brush it aside. It's always inside you, wherever you go.

Pepa Oh, listen to you! Knock that out of your head. It's done with. You're lucky, you got yourself out quick. (*Miserable.*) Me ... I can't even remember how long I've been there. (*Pause.*) And I'm going to die there. And then they'll bury me behind the fence. With people like me, you know, they don't stand on any ceremonies—you lived in the swamp, they bury you behind the fence.

Judith "You lived in the swamp, they bury you behind the fence ..."

Pepa   You know what? I can't stand it upstairs anymore. I've been so lonely since you left. Sometimes I just wish it would all end, and that people like me would never be born anymore ...

Judith   You silly ... Things could get better for you too! You're still young, you're pretty ... (*Pause.*) You know ... I've always been fond of you. You're also different from the rest. You were the only one I could really talk to, pour my heart out to. And not just once ... You know what? Come back home with me. I'll bring you—I have enough money for both of us. If you'd just get yourself out of there, you'd find a better way to live. Back home nobody will know who you are, or who you were.

Pepa (*laughs*)   "Nobody will know who you were." You're wrong. Look at me. (*Stands up straight.*) Look at me. Don't you see it? It's engraved on my forehead, who I am. It's permanent. What could you make out of someone like me? Could girls like me pass themselves off as respectable people? We'd never stop shaking. Why would you want to drag my past along with you? My ... awful past ... (*Drops her head.*) I've been away so long from where I came from that it's like I didn't really come from anywhere, that I was just born like this ... And I don't think I could live any other way ... Drunk every night ...

Judith   God! Drunk? You never used to do that ...

Pepa   Yes, oh yes, I get drunk, that's the only thing I have now. (*Beat.*) Getting drunk—that's important.

Judith   Oh, no, what are you doing? I don't remember you drinking at all.

Pepa   When you were there I kind of had a taste for it. But then I was afraid to, because of you, afraid you'd think I was getting ugly. While you were there, I could take care of myself, I thought. That's all gone now ...

Judith   Why are you doing that? You're destroying your soul and your body, you're –

Pepa   I do it. I have to do it. It's the only thing that helps me forget, at least for a while. Forget who I am, forget what's going on around me … Then it seems like this is all there is. There's nothing else … There's no God … There's no swamp, no fence, there's nothing, really nothing, I mean it! When we were together there, I felt different. Not that I blame you for getting yourself out of that hellhole, not a bit …

(*Long pause.*)

Judith   When you slip the first time, you think you've learned a lesson for your whole life. But that's not true. You're not even aware of it, but you stumble, then you fall, and you get deeper and deeper … (*Remembering.*) It was so fast, how it happened … Before I could turn around. Unbelievable. When I left my father's house, from the first minute, I lost the ground under my feet. When I was fired from that restaurant—I was waiting tables, and I … insulted a customer—he was rude—I'll never forget that moment … I found myself on an empty street, outside the city. There was nobody there, just me and a cloudy sky. I cried out to my mother, in her grave, that she should do something for me, she should look out from her grave and see what's happening with her favorite child, the child she saw herself in … (*Sadly.*) But no, no, she didn't do that, and before I could even look around me, I was lost. (*Stares off; pause.*)

Pepa   What do you think you'll do about the child? Listen to me—leave her with us. If you knew how the Mister and Missus love that child! Everyone says she looks just like you. (JUDITH *shivers.*) The other day the old prefect of the city was at our place—you remember him, right? He was one of yours—he also said she looks like you.

Judith   That old drunk still comes around?

Pepa   Now he goes to Franke, the dark one. He's one of her regulars. (*Beat.*) I had a little run-in with her. Imagine how low—I'm ashamed even to tell you—you know what kind of nerve she has? She had the gall to—She said that certain parties told her that you used to slip money out of the prefect's pockets. I slapped her right down to the ground! Running around telling lies like that …

Judith   God, why did you hit her? It's not her fault—I did do that. Many times. I'd slip out a few hundred rubles. But only from him, not from anyone else.

Pepa   You did that? Really? No, no, I don't believe it. I don't. Not you. You're too honest. It's a joke!

Judith   You can believe it, I used to do it all the time, no hesitation at all. (*Beat.*) He used to have city-money with him, and we were part of the city's support system. They needed us—we were the only ones the city would allow to do that kind of work. So, I thought the city should pay me well for it. I held onto that money for something important … You shouldn't have hit her. It's true.

Pepa (*amazed and disappointed*)   I wanted to kill her when she said that … (*Beat.*) Oh, yes, we were talking about the child. So? Well? Leave her with us. She's good there, she's raising herself, it's beautiful. And you can take her back whenever you want.

Judith   No, dear, you have to leave her here now. She mustn't go back there anymore. What would she end up as, another "part of the support system"? I can't allow that, that would be criminal, just criminal. (*Beat.*) I don't love her. She's a stranger to me. I feel more drawn to any child on the street than I do to her. She reminds me of my past—but I can't leave her there.

Pepa   You 'll take her with you?

Judith (*stands and considers*)   Yes, I will. But please, dear, don't tell them upstairs. Say she's staying with me overnight.

Pepa   They'll tear my head off. And the child will miss us. (*Sadly.*) Now I'm really alone. You're going back home, like you ought to, and I … I … (*Beat.*) Will you even remember me there? Write to me sometimes, will you? (*Kisses her.*) Have a nice trip. Good luck.

Judith   Pepa, maybe you'll take my advice and come with me?

Pepa   I can't change my life. For me that's all there is. (*Suppressing tears.*) Good luck, Judith!

Judith   I still hope that you'll be able to save yourself, like I did. And I won't give up on you. I'll keep my eye open, maybe I'll be able to get you out of there.

Pepa   Be well, Judith. Don't forget me. (*Calls.*) Bobbi! Don't forget me, Judith. (*Kisses her firmly.*) Have a good trip. (*She exits.*)

Judith (*following her to the door*)   Good luck! (*Sits; covers her face with her hands. Beat. She starts suddenly, calls off.*) Tanya!

Tatiana (*enters, kisses Bobbi, and looks around*)   Where's Miss Pepa?

Judith   She left.

Tatiana   Oh? (*Pleased.*) She left the child! Oh, will Bobbi stay with us then? (*Kisses Bobbi.*)

Judith   You love her that much?

Tatiana   Like my own life.

Judith   Tell me, would you like to have her stay with you for a bit?

Tatiana   Madame is making fun of me. How can I take her in with me when I live here with you?

Judith   You see, I'm going to visit my home. I can't take the child with me. I'll leave you some money for food.

Tatiana   You're joking.

Judith   I mean it. You're a very honorable person, and I'm happy to leave her with you.

Tatiana   Could that really be true? (*Doorbell rings.*) That must be the gentleman. (*She runs out.* OFFICER *enters.*)

Officer   Oh, Judith, dearest, how are you? These last four days felt like four years. Four days away from your silken hair, four years out of your beautiful arms. Oh, Judith! (*Lowers his head.*) You may claim the head of your Holofernes. (*Sees Bobbi.*) Look who's here! Hello, Bobbi, how are you? (*Kisses her; to Judith.*) So you do listen to me! Oh, you're a gem. She'll be staying with us? What are you planning? I don't care whose daughter she is—she's your child, and she's just as pretty as her mother. (*Sits on the sofa between* JUDITH *and* BOBBI *and pulls both to him.*) What a pair of beauties! One is a rose in full bloom, and the other's a little bud on her side. (*Sniffs them.*) And you both smell just as sweet! Now go to sleep, and I'll sing you a Russian song. (*Sings.*) *Skoro li polnotsh nastanyet,*
Skoro'l dozhdusya tyebya …
(*Sits quietly holding them for a moment; then*) You know what? We'll go to Vyaltseva's concert today! And my beautiful lady will sit enchanted listening to Vyaltseva's singing. We'll make an evening of it. Just put the baby to sleep. (*Beat.*) You know those four days of maneuvers got me so worked up. Unbelievable! You can't imagine how angry I kept getting. I couldn't stop screaming at them. I was like a madman. I drove them all so crazy that the maneuvers went like "Blind Man's

Bluff"! (*Chuckles.*) It was a mess. What did you do for four whole days? Promenade?

Judith   You know I don't like to walk on the street.

Officer   I don't like to hear that. Four whole days inside in this heat? It's unhealthy. You're going to have to pay for that. From now on you and Bobbi are going out every day for a constitutional. (*Beat.*) Has she been here long?

Judith   Just since today. Pepa brought her around, like she always does.

Officer   She's a very nice young woman.

Judith   She's lost, unfortunately … It's very sad.

Officer   Oh, I almost forgot to tell you—it's not important, really—I had a bit of a run- in with Ivan Alexandrovich. Imagine, he got himself good and drunk, and just babbled on and on about you. And when I told him I'd shove it back down his throat, well, one thing led to another, and he gave me to understand he plans to inform on me to my father.

Judith   So? Are you afraid of your father's finding out about us?

Officer   No, it's not that. But he might tell my father you're Jewish.

Judith   And then?

Officer   You know that as the mayor he can order you to leave the city within twenty-four hours.

Judith (*indifferent*)   For what?

Officer   I'll explain, sweetheart. A Jew, you see, who is not working at the job listed on their residency permit loses the privilege of living outside the Jewish zone.

Judith   Oh really? (*Laughs.*) So when I was still up there, I, as a Jew, could stay in the city for years, but not anymore!

(*A nervous chuckle.*) So it seems your father's job is to throw decent people out of the city and keep *in*decent ones in … You'll probably be the mayor yourself someday, and I'd advise you not to uphold that law.

Officer   What's the matter with you? You're so easy to upset … It really bothers me that you can't just get over things. But you don't have to worry, there's a way out. I'd already been thinking about it—we'll get married! (*Beat.*) Did you hear, Judith? (*Kisses her.*) We'll get married!

Judith   Married? How? You're a Christian, and I'm Jewish.

Officer   You know, sweetheart, what has to be done in that kind of situation—one person has to convert. It's against the law for me to become a Jew, so you'll have to become a Christian.

Judith (*stiffly*)   Absolutely not. That I will never do. I could lie to every person in the world, but to fool God himself— that, I'm not capable of.

Officer   That's just childish. When you love someone you do everything for them—it's no sacrifice. I know you love me, at least a little … (*Looks her in the eyes.*) You do love me?

Judith   Yes. You're the first person that ever had a hold on my heart. But to convert … (*Turns away*) No. Definitely not.

Officer   Well, my love, we'll see. You just take it easy, and we'll deal with that later on. (*with arch formality*) Just now, with inexpressible regret, it behooves me to inform you that we must part—I have to go down to the regiment and present a report. You, darling, get yourself ready, you'll want to look your best, we're going to a concert. Put on your white dress. By 7:00 I'll be back at your feet. And take good care of Bobbi for me. (*Laughs.*) You must treat her with respect. Bobbi, in a little while I'm going to bring you some very fancy chocolate!

(*Kisses her.*) Now you be a good girl here. (*Kisses* JUDITH. *Buttoning his tunic*) J'ai l'honneur de vo saluer. (*Exits. Pause.*)

Judith (*rises, seems to "brush something off," calls*)   Tanya! Tanya!

Tatiana (*entering*)   What do you wish, madame?

Judith   Tanya, what do you think about what we discussed earlier?

Tatiana   Oh, madame, is it possible? You never mentioned that you might leave. Perhaps, madame, you might put it off for a while? It's a pity, for the gentleman's sake, really a pity. He loves you so.

Judith   No, Tanya, nothing in this world could delay me. I must go there, my father is very old, and that's why I'm asking this of you. It would be a great kindness if you would take in the child. I can't take her with me, and leaving her up there would be terrible. (*Beat.*) You needn't worry that you'll be raising a Jewish child … (*biting her lip*) God alone knows what that child is … (*Pause.*) Will you do it?

Tatiana   Madame, I'm very sorry to see you go. You are such a kind person. But if God wants me to bring up your daughter, then I will bring her up just like she was my own child. You won't have to worry. God forbid I should do her any harm –

Judith (*goes to her wardrobe and takes out some expensive dresses and furs; takes off her earrings and rings and hands it all to* TATIANA)   Sell all of these, all together it will add up to a nice amount. (*Takes out a purse from a drawer in the wardrobe.*) And here's money. This should last you a while.

Tatiana (*stunned*)   Madame, in my village, with God's help, this could last a lifetime!

Judith (*taking off her robe and putting on a black dress and hat*)   Please, Tania, just take it. Pack my clothes and the laundry from the dresser into the wooden trunk that's in the hallway. But quickly, please, we have to rush, we have to leave here as soon as possible, the train leaves at five. Hurry, Tania, hurry! I'm going to change.

(TATIANA *quickly packs.*)

Tatiana   It's done, madame.

Judith   Good, good. Now get your things and dress the child. Quickly!

(TATIANA *takes BOBBI and exits.* JUDITH *sits at the desk and writes.*)

Judith   "I beg your forgiveness. Don't think badly of me. You're young. There is a great world out there … Judith." (*Pause.* TATIANA *enters with* BOBBI, *both dressed to leave.*) Ready? Very good. Now call the custodian.

Tatiana (*opening the airshaft and calling*)   Vasili Nikolaevich!

(*The* CUSTODIAN *enters.*)

Judith   Take all these and go to the Varshavski Station. And fetch a coachman. (*He takes out the boxes.* JUDITH *looks around the room.* TATIANA *takes* BOBBI's *hand. Pause.*) Tatiana, bring her up to be an honorable person. God will thank you for it. (*to* BOBBI, *holding her*) You are a child of the world. You come from somewhere in the world (*shaking her head*) … Now go back to the world. Maybe it will grant you a better fate than your mother's. Your mother's past would have only done you harm. It's better for you to be far away … from your mother's sad history. Far away … (*Beat.*) Swear to me, Tania, that you will never tell her who her mother was.

Tatiana (*teary-eyed, kissing* JUDITH's *hands*)   Madame
… Madame … (*crosses herself*) I swear to you that she will
never find out anything from me.

(JUDITH *kisses* TATIANA's *forehead. The* CUSTODIAN
returns.)

Custodian   The coachman is here, ma'am.

Judith   Come, Tania, quickly!

(*She runs out quickly, followed by* TATIANA *and* BOBBI.)

CURTAIN

END OF ACT II

ACT III

(At the Zaltsmans' house, the same room as Act I.
Three months later. SAUL, who has aged considerably,
sits with SHEYNDL.)

Sheyndl   Believe me, Saul, my life was not so happy like you
suppose. How many times did I think, "What's doing with
him over there? How is *he* feeling?"

Saul   Why didn't you try to bring us back together?

Sheyndl   You don't know how it is … It's embarrassing, in
a situation like that. It's not appropriate for a woman … for
her to be the first.

Saul   Oy, Sheyndele, Sheyndele … A husband and wife
shouldn't think about such nonsense. I'm the first, you're the
first … All I know is the angels brought Judith back home.
Lonely like I was, I wouldn't've lasted much longer. Two
years I walked around alone, I hated being alive … Besides,
the minute you left this house, my luck turned, everything
started to go bad for me. Judith, when she was here only a
few days, she noticed, she said how it's hard for me to live.

One time she turned to me and said, "Father, it seems to me
you're missing your wife. Look at yourself, there's nothing
left. I think we'll have to make peace between you." Smart
she is, bless her. That you can't take away from her, how
smart she is.

Sheyndl   When she came into my house, I got very scared.
Her, in my house! She just stood there, and she said, "Don't
be frightened, Auntie, I came to make peace between you.
My father can't live without you. This anger between you
has gone on long enough." She wouldn't let me go. She kept
trying to bring me around, I couldn't do a thing, she would
not leave until I promised I'd move back in with you. (*Beat.*)
And from now on, that'll be it. "Until a hundred and twenty."
(*Beat.*) I'll tell you the truth, Sauly, for me those two years
were like two thousand years. (*Coquettish.*) Oh, you should
hear how many times people tried to put me together with
someone. Some very nice matches, I'm telling you! But I said
to myself, "No, I'm not doing that again." And second, I
had Pesele to deal with the whole time. You know how hard
it was for me to find her a match. And the minute she got
married, she started getting sick, and on and on.

Saul (*smiling*)   She is nothing like her mother. (*Pinches her
cheek lightly.*) You, *kinahora*, are a fine Jewish lady with
pretty pink cheeks!

Sheydnl (*pleased*)   She takes after her father, may she be well …

Saul (*stands, brushes his beard*)   But I'm still not too bad,
right? What do you think, Sheyndele, have I changed that
much?

Sheyndl   Of course you've changed. Your stomach is
completely gone, your beard is all gray … (*Smiles.*) But don't
worry. You're still the only one I like.

Saul (*pleased*)   My little Queenie!

(The MATCHMAKER *appears in the doorway.*)

Matchmaker   Good evening, good evening! (*Catching her breath; talks fast.*) *Nu, Reb* Saul, I went over there and everything is taken care of. They agreed to everything. So, could we have a meeting today?

Saul   If they're agreeable, I am too. So. We can have a meeting today.

Matchmaker   And maybe today sign the betrothal?

Saul   If they'd like to, then I'd like to, absolutely.

Matchmaker (*pleased*)   *Oy*, is this a match for her! The groom has been offered maybe a thousand different matches, he don't have to go around asking. Oh, I should only make a living as good as this match is! All of Warsaw will be jealous. There's not another young man like this in the world. I should only live to see my own children under the *khupe*, please God, as this match is right for your daughter. You can see it comes from God! Because *he* had to go serve in the military, and *she* had to spend such a long time away from her home—

Saul   It's from God, no question.

Matchmaker   It's sent from above, definitely. Plus I also helped. What then? You had Berl Tslap running after you, could he offer you a match like this? He would drop dead before he'd have the sense to put this together. Wherever he goes, it's a flop. Everything falls apart, I'm telling you, it falls apart. What happens with Rubinshteyn's match? With Grosslik's? With Boymritter's? May a black funeral chase after me if one of my matches fell apart like theirs!

Saul   Please, lady, that's enough, just go do what you have to.

Matchmaker   Oh, bless you *Reb* Saul, how wise you are! "Just go do what you have to." And may God help me that this match will go through. (*Beat; sadly.*) I forgot already what a matchmaker's fee looks like. Please, God should help me with this. (*Looks ready to cry.*) I'm a widow with small children! (*Waits a beat; then, hearing no response.*) So they should come?

Saul   Have them come around eight. Then, the betrothal ... (*to Sheyndl*) We'll have to put something out.

Matchmaker   Of course, of course! I'm going to run over there right now and tell them "around eight"! Meanwhile, goodbye! Goodbye! (*Exits.*)

Sheyndl   Goodbye! Be well!

Saul (*resigned*)   A soldier ... A Jewish boy, and he decides to go off and join the Czar's army ... But what can you do, what can you do ...

(JUDITH *and* REYZL *enter.* JUDITH *is all in black.*)

Judith (*taking off her hat*)   Well, Auntie, so how do you feel in your fresh-start life?

Sheyndl   Thanks to you, very good.

Judith   And you, Father, look at you, you're beaming! You're the master of the house again, a husband, a breadwinner. (*Beat.*) May God grant you all the best.

Sheyndl   Judith, Reyzl, would you like some tea? You both look absolutely frozen.

Judith   Don't bother, Auntie, I'll make it myself in a minute.

Sheyndl   No, no, I'll bring it right in. (*Exits.*)

Reyzl (*to Judith, who has seated herself*)   You look tired. It's no wonder, sitting in the cemetery that long. You know, Judith, he did a very nice job, cleaning up Mother's stone. (JUDITH *doesn't seem to have heard.*) You had that same look on your face at the cemetery. At least here it's warm.

My teeth were chattering, and you stood there like you were under a spell or something.

Judith It's true, like under a spell. It was so beautiful today at the cemetery! Very different somehow. The whole cemetery covered with a blanket of snow … The headstones draped in snow like wedding gowns, and it was all so perfectly still. You know, Father, everyone there lies next to each other in peace. People don't cause trouble for each other. Quiet, quiet … It's beautiful. There's no pride there, no hate, no lies … In birth and death people are together. We all come from one place. Then life pulls us apart, makes us distant from each other … but after death we all go to one place, to the earth. There are no passions there, no tears … You're freed from everything that's human. And you're as pure as the thoughts of a newborn child.

Saul (*interrupts*) You've been like this your whole life, you don't know what you're saying. Let my *enemies* go into the earth!

Judith You see, Father, that's wrong of you. An enemy might someday become a friend. You shouldn't curse an enemy.

Saul (*spits*) She's lost her mind!

Judith Believe me, Father, it's better to be dead than to live a lie …

Saul What's gotten into you? Who's living a lie?

Judith All of us. Everyone in this world.

Saul (*annoyed*) Whoever wants to live with truth, lives with truth. And whoever wants to live with lies, lives with lies.

(SHEYNDL *enters with tea.*)

Let's stop talking nonsense. Reyzl, after you drink your tea, maybe you can go pick up a few things? We may be signing a betrothal here today.

Judith   You're still determined, eh? You're going to make me a match? (*Beat.*) See, this is your truth. You're forcing me to commit a crime that everything inside me is fighting against.

Saul   Naturally, it's a "crime"! You can't even talk to her!

Sheyndl   I don't want to mix in—in ten seconds someone will say "a stepmother, she sticks her nose in everywhere"— but from what I've heard, it sounds like a wonderful match.

Saul (*getting angry*)   Sheyndele, please, don't talk. It's a short day, it will be night soon, we need to buy a few things. Let Reyzl go buy things.

Sheyndl   I'll go myself, Sauly.

Saul   So go, darling, go. Here's money. (*Gives it to her.*)

Sheyndl   I'll go right away, I just have put something on. (*Exits.*)

Reyzl (*to JUDITH*)   Believe me, Father's not trying to hurt you. He's right. Why make people talk? Make them close their mouths—period!

Saul   Just a ceremony. That's all I want. A wedding ceremony. I've had enough troubles from you. Just go through with the ceremony, and after that, whatever God wants, he'll do. Maybe it will work out for the best.

Reyzl   Father knows what he's doing. (*JUDITH sits frozen by the window.*) Judith, maybe you could lend me a blouse for today? Honestly, I have nothing to wear, everything I have is so old-fashioned.

Judith (*goes automatically to a wooden trunk full of clothing, opens it and pulls out a blouse. Several photographs fall to the ground, having been caught on the blouse. JUDITH shivers; to herself*)   Where did those come from? Oh, Tania … She packed my past … (*Tosses the photographs back in the trunk. Hands Reyzl a blouse.*) This will look good on you.

Reyzl Thanks! Well, I'm going, I've wasted too much time already, I'll probably catch an earful. Goodbye, Papa!

Saul Don't come late. And tell your husband to go to the scribe and pick up a betrothal contract, all prepared, just without the names written in. I'm sure he'll have one. We may need it.

Reyzl Alright, Father. (*Exits.*)

Saul Judith, if you like you can invite your friend Brontshe and her husband. From our side there won't be anybody except for Reyzele and her husband.

(*A knock is heard on the door.* GOLDMAN *enters.*)

Goldman Good evening.

Saul Good evening! Here you are in the flesh—I just mentioned you! I should have mentioned Elijah the Prophet! I just said we need to invite you—there's going to be a little celebration here this evening. Judith may be signing a betrothal.

Goldman (*thrown*) A betrothal?

Saul What, she's not ready yet? Judith, why don't you ask him to sit down?

Goldman Thank you. (*Sits.*)

Saul Come tonight with your wife. Do come. I haven't invited any family, just you, but, you know, Judith and your wife have been friends since childhood. (*Turns to go, turns back.*) Mr. Goldman, did you have some business with me?

Goldman No, not a thing. I was just passing by and thought I might drop in.

Saul You'll excuse me, I have to step out for a bit. But you must definitely come back with your wife. (exits. Pause)

Goldman Well, you're signing a betrothal today?

Judith   As you heard.

Goldman (*approaches her; she moves away*)   I haven't seen you in days, I can't bear it …

Judith   Really?

Goldman   It's wrong of me to come here and tell you that— but I don't know what to do with myself! And you, since I told you how I felt, you've been avoiding me …

Judith (*ironically*)   And you still feel the same way, even after everything I told you.

Goldman   Not only do I still feel it, it's growing. And it gets stronger every day.

Judith (*laughs bitterly*)   You should be ashamed. (Pause.) Why are we even talking? I've said this to you many times:she is a wonderful human being. (*Pause.*) And she is a beautiful woman.

Goldman   It's true, what you're saying. Still, since you came here I don't see any of that—not her goodness, not her beauty—I only see you. Now she's like a stranger to me. I used to see the whole world in her. But now … sometimes … I hate her. (*Beat.*) Your image tears at me wherever I go.

Judith (*frightened*)   It's gone that far, there are times when you hate her? That's really … very … sad. (*Beat.*) Listen. I forbid you to tell me such things. You know that Brontshe is my only friend in the world. I love her. I treasure her. You're a very foolish man, to have a wife like her and to forget yourself so.

Goldman   Who cares about my wife! She doesn't have to know a thing.

Judith   She doesn't have to know? (*Drops her head. Long pause. Straightens up.*) You know, Goldman, that girls like me, I mean, no longer so very young … We can't take any chances, you understand, Goldman? I can't involve myself with a married man. I have to consider my future.

Goldman   So what should I do? What?

Judith   I'll tell you what. Go home. Live with your wife, and be happy.

Goldman   That's not going to work.

Judith (*changing her tack*)   If you were a widower, or divorced, then maybe we could talk. But like this?

Goldman (*impassioned*)   Tell me, dear, do you want me to get a divorce? I'll get a divorce!

Judith   You could divorce her?

Goldman   Of course.

Judith   And if she's not willing?

Goldman   I'll do whatever it takes to get her to divorce me. I'll force her.

Judith (*frightened*)   Whatever it takes ... (*Beat.*) Look, Goldman, it's fine to say you'll get a divorce, but it has to look like there was a reason. You want people to be on your side.

Goldman (*pleased*)   That can also be done. I can give her the sort of runaround that she'll have to leave Warsaw from the embarrassment.

Judith (*a slight shiver*)   And that can also be done ...

Goldman   Of course, absolutely.

Judith   So because of your desires you will divorce your wife. You'll slander her. (*Beat.*) You are filth.

Goldman (*thrown; stammers*)   Judith!... Judith ...

Judith (*very upset and angry*)   You—shameless!—go home and kiss the ground in front of your wife! You are a disgusting piece of garbage! And Brontshe's as innocent as a child. (GOLDMAN *tries to interrupt.*) Don't you dare! Go home and prostrate yourself before that poor woman that fate tied to you! Get out!

(*She pushes him out. He runs into* SAUL *as he goes.*)

Saul   What happened here? Why were you shouting?

Judith   Nothing, nothing. We were just … talking loudly.

Saul   Just … talking loudly. So *he* was talking loudly?

Judith   What do you mean, Father?

Saul   What do I mean? I mean that I overheard, not on purpose, what *you* were saying so loudly.

Judith   What, you were eavesdropping? That's really inappropriate for a man your age.

Saul   Oh, daughter, daughter … It's easier not to reach this age than to have to listen to a married man talk to your child that way … (*Beat.*) I know it's not your fault, but that's how it is. (despondent) Every vulture will come after you … Now you should understand why you have to get married … It doesn't matter to who, so long as you're married. (*Goes to* JUDITH.) You hear? You have to get married, and as quickly as possible!

Judith   Father, you're trying to make me do something that God knows where it will lead. You talk to me about marriage, and here, just a minute ago, you heard what can happen to a wife when her husband no longer cares for her. Don't think he's the only one. There are a lot of Goldmans in the world.

Saul   That, my child, has to do with luck, with fate … Everything is up to God.

Judith   But I don't believe God decides things for me. God has forgotten me, I think. Completely.

Saul   You can't know what will be.

Judith   Father … Why are you forcing me to do this? I can't! No matter what I was, there's still some decency left in me. (*Beat.*) When I came back home, I burned every particle that remained of that life. I thought that if I just carried myself respectably I could escape from those pressures that were pushing me down, that made me feel I didn't even own myself … But you also give me no peace. (*Getting upset.*) You're forcing me to—to tie my soul to a man who maybe deserves something more respectable … And you're forcing my body to be the property of someone who might be a stranger to me my whole life. Isn't that *also* "selling yourself"?

Saul (*spits it out*)   You already convinced yourself, eh? I don't like that kind of talk, you know that.

Judith   Father, you have to listen to me now. I didn't think it would come to this, but you're making me do it. You, Father, pushed me into all of that. I was a naive young girl and you forced me out of my home. You, Father, made me wander around, lost, out there, in that big world, that vicious world. You, Father, you didn't consider, when you threw me out of my home, that you might have to take *that* on your conscience. You—(*Falls onto a chair.*) No, Father, I don't have the strength to blame you anymore.

Saul (*pacing the room*)   She is just impossible! You think of where all her talk brought her to, but nothing, it's hopeless. Whatever comes into her mouth, she says. (*Beat.*) She couldn't care less that people won't let me walk down the street. I can't look anyone in the eye. Is this how I'm supposed to end up? Me? Any ordinary tramp has at least a little pride, a little pleasure, and me, in my old age, I'm miserable. How much scorn, how much humiliation I've had to put up with because of her all these years! (*Wrought up.*)

This is my old age. This is my old age! … God in Heaven, why do you test me like this? Have I done so much wrong? I don't know what I'm supposed to do now. How do I make it up to you, God? To hear such talk from my own child at this age …

Judith (*crosses to him and embraces him. He pulls away*)   I've hurt you. Forgive me. I won't make you suffer. Ever. I will live a decent life. But I worry that my sensibilities … I don't want anything bad to happen. Papa, don't make me sin against you with words anymore. You have to know how dear you are to me, and … When I'm with you, I feel so protected. Papa, let me stay like that!

(SHEYNDL *comes in, loaded down with packages.* SAUL *springs over to help her with them.*)

Sheyndl   Oh, everything today is so cheap! I bought such beautiful oranges for eight kopecks. What do you think, Sauly, nice, huh?

Saul (*recovering with effort*)   Shopping you can do, this I know.

Sheyndl   May we live to do it for grandchildren!

Saul   *Omeyn.*

Sheyndl   Listen, Judith, I ran into Brontshe. She was very glad to hear you'll be signing a betrothal. She wondered why you didn't tell her yesterday. So I invited her tonight in your name. She promised she would come. Did I do the right thing, Judith?

Saul   You do everything right. Does she know who it's with?

Sheyndl   Yes, I told her. She said she knows his parents. Very fine people. She said they used to be rich. But the groom she said she doesn't know. She says he's probably also a fine person. All right, everything looks good …. But it's getting dark outside, Judith, we have to get to work. We have to get dressed.

Saul   You're right, Sheyndele. Don't take too long.

Maid (*enters bringing a lamp*)   Judith, are you going to change? Somebody might come early. I put everything in order here. (*Cheerful.*) I lived to see Judith's engagement, and with God's help I'll live to see her children's *simkhes*. And may her mother, please God, intercede for her up there, *omeyn*! (*Goes to* JUDITH, *who sits deep in thought; she kisses her on the head.*) My beautiful Judith! When I first came here she was still a young girl, maybe thirteen years old, and she grew and grew, overnight, *kinahora*. Her mother, may Judith live longer than she did, used to say "We have to let down the hem of her dress again, it's embarrassing, you can see her whole feet!"

Sheyndl   Don't talk, don't talk, just do your work.

Maid   Right away, right away, everything will be taken care of.

Sheyndl   Sauly, maybe you'll lay down on the couch inside? We'll be sitting up late and that's not good for you.

Saul   You know what, sweetheart, you're right, I'll go lay down for a bit. (*They exit.*)

Maid   This is a very good match, they say. I overheard what the matchmaker was saying. She swore up and down that it's lucky ... Judith, I can't look at you sitting there so ... Please, for my sake, (*kisses her*) don't be so sad.

Judith   What, you want me to marry?

Maid   Of course, why not? With God's help I'll have some place to go to—one Shabbos to my son, one Shabbos to Judith's. Or maybe Judith would like me to work for her?

(*Doorbell rings.* MAID *exits.* REYZL *enters with her* HUSBAND.)

Reyzl   *Nu*, Judith, you're not even dressed yet! Or are we that early? My husband said he has something to discuss with Father. You know they're always talking and talking … Where's Father? Where's Auntie?

Judith   I think Father's resting, and Auntie is probably in the kitchen.

Reyzl   You have to get dressed, somebody might come in. I'll go help Auntie. If Father sees you're not dressed yet, he'll get angry. You always have to get him angry. Are we interrupting? So we'll leave. (*They exit.* JUDITH *gets a black dress from the wooden case and puts it on.* BRONKE *bursts in, clearly upset about something.*)

Judith   Brontshe, you're here!

Bronke (*stammering*)   I came here to tell you, Judith, that I can't come to your engagement party tonight, even though I promised your Auntie … I … I can't.

Judith (*shaken*)   Look at how upset you are.

Bronke   Yes, I am a little upset.

Judith   You got some bad news?

Bronke   Yes. (*Sympathetically.*) I wish I could come to your engagement. But God bless you. I wish you the best of luck. (*Not looking at her.*) Goodbye, Judith.

Judith   You're leaving already? Why? I don't want to pry, but you're worrying me. (*Looks her in the eyes.*) Something happened to you today. But if it's private, you don't have to tell me, certainly not.

Bronke   You're right. There is something that's upset me. More than anything in my life. (*Beat.*) Goodbye, Judith. (*Starts to go.*)

Judith   Goodbye, Brontshe. But please, whatever it was, don't take it so much to heart.

Bronke (*turns back, fall on Judith's shoulder in tears*)   Judith, Judith, I have to tell you—I was forced to—you mustn't come to my house anymore. (*Beat.*) My husband says I can't speak to you …

Judith (*shaken; beat*)   It's not important. Don't let it upset you so. Your husband probably knows what he's doing.

Bronke   I don't know if I can do that, living in the same city as you. To run into you on the street and not even say a word! That's awful! I don't know what's gotten into him all of a sudden. (*Looking in her eyes.*) I know what a good friend you are, how … how devoted … My husband used to say that too, but now … Did somebody tell him some story about you? He burst into the house like a madman, and he started ranting, about you, all kinds of things … Can it be true, what he said? Could any of it be true? It's terrible. What am I supposed to do? He says he'll tear the house apart if he sees you there … (*Decided.*) But I won't listen to him. I'll see you every day, every day! Any place you want. I'm afraid to come here—I don't want to start in with him. But I'm going to see you every day and that's that! (*Beat.*) That's all lies, what he said about you, some nasty piece of work talked it all into him.

Judith (*warmly*)   No, don't do that. Don't go against your husband. We're not going to meet anyplace. Your husband is right. Everything he told you is true. (*Beat.*) You shouldn't … You mustn't have me in your home.

Bronke   Oh, God, what are you saying?

Judith (*with effort*)   Go away, Brontshe. Go home. He might look for you here. He's right in what he says.

Bronke (*taken aback*)   You're right, he might come looking for me. But please, just say that everything he said about you is a lie, and that we'll get together someplace tomorrow, and you'll tell me how you liked the groom.

Judith (*bitter*)   No, no, we're not going to see each other anymore, we're not going to meet anywhere. Don't defy your husband. Go along with what he says.

Bronke (*almost weeping*)   Goodbye ... then ... May God bless you. (*She runs out.* JUDITH *falls into a chair. The* MATCHMAKER *reenters, dressed loudly.*)

Matchmaker   May everything go with good luck for you! With God's help, the same for my children, oh, God of Mercy!

(*Enter* SHEYNDL, *The* MAID, *and* REYZL. *All carry trays of sweets, which they put on the table, then exit. The* MATCHMAKER *makes sure* JUDITH *isn't watching, then takes a few things from the trays and slips them into a pocket in her petticoat. Reenter* REYZL *with her* HUSBAND, SAUL *in a silken coat, and* SHEYNDL *in a satin dress.*)

Saul (*looking at Judith*)   You're dressed in black? And you're crying?

Sheyndl   So she's dressed in black, leave her be, Sauly.

Matchmaker   It's fine, let her cry, it'll give her good luck.

Sheyndl (*lighting the lamps*)   Keep calm. You see how she's calm? (*Looks off.*) Oh, the in-laws-to-be are here, and the groom—

(*The* PARENTS, *the* GROOM *and his* SISTERS *enter. The groom has a military manner. General greetings, "good evening," "how are you," "please sit down," etc. All sit.*

JUDITH, *seeming very uncomfortable, stares out the window.*
REYZL *encourages her to come to the table, and she does,*
slowly, sitting down and staring at everyone. The MAID
brings in a tray with tea, then watches from the doorway.)

Sheyndl   Please, have some tea, please, and you must taste
the *bodyankes*! Those are *very* good. Please drink some tea,
you must be frozen. Though it was a beautiful day.

Groom   The frost now is just as it was in 1812, when
Napoleon and all his forces froze outside Moscow.

Saul   Please, drink something, eat something, don't make us
keep asking! (*To the GROOM*) You must be fond of tea—in
the military they drink a lot of it.

Groom   Oh, yes. Why, I can drink fifteen glasses of tea at
one sitting. In the regiment we used to bet who could drink
the most tea, and I would down something like thirty glasses
in a row. Those were the days! You could buy it from the drill
instructor for a ruble, and we would sit whole days and not
do a thing except drink tea and play cards. And I didn't lack
for the rubles. They'd send me a little from home, plus twice
a week I played a flute in the officers' club, and I'd pick up a
little something from there too—

1st Sister   (*to Judith*)   Why don't you say something? And
don't want your tea?

Groom   Have some, it's good for you. (*Cheerfully.*) You
know, if Russia would drink more tea instead of vodka,
things might have come out better with Japan ... What do
you think?

Judith   I don't mix in with politics. I don't like to talk about
those things.

Groom (*amazed*)   Who isn't interested in politics?

2nd Sister   What do we need it for? We have our own politics. Let's talk about things a little closer to home.

Matchmaker   Absolutely.

Saul   Why do we need to talk? You must already know it all. I'm sure the matchmaker told you the details.

Matchmaker   Naturally, naturally. A gold watch with a chain! What's to discuss? Let it be in a lucky hour, and that's that!

Saul   If the two of them are happy, and the in-laws are happy, then good luck to them, and that's that. We just have to ask the groom what he thinks. Now what do the in-laws say?

Groom's Father   Of course! If my son is pleased, then good luck to them.

Matchmaker   What then, he wouldn't be pleased? I should have a year as refined as this young lady is, as graceful. So what do you say, young man?

Groom   What should I say? If my parents are pleased, then I am too.

Matchmaker   So we have to sign a betrothal contract, may it be in a lucky hour. Why put it off? Better to do it now.

Saul   So what do you think, in-laws, should we sign it now?

Groom's Parents   All the same to us.

Saul (*to* REYZL'S HUSBAND)   Yankl, maybe you could go out and pick up a betrothal contract?

Reyzl's Husband (*signaling to* SAUL *that he has it already*)   I'll go right now.

(*He exits. The atmosphere becomes more informal.*)

Saul (*to the* GROOM'S FATHER)   Yes, in-law, that advertising cost me more than you'd think …. Quite a lot, believe me.

Sheyndl (*to the* GROOM'S MOTHER)   Tell me, Mrs. In-Law, how is it working out with your new servant?

Groom's Mother   She's very good. And not expensive.

(*The chit-chat continues for a moment, and then* REYZL's HUSBAND *returns with the document.*)

Matchmaker   Now we can sign it, may it be a lucky hour.

Groom's Mother (*ready to cry*)   Yes, dear God, in a lucky hour.

1st Sister (*to* JUDITH)   What kind of sickness did your husband have?

Judith   Sickness?

2nd Sister   No, he didn't die. I think the matchmaker said they got divorced.

Judith   The matchmaker lied to you.

Both Sisters   What's that?

Judith   The matchmaker lied to you. I've never had a husband. (*Suddenly springs over to the trunk; grabs the photographs and throws them on the table, pointing to them and shouting.*) But *he* was like a husband! And him, and him, and all of these, and more, many others, quite a lot of them! (*All leap up from the table, stunned, murmuring.*) Oh yes, oh yes. You needn't look at me like that. It's the truth, that's how it was. My husband was every one of them.

(*Pause.*)

1st Sister   What, is she not feeling well? I noticed it right away, it was how she was sitting, you'd think that—

Matchmaker (*stammering*)   She is, she took sick, it just happened.

Sheyndl   She's been upset all day. She was visiting her mother's grave today, and she's just not herself.

Matchmaker   Absolutely. Absolutely.

Groom's Mother   We'll sign the papers another time.

All   Yes, another time, put it off ... (*etc.)*

Matchmaker   Saturday night, with God's help.

All   Yes, a small delay, good night (*etc. The visitors exit slowly. A long pause.*)

Reyzl (*to* JUDITH, *who stands lost in thought*)   Why did you do that? What good did it do you?

Sheyndl   Honestly, who tells people about such things?

Saul (*pacing about, the words sticking in his throat*)   She ... murdered ... her own father ... The disgrace ...

Judith   There was nothing else I could do. You should have told them the truth ... And you should also have told them that back there, where I was, I left proof, living proof ... Yes, Father, I was silent about that, I kept it from you. But now you know. I left behind a child.

Saul (*leaping at her*)   You ... trash! You monster! Why don't you just die already? You can't stay in this house another minute! Get out, you hear me? Get out!

Sheyndl/Reyzl   Saul/Papa, get a hold of yourself! Let her talk, it's just her nonsense, you should be used to it by now ...

Saul   I can't bear this ... That, what she was back there, that's not enough, she had to leave a bastard behind her ... Dear God, a bastard! Why didn't—you monster—why didn't you tell me right away?

Judith   I didn't tell you enough. But I couldn't tell you that too. I … didn't have the words.

Saul (*ironic*)   You didn't have the words! *She* didn't have the words!

Judith   I couldn't.

Saul   You could have just choked on it—and not said anything now either.

Judith   No, Father, I had to! (*Firm.*) You can't play games with somebody else's life. I had to tell them the truth—if I hadn't, someone else would have turned up sooner or later and told them everything.

(*Pause; collecting herself.*)

When I was back there, I only wanted one thing: to come back home, to hold on to you, to kiss your gray hairs, every day. Back there, I hoped that someday I'd be buried in that cemetery where my mother is … and not somewhere behind a fence. But it's like you say, Father—"It's not to be." So what now? Here, you tell me, I can't remain, and I can't go back there either … Where can you go when your soul is torn? … But I have to leave. I have to find a place that you never come back from. (*Thinking.*) Never. Father, we have to part now. (*Paces the room.*)

Sheyndl   You should be ashamed to say things like that. How does that get into your head? Where can you go? You've gone enough.

Saul (*angry*)   Sheyndele, please, don't butt in, she knows herself what she has to do.

Judith   Don't yell at her, Papa, she's not keeping me here. (*Firmly.*) I'm leaving. (*Goes to the trunk, takes out a black shawl, and puts it on, then a coat; stands in place for a moment, looks around; drops to the ground and kisses the* *floorboards.*) Here, Mama, here you lay, eight years ago, here, on this floor … (*Kisses it again.*) Your shadow was here. (*Kisses the wall.*) Eight years ago. I remember like it was today.

Now I say goodbye. (*Slowly rises. Softly.*) Now I say goodbye … (*Weeps. Crosses to SAUL and tries to kiss his hands. He pulls away from her.*)

Be well, Father. If I've done you harm, please forgive me. Stay well, Auntie, and be a good wife, he loves you.

Don't cry, Reyzl.

(*She runs out. SHEYNDL, REYZL, and the MAID follow, calling after her.*)

CURTAIN

END OF ACT III

ACT IV

(*Russia. Four years later. A large, antiseptic, institutional-looking room on the outskirts of a city. Judith sits at a desk, examining papers. Beds along the walls, with starched white bedding. A few windows sit high off the ground. Open double doors lead to a second room, in which we see a large dining table with young women sitting around it wearing black dresses with white collars. They are getting up from lunch and start clearing the table. We hear from within:*)

Seamstress   Today it's your turn to do the dishes.

Down Collector   I can't today, I hurt my finger.

Seamstress   That doesn't matter, it's your turn. Everyone has to do their job.

(*They start coming through the door.*)

Embroiderer/Franke   Judith, please, let us take a nap after lunch.

Judith   No, girls, you can't, it's absolutely forbidden. You know very well that each of you has work to do right after lunch. And we go to sleep early. Now what would the chairwoman say if she came in and saw the beds not made? No, girls, it won't do. They are making a great effort for us, and we must follow the rules. And the work we've been assigned is so needed, so important for mankind, that even if we lose a few nights' sleep, it's worth it. (*Sits at desk.*) So, girls ... (*Looks in a notebook and calls.*) Bandage-Nurse! (*She approaches;* JUDITH *looks at her.*) Are you not feeling well? Why so gloomy?

Bandage-Nurse   It's nothing... It's just that the last patient had such awful wounds that I couldn't come near him. The wounds were so painful. I can't look at that ...

Judith   You should be used to it by now. You've been tending to the patients more than six months already.

Bandage-Nurse   But he screams when I touch him. It's awful.

Judith   So be more careful, then. Gentler.

Bandage-Nurse   I'll try. (*Exits to second room.*)

Judith (*looks in the book*)   Embroiderer! (*A woman enters holding a piece of embroidery, which she hands to* JUDITH.) Your work is going very slowly.

Embroiderer   It'll be ready in time.

Judith   Time is short. I'm afraid you might have to go a few nights without much sleep. Work faster. Please.

Embroiderer   All right. (*Exits.*)

Judith (*looks in book, calls*)   Down Collector! (*A young woman approaches, keeping her face turned away.*) Why are you turning away like that? (*No response.* JUDITH *comes over and looks at her.*) Make-up again, eh? That's inexcusable! If anyone came in and saw that! (*Calls.*) Pepa! (PEPA *enters from the other room.*) Where did she get that make-up?

Pepa   She probably found a piece of red paper in the street somewhere.

Judith   Please, Pepa, let this be the last time. You have to watch out for everything, you know that. Something like this could bring us a lot of unpleasantness.

Pepa   She knows herself not to do it again.

Judith (*to* DOWN COLLECTOR)   Will you promise not to do it again?

Down Collector   I don't see how it could hurt anybody.

Judith   God, it's embarrassing for you yourself!

Down Collector   If it's embarrassing for me, then it's not going to embarrass anybody else—

Judith   Please, try to show some self-control. Now return to your place and go back to work. (*Beat.*) And wash your face, right away. (DOWN COLLECTOR *exits.* JUDITH *looks in the book, calls.*) Seamstress! (*a young woman with a sluttish walk approaches, carrying clothing*) Let's see, what have you done since yesterday? (*Looks, pleased.*) Oh, three shirts, two dresses … You've done beautifully! Mankind will bless you for this. But you sit for days on end indoors, and you look very pale. You know what, I'll take you with me today. I have to deliver a report to the Committee.

Seamstress   Thank you, very much! (*Walks away.*)

Judith (*calling*)   Pepa!

Pepa   Yes?

Judith   Send in those two unfortunates. (*Two unkempt-looking women come in. One's hair is extremely disheveled. Firmly, to that one.*) Tell me, why did you not comb your hair again today? (*The woman doesn't answer, just stands there picking her nose.*) You're a problem, you two. Letting yourself go like that, it's very strange … Are you feeling all right?

1st Melancholic (*muttering*)   All right.

Judith   Are you getting enough to eat?

1st Melancholic   Yes.

Judith   Would you like to go for a walk? (*No reply; then.*)

2nd Melancholic (*staring at the ground*)   I had a bad dream … My mother and my dead sister came to me … They said they were burned in a fire …

Judith (*sympathetically*)   You shouldn't believe in dreams. I'll write a letter home for you … You can go back to your places. (*They exit together. Calling.*) Pepa!

Pepa   What do you need?

Judith (*leaning in to her*)   You know, Pepa, we're going to have to send those two to a hospital. That's what the administrators have ordered … and really … they get worse every day …

Pepa   Whatever you think is best.

Judith   The others know too, eh? (*Rises; to all.*) So. Is everyone happy with the meals? Is everyone feeling all right? Who would like to write a letter?

2nd Melancholic   I want a letter.

Judith   Good, good. I'll write it for you as soon as I get back. (*Calls.*) Seamstress, get your coat!

Seamstress   Yes, ma'am.

Judith   So, girls, everything seems to be in order. I'm going out for a bit.

Pepa (*bringing* JUDITH *her coat*)   Please, Judith, make it quick.

Judith   I never take very long.

Pepa   I know, but when you're not here …

Judith   … Yes?

Pepa   Nothing, nothing.

Judith   You're hiding something? There's something you don't want to tell me?

Pepa (*turns away*)   No, no. (*Exits to second room.* JUDITH *and the* SEAMSTRESS *also exit. Several young women peek out the window after them.*)

Embroiderer (*overlapping*)   Finally! You just can't get rid of her!

Bandage Nurse (*overlapping*)   A whole *day* she didn't leave the place.

Down Collector (*overlapping*)   She's walking up the street.

Embroiderer (*to* DOWN COLLECTOR)   Who's that letter for? The one you found today?

Bandage Nurse   If she knew …

Down Collector   The custodian gave it to me, he said, "*Khozyayka, pazhalusta, adayte Rivke Burak.*" (*She hands a letter to a girl walking by, yawning.*) Please, Franke, read it to me.

Franke (*sits on the ground in the middle of the room. The others crowd in around her as she reads*)   "My dear little viper! First I want to say that thanks to—"

Several   Who could that be from?

Franke   Wait a second! And stop crowding, I can't even breathe! (*Reading the signature.*) Yitskhok-Leyb Charb.

Several   Hoorah! It's Charbie! He didn't forget!

Down Collector   Read some more.

Franke   I lost my place. "My dear little viper. First, I want to say that thanks to myself, plus also to Russia, who fed me well with rye bread and cabbage while I was in their little dormitory, I am in the best of health, and hoping to hear the same of you. Second, I want to tell you that as soon as they let me out I ran straight upstairs, and you can't imagine my amazement when I didn't find you there. The old man and the old woman sit there yawning, and they look, I hate to tell you, like it's just after Yom Kippur. Right away they told me their sad story—that she, the one you called 'Princess', yes, her, who the devil brought over from Warsaw, talked it into all of you to leave there with her, and you'd all go into some other business. I'm not going to say that upstairs there the poverty is blowing through every crack, but to do such a thing, to just abandon people with no way to earn a penny, well, nobody with a Jewish heart would do that."

Embroiderer (*overlapping*)   Oh, they can't even make a living …

Bandage Nurse (*overlapping*)   He's absolutely right. It's a terrible thing to do.

Franke   Will you let me finish? (*Reads.*) "… nobody with a Jewish heart would do that. If I ran into that Warsaw girl, I'd break her legs."

Down Collector Oh, yeah, he could do it, too.

Franke Will you let me read or not? "And you, little viper, I have to tell you—really, my mother should live so long—what you did was very stupid. We should both have a year as good as the business that could have been done upstairs."

Down Collector You hear that? But no, we have to be here with her! This is nowhere!

Embroiderer (*overlapping*) Stop interrupting!

Bandage Nurse (*overlapping*) Let her finish!

Franke Right … "… could have been done upstairs. The chicken man isn't what he used to be up there, so there are opportunities. So, lambie, when you get this letter, don't be shy, tip them all off and get moving."

Down Collector He doesn't have to tell me twice. I'm rotting here. What kind of life is this?

Bandage Nurse Let her read it!!

Franke "You can forget how it used to be. What I mean is—the rough stuff is gone. Believe me, I swear to you, all the Jews should live so long, beating just doesn't go anymore. Stay fresh and healthy. I kiss your rosy cheeks … Are they still rosy? From me, your bridegroom, Yitskhok-Leyb Charb."

Bandage Nurse What do you think of that?

Down Collector Bless him! Bless him! Well, what do you say, who wants to get going?

Embroiderer I'm the first! Girls, it's a new world. We have to get out of here or else we'll go crazy too. (*Beat.*) I have a secret: we can even drink to our future—Look at this! (*Pulls a bottle from under her bed.*)

Franke Where'd you get it?

Embroiderer   What kind of question is that? I didn't *steal* it! (*Drinks from the bottle.*) Sisters!

(*The bottle passes around; several girls drink from it.*)

Several (*hollering*)   Good for Charbie! Here's to Rivke Burak! Hurrah!

Pepa (*comes in and sees it all, terrified*)   Oh, God, what's going on here? Oh my God! When Judith comes back, she'll go berserk!

Embroiderer   Look at her, the yellow-belly! (*Laughter.*)

Franke   Come here, little sister, you used to like a drink or two. (*She puts her arm around PEPA, who pulls away.*)

Pepa   Let me go, please. Stop, you'll ruin everything—(*The* EMBROIDERER *grabs* PEPA *and forces liquor down her throat.*) I don't want it! (*She drinks anyway.*) You're crazy! (*The* DOWN COLLECTOR *runs to* 2ND MELANCHOLIC, *who is sitting cramped in a corner, humming to herself; she pulls her to the middle of the room and tries to pour liquor into her.*) Let her alone!

Pepa   Go away, I don't want it.

Down Collector   She has to! She has to! (*Pours liquor down the girl's throat.*) Now, girls, we're gonna dance.

(*The girls form a circle and make* PEPA *and the* 2ND MELANCHOLIC *join them. They dance around and sing.*)

Several   "Dance, Yasha Morningstar

A girl can go so very far

A girl can be most anything—"

(*hollering*) Dance! Dance!

(2ND MELANCHOLIC *falls; the* DOWN COLLECTOR, *drunk, falls on top of her. Others ignore them, dance, scream, whistle …* JUDITH *and the* SEAMSTRESS *appear in the doorway and watch, unseen. The* DOWN COLLECTOR *drags herself back up and stands on a chair.*)

Down Collector   So, girls, who's going with me to my wonderful Charbie?

Franke (*overlapping*)   Me!

Embroiderer (*overlapping*)   We're not going to stay here!

Bandage Nurse (*overlapping*)   We're wasting away, we're young, we can live –

Down Collector   So, tomorrow, when the witch sends us out, that'll be the last time she sees us. She should drop dead, the way she dragged us here. She wants us to behave like little judges. And she's *our* judge –?! No, we have to live! We have to live!

Several   Yes! Hurrah! Yes! Let's dance!

(*singing*) From the head down to the toe

Nothing to be ashamed of, Joe

Dance, Yasha Morningstar

A girl can go so very far—

Pepa (*sees* JUDITH)   Quiet down! Oh, God …

(*The girls see* JUDITH *and run off.* 2ND MELANCHOLIC *remains lying C, moaning.*)

Judith (*as if she hadn't seen a thing*)   How are you, girls? (*No response.* JUDITH *helps the* 2ND MELANCHOLIC *into a chair. Passes her hat to* PEPA, *whom she studies closely.* PEPA *takes it, eyes lowered. The light outside is dimming.*) You know what, girls? I've decided that those who are on the schedule to help in the infirmary tonight will not go …

It's such a sad day today. You know, I just got up from sitting *shiva* for my father ... So girls, we'll all stay here. We'll talk about our homes, about our childhood. What do you think, would you like to do that?

Embroiderer (*overlapping*)   Yes, yes, it won't do any harm if we don't go one time.

Bandage Nurse (*overlapping*)   Taking a night off is a good idea.

Franke (*overlapping*)   Let the administrators help the patients for one night—see how they like it.

Down Collector (*overlapping*)   Nice when you can get someone else to do things for you.

Judith   So you'd like to? Good. Pepa, ask them to start on dinner while we talk. So who's first? Embroiderer, why don't you start, you were always a good storyteller.

Embroiderer   What do I have to say? I've told it a hundred times already ...

Bandage Nurse   So what? Tell it again.

Embroiderer   ... My mother was widowed very young. She was very successful. She used to sew beautifully, for ... women like we used to be. She used to send me up there to deliver work. I was thirteen, and my mother thought I didn't understand anything yet. But I understood a lot ... Every time I was upstairs, the madam showed me how well they lived there. They had fancy food ... She told me they danced up there every night. I used to love watching people dance ... One night I snuck out of the house and went over there to see the dancing ... I never went back home. For a long time they used to hide me when my mother would come by with her work. She cried right in front of the madam—the madam told me—because she didn't know where I was. But maybe six months later I bumped into her there—we saw each other.

She didn't say a word, she just went white, and she ran out screaming ... I never saw my mother again ... I found out later that she'd died ...

Judith   Sad story. Sad story ... Who will be next?

Down Collector   I have nothing new to say. You heard it all already.

Bandage Nurse   Tell it. It's not gonna hurt you ...

Down Collector   I'd like to know if maybe they finally got killed somewhere, the people who brought me into everything ... That was my own family. They did it.

Judith   Every one of us was brought to it by something. But that doesn't matter. It was mostly we ourselves who brought us there. We're more to blame than the people who pointed out the way. To point is just to point, but to actually go ... When you see where that road leads, (*to herself*) you have to turn yourself around ...

Franke   You turned yourself around, but then later you went back to it ... They said you were "saved from death"—but if it's fate, it doesn't matter how much you struggle, you have to keep on doing it.

Judith   Yes, I went back, and that was my fault too ... One time I *was* "saved from death," but the second time ... I had no strength left. I wandered a while, then I stumbled again ... (*Beat.*) But I did have the strength to find a new path for us. Thank God, the danger is over, we've found the right road. (*Several girls laugh.*) Why are you laughing?

Franke   You think this is the right road ... (*Laughs.*) They put us in a cage and they feed us! (*Sarcastic.*) Isn't that wonderful, they feed us!

Judith   Dear God, you think that's nothing? You've got a clean place to live, you eat regularly, you're away from temptation—what else do you need?

Franke   What do you think, because we don't do anything wrong here, people look at us differently than they used to? The Society saved us, they threw us a bone. Fine, who are we now? They're just as horrified by us as they were before. That Society isn't interested in *us*, what we went through, what we're going through ... They took away our words. We don't have the right to speak. The same people that allowed our bodies to roll around in garbage, now they're doing us a favor, they're feeding us. Well, I don't have any gratitude for them, none. Just a curse, that's all I have for them.

Down Collector (*stretching; sarcastic*)   You think one of the administrators would let you marry her son? (*Laughs.*) Sure, why wouldn't she? We've all turned into "Little Mrs. Rabbi"!

Seamstress   What more do you want? What do you want from them? They're strangers! My God! Do our own families even want to know us? Do we ever hear from a brother, a sister?

2nd Melancholic (*quietly, almost to herself*)   My little sister, Rachel ... I used to braid her hair, and ... I'd tie it with blue ribbons ...

Franke   Look at her, how she ended up. (*Long pause. PEPA enters.*)

Pepa   The dinner's on the table. (*She lights the gas lamps as the girls go off into the other room.*)

Judith   Pepa, stay here a minute.

Pepa   What do you want?

Judith   What's this? I hadn't noticed before—you can barely stand up ...

Pepa (*downcast eyes*)   I'm listening. I'm not drunk.

Judith   I want you to have all the shutters closed tonight. That is, you yourself should see to it that they're all closed tight, and fill the cracks. (*Beat.*) Here's an idea—stuff them with the down.

Pepa (*stares at her, amazed*) It's not cold outside. And it's so stuffy in here.

Judith Do what I told you! *I'm* not drunk. (PEPA *exits. JUDITH looks around for a moment, then sits at the desk. Joking and laughter are heard from the other room. JUDITH takes paper from a drawer, thinks for a moment, then starts to write.*) "Dear Honored Administrators. It is clear to me that we are unable to show our gratitude for all your effort and generosity. I can also see that our lives cannot be of any real use to anyone. It is better that what will happen to us this night should happen.

Please pardon my boldness, but I will pass along one observation your objective is beautiful, but it would be still more beautiful, as well as more practical, if instead of establishing homes for women who have fallen, you could create institutions that prevented their falling in the first place." (*Signs the letter, then puts it in an envelope, and writes an address. Takes out another piece of paper and writes.*)

"I have one more request of you. Knowing your kind hearts, I will be so bold (*cont'd*) as to ask you to follow those hearts once again and take under your protection a child born of a Jewish mother who is being brought up by a Christian woman named Tatyana Nazarova in Tverer Province, Village Kazyonke. To prove this came from me, mention Tatyana's pledge not to tell the child who her mother is. With deep respect, Judith Zaltsman." (*Signs the letter, puts it in an envelope, and writes an address. Calls out.*) Girls, have you finished eating? (*They start coming back.*) It's time to go to sleep.

(*The women start getting into beds, talking across to each other, joking. The 2ND MELANCHOLIC remains sitting on the ground, talking to herself.*)

Down Collector   The crazy one's making a speech.

Judith (*calls*)   Pepa, help her undress. (PEPA *tries, but the girl won't let her.* JUDITH *kneels next to her, holds her head, and starts stroking her hair. After a while.*) Go to sleep.

2nd Melancholic   Write my family a letter.

Judith   What should I write?

2nd Melancholic   Write that I'm fine, that the whole world is fine, that I'm coming home soon, and that I'll bring a lot of ribbons for Rachel's braids …

Judith   Good, good, go to sleep. (*Leads her to her bed, helps her undress. Snoring is heard from other beds.*) Pepa! (*Hands her the letters and some coins.*) Give these to the custodian. Tell him to deliver them tomorrow to those addresses.

Pepa (*exiting*)   All right.

Judith (*goes to each bed and makes sure the girls are asleep.* PEPA *returns*)   All right, now you can go to sleep.

Pepa   You've been so downhearted lately. (*Looks at her.*) You know, as long as I know you, I've never seen one real smile cross your lips …

Judith   There's nothing to be so happy about. Tell me, Pepa, why did you never tell me that they … that they're so unhappy with the situation?

Pepa   I knew it would upset you.

Judith   What about you? How do you feel here?

Pepa   For me it doesn't matter, as long as I'm with you. I wouldn't be able to hold myself together for a minute without you. (*They kiss.*)

Judith   Go to sleep.

Pepa   I really am tired tonight, much more than usual. And you, why don't you lie down?

Judith   I'll go to sleep soon too, I just want to look at the accounts.

(*PEPA turns off the gas lamps except one and goes to sleep.*)

Pepa   Good night, Judith.

(*JUDITH doesn't answer. She slowly rises and locks the doors, then puts the keys under the pillow on her bed. She sits at the desk again. Pause. She rises and goes to each bed again to make sure that they're all asleep. Some snore. Some talk in their sleep.*

She goes to each lamp, takes off the sconce, and turns up the knobs, then turns off the one that's lit.)

Judith   If there really is another world, we'll see each other soon, Mama.

(*She goes quickly to her own bed near the desk and lies down. We hear the gas hissing from the pipes in the lamps.*)

SLOW CURTAIN

END OF PLAY.

Translator's Note by Miro Mniewski

How thrilling it was to be handed an old yellowing notebook, the pages so fragile that handling them might cause them to crumble. And so archival gloves came to the rescue in order to peruse the pages of Lena Brown's early-twentieth-century college notebook.

The upper corners of each page were stamped with numbers in sequential order starting from the left side of the notebook. But Lena Brown's play *Sonia Itelson or A Child ... A Child ...,* opened with Act I at the back of the notebook, to read from right to left as is customary in Yiddish text. The four dramatic acts of the play were handwritten, culminating at the front of the notebook, with the final curtain of Act IV.

What a surprise it was to discover that this ancient-seeming artifact, written sometime in the early 1910s, was, throughout, a feminist play, a family drama, intimately tracing the arc of its female characters from bold, independent-minded women, to their tragic downfall. In fleshing out that process many themes relevant to women's lives to this very day came to the fore: rebellion against gender roles, rejection of society's mores, the shame of abortion, and the tragedy inherent in not being seen and heard by family members. And all of these themes reflect the struggle to communicate honestly in our most intimate relationships.

Set in the middle-class living rooms of our two anti-heroes, Sonia Itelson and her sister Fanny, the play reveals personal and intimate tensions. The dialogue is, at times, poignant, and at times sarcastically humorous. This back-and-forth banter rang so clearly in my head it wasn't difficult to transform the sometimes archaic, Germanic Yiddish to current American vernacular.

As a nonbinary identified translator, the play initially attracted me because it was so conducive to queer interpretation. The main character buckles at what I might suggest we refer to as "their" assigned gender, and both sisters rebel against societal pressure to bear and nurture children, albeit in different ways. What's more, Sonia's boyfriend, whose name is provided as "Leo Edit" at the top of the manuscript is referred to by his last name "Edit" throughout. At first, I mistook him for female as I thought the character's name was a Yiddish version of the English name "Edith." When I considered referring to him by his first and more conventional masculine name Leo—all other characters are referred to by their first names—I decided against this. I translated Brown's words as she set them down and the choice adds to the curious gender-bending slant of the play.

Lena Brown, the playwright, was a married woman, living on the Lower East Side of Manhattan at the turn of the twentieth century. She was to have one child, a son, David Brown, who kept her notebook until his death. According to Jeffrey Brown, David's son, Lena Brown kept to herself. She demurred socializing with her husband's friends, and instead frequented the Yiddish theater by herself. Jeffrey Brown came across the notebook while cleaning out his father's house on Long Island. He was curious as to what it contained and serendipitously connected with me to translate it. How lucky for me that it fell into my hands! And how wonderful that Alyssa Quint recognized its merit to bring it to publication!

Thank you to my partner in life and in our research and translation business, my beloved Chana Pollack. We had the greatest time reading through the play together.

Sonia Itelson or A Child ... A Child ...

a drama in four acts

by Lena Brown

Characters

SONIA ITELSON

FANNY: Her sister.

Dr. DAVE ITELSON: Her brother.

SIMON RABINOV: Fanny's husband.

LEO EDIT

IDA: Sonia's friend.

WOMAN

LILLY: An eight-year old girl.

MRS. GOLDEN

A BABY, NEIGHBORS

ACT I

Winter in New York
A richly furnished dining room in Rabinov's house.
Stage right: library w/ bookshelves
Stage left: fancy bedroom
It is Sunday afternoon. FANNY *is in a housedress*
cleaning the furniture with a duster.
She is twenty-two years old but looks much older,
sickly and pale.
Doorbell rings.
She goes to the door w/ duster in hand and
presses the button.
SIMON *enters. He is a handsome, life-loving young man,*
wearing sports clothes.

Simon   *Happily.*
Fanny, Faninke, I got tickets, look, Balcony B, Center.
Gives her two theatre tickets.
She doesn't take them.

Fanny   *Indifferent.*
I believe you.

Simon   *Insulted.*
Talks to himself.
It's impossible to make her happy. I push through a crowd
to get good seats so she could sit like a lady, but she could care
less. She only wants to stew.
Regretfully.
You're not even dressed yet? You knew I was going to get
the tickets.

Fanny   *Sarcastically.*
I didn't believe you would get good seats for today.

Simon   Is that why you're hanging around in an apron holding a duster in your hand?

It's already one o'clock. When do you plan on getting dressed?

Fanny   I can be ready in fifteen minutes and to walk over to the theatre shouldn't take long.
Exits to bedroom.

Simon   *Looks in the mirror.*
Fanny! What are you going to wear?

Fanny   I'm already dressed, you'll soon see.
Comes out in an elegant walking dress, combing her hair.

Simon   *Checks her out critically.*
This is what you're wearing? And you put it together so quickly. You didn't even put fifteen minutes into it. That's how much you care about it.

Fanny   It'll do.

Simon   *With a tone.*
Oh yes, I can just imagine what you're going to look like.

Fanny   I can't do anything about your imagination. You know that I never liked spending too much time in front of the mirror

Simon   I know, you're just like your sister; it takes her five minutes to get ready, as if she weren't even going to a theatre, concert, or the opera. That's why you two never look like ladies.

Fanny   We want to look like people, not like ladies. First of all, you only like women who wear the latest fashions. The ones that please you, wear only what's in style, not what looks best on them. All those promenading around in the latest hats and dresses don't care whether they look good in them or not. The only thing they care about is "the latest style."

Simon   *Impatiently.*

That's enough. If you continue I'll think it's Sonia talking. Fine, let her take you over then. You don't need much more to turn you into the little lady philosopher that she is. I'm not happy about it. The less I hear from her the better.

Fanny   Settle down, it's not doing me any harm.

Simon   Oh, it's done plenty of harm already.
Looks toward library.

If it weren't for her we'd have a beautiful parlor here. What do I need a library for? Oh, "I beg your pardon," a library. As Sonia would say, "When you speak Yiddish, speak a clean Yiddish, it's not nice to throw in English words."

Fanny   And you think it's okay?

Simon   Oh, would you like me to speak the way she does? Like a greenhorn just off the boat?

Fanny   Don't let her way of speaking bother you. Nobody's preventing you from speaking the way you want to.
She gives him her coat. He helps her on with it and gives her an ebullient smile.

Why don't you get ready. You're complaining we're going to be late.

Simon   *Takes her hand.*

This time my wife, you deserve credit. You got dressed quickly and you look beautiful.
He tries to kiss her, but she pushes him away capriciously.

Simon   Ah, you cold fish. You're not going to get your way with me.
Kisses her.

You beautiful, frigid soul. In this you are not yet as skillful as Sonia.
Faint ring.

Here she is now—that's her ring.

Fanny   *With a tone.*
   Her ring?
   Opens door.
   Enter SONIA, *a thin, cordial young woman, very well dressed, in her twenties.*

Sonia   You look all dressed up to go out. It's a good thing I got here in time. I don't have my key.
   Takes off her hat and coat.

Fanny   I found your key on the floor. But rushing to go out to the theatre I forgot about it.

Sonia   What are you going to see?

Fanny   *Bored.*
   I don't know, Simon's the one who really wants to go to the theatre. He said that if there were good seats he would get tickets.

Sonia   *Smiling.*
   You must have gotten good seats then, huh?
   Turns to SIMON.
   Where did you get them?

Simon   At the Grand Theatre. I don't know what's playing there. There was such a crowd when I got there that all I could do was push my way toward the box office.

Sonia   Well they must be playing something good then if Simon had to push his way in.

Fanny   *Curiously.*
   What?

Sonia   Elisha Ben Abuya by Jacob Gordin.

Simon   What did you say was playing? What?

Sonia   Elisha Ben Abuya.

Simon   *Upset.*
What kind of play is that?

Sonia   You'll see.
An aside.
And afterward you won't know either.
Before you push your way to the box office why don't you take a look at the poster.

Fanny   Today it makes no difference that he didn't look.

Simon   *Insulted.*
Take a look at your watch, it's already half past one. Enough philosophizing, let's go.

Sonia   Yes, it's time to go.
Turns to FANNY.
Have you eaten dinner?

Fanny   We had breakfast at eleven.

Sonia   *With a gentle reproach.*
Fanninke, I don't like that. One must eat regularly, especially you.

Simon   Especially her? What's wrong with her? Are you trying to talk her into being sick again? And if you think so, why don't you listen to me? Instead of spending so much money on a wet nurse we could get a good housekeeper to attend to everything: the baby, the house. Then she could be a lady! She woke up this morning very early and worked non-stop till just a little while ago.

Sonia   Fanny, how many times have I told you not to do anything except prepare food.

Fanny   Leave me alone, please, I cannot take your worrying about me. He complains that I work too hard. It's not that bad, working around the house will not harm me.
Sarcastically.
All we need is a housekeeper.

I wouldn't keep a servant even if I brought the baby home from the wet nurse.

A worker's salary is nothing to sneeze at.

Simon   What are you complaining about? Aren't my wages good enough for you? And you're calling me a worker—you're calling a foreman in the cloak industry a common worker?

Sonia   She didn't say you were a common worker or that you don't earn enough for her. But a foreman is also a salaried worker, and like everyone else not immune to slack, as you call it.

Simon   *Proudly.*
   I, like all foremen, have steady work.

Sonia   Really, is that why when a foreman loses his job it's much harder for him to get another one, unlike a common worker. For that reason it's not generally advisable to spend one's wages on servants. But it's different for us. Fanny and I should be sharing the housework, but she doesn't allow it.
   Turns to FANNY.
   You worked all morning?

Fanny   I did very little, Sonia, I just made breakfast and dusted my bedroom. You cleaned all the other rooms yesterday, and you have half a day off today, I don't want to rob you of it?

Sonia   *Moved. Takes* FANNY's *hands and kisses them. Tenderly lets go and opens the door.*
   Go dear ones or you'll be late.

Fanny   *Smiles.*
   Good-bye Sonia.

Simon   Bye-bye

Sonia   Good-bye dear.
   FANNY *and* SIMON *exit.*

Sonia   Watches *them from the window. Sits down in a chair and sighs. A knock at the door.*

Sonia   Come-in!
   EDIT enters, a handsome, thin man sophisticatedly dressed, twenty-three years old.

Sonia   *Surprised.*
   Oh, Edit!
   Goes to greet him.

Edit   *Squeezes her hand.*
   Unexpected, huh?

Sonia   For sure. Could I have waited longer?

Edit   I've told you several times that you not allowing it won't stop me from visiting you.

Sonia   *Enlivened.*
   And you kept your word! You deserve credit for that. Let me take your hat and coat,
   since you're already here, be my guest.

Edit   Thank you. Here I am your guest. But don't bother with my hat I can hang it up myself.
   He does it.

Sonia   *Pulls a chair up for him. He sits down. She sits down in the rocking chair.*

Edit   I ran into your sister and her husband in the hall. She opened the door for me and invited me to go up to you.

Sonia   *Surprised.*
   I don't understand. You two know each other?

Edit   Hasn't she told you?
   Smiles.
   That was nice of her. Now I must confess that this is already the second time I've come here to visit you.

Sonia   When were you here?

Edit   Wednesday evening. I was disappointed you weren't home but I didn't want you to know so I asked your sister not to tell you.

Sonia   And she agreed.

Edit   She did.

Sonia   Were you certain she'd keep her word?

Edit   Yes, she made a very good impression on me in the short time we spent together. But if I'm not mistaken she seemed unhappy, sad.

Sonia   That's nothing new for her. Can a sick person look any different?

Edit   You told me a few months ago that she was in the hospital. Is she still sick?

Sonia   I hope not. It's already time she were well.
Absorbed in thought.
Not even twenty-two years old and has already managed to have twins. And to make matters worse she's married to a common, happy-go-lucky, kind of guy.

Edit   Don't be so distressed about everything. You're making it worse than it is.

Sonia   What can I do if that's how I see things? And anyway, no one else would see it differently in this case.
Speaking heard through the door: "Most likely her sister is home. I saw her leave a little while ago"

Sonia   *Opens door. Wet nurse enters with baby. Happily.*
Oh it's you, Mrs. Golden.
Hastily grabs the child into her arms.
Dear sweet, little girl.
Kisses her and presses the baby to her breast.
Darling dear one, what a guest.

Turns to the wet nurse.

Thank you, Mrs. Golden, I haven't seen you in so long. I worked all week till nine and didn't want to visit you that late. Sit down.

Pulls the rocking chair over for her.

Mrs. Golden *Sits down.*

Mrs. Golden You should live and be well. There's nothing to be afraid of, no one is ever asleep at our house, even if you come at midnight.

Sonia *Worried.*

It's not very good when everyone in the house is up late. It makes it hard for a child to sleep soundly. But I guess it can't be helped. You can't expect people to go to bed earlier than they want to, or are used to, on her account. But I wouldn't want to disturb her. When I see her I want to pick her up and kiss her, dance with her, just like now.

Dances and sings tra la la la from Carmen. Stops dancing and looks at the baby, enchanted.

How beautiful and lovely she is.

Edit Attentively *observes the scene under* MRS. GOLDEN's *gaze.*

Mrs. Golden As you can see she's always overjoyed when she holds the baby. What a little weakling she is, *nebekh*, I don't want her to get too shaken up—she should be big and fat by now! It's not as if she's lacking for anything.

Looking down at her large bosom.

Sonia God forbid, she certainly isn't lacking for anything in your care. But she's asleep now, the little one. Please, take her.

The wet nurse takes the baby and sits down in the rocking chair.

Sonia Ha, ha, my tra, la, la put her to sleep.

Edit   You really love *Carmen* don't you. You've been singing from that opera ever since you saw it.

Sonia   Yes I'm more taken with Carmen than any of the other operas I've seen. Especially the second act. The beginning of it is so dynamic—girls dancing, Carmen on the table with a tambourine, her girlfriends accompanying her in song—tra la la la la la la la la la.
Enthusiastically.
Tra la la la la la la la la la.
Suddenly interrupts her singing with laughter and turns to EDIT.
Ha ha ha ha ha
I'm not putting you to sleep, am I? I suddenly realized in the middle of my singing that I might be putting you to sleep.

Edit   Don't you think I'm as much of a connoisseur of music as your little niece?

Sonia   I hope you don't think I meant to criticize your taste in music.

Edit   If you're talking about your singing—you're not that bad of a singer.

Sonia   Ha, ha, not that bad is right.

Mrs. Golden   *Rocking in the chair.*
Ha, ha, ha.

Sonia   Did she wake up? Did I wake her?
Nu, in that case I'll rock both of you until she wakes up.
Rocks them.

Mrs. Golden   I'm the one to rock since I've already rocked all my children and those of strangers.
Looks at the baby.
She's sleeping. I'm going to put her in her carriage.
Stands up.

It's time for me to go. It's too bad Mr. and Mrs. Rabinoff weren't in.

Sonia   They're planning on visiting you later.

Mrs. Golden   In that case, I bid you good day.

Sonia   Kisses *the baby.*

Mrs. Golden   It's not good to kiss a sleeping child.

Sonia   I don't imagine it will do her any harm.
Looks deeply at the child one more time.
She looks like an angel.

Mrs. Golden   *Keyn ayn hore*, may the evil eye not befall her.
A good day to you again.

Sonia   Bye. Go in health.
Wet nurse exits with baby.

Edit   I never would have believed, Sonia, that you could so love a child.

Sonia   Why? Do I appear so bad to you? They say that bad people hate children.

Edit   I most certainly never thought of you as bad. I didn't think it about you when I thought you didn't like children. But I've so often heard you express opposition to bringing them into this world that I'm surprised at this great love you've displayed for this baby.

Sonia   I could answer you plenty on this but I'm not in the mood.
With a smile.
I'm not in the mood for a discussion.
Looks at him cheerily, full of life.
Let's have fun.
Takes his hand.
Let's go for a walk.

Edit   *Stands up. Contemplates her with love and delight.*
   Ach, it's so great to be with you when you're in such a good mood, Sonia, when you want to have a good time. Shall we go somewhere?

Sonia   *Happily.*
   Where?

Edit   That I leave to you. Pick one of your favorite places.

Sonia   In that case, let's go to the skating rink in Prospect Park.

Edit   Skating rink? Why would we want to go there? We don't skate.

Sonia   *Enthusiastically.*
   It's delightful to watch the flying couples zooming on the ice, holding each other tightly while gliding back and forth. Their cheeks aflame, looking into each other's eyes so lovingly.

Edit   *Smiling.*
   If it's truly how you describe it then let's go and have a look.

Sonia   It all depends on how one sees it. But I can tell, you're not that interested in going there. Shall we go to Coney Island instead?

Edit   Now that's much more interesting but it's not that great in winter. It's calm and peaceful but the air is raw. Mostly there's not much to do there but stare at the waves.

Sonia   *Laughs.*
   You can do that in the summer too if you don't feel like doing anything else.
   Puts on her hat.

Edit   Dress warmly, it's really cold today.

Sonia   The colder it is the more I love being at the ocean.
   Fantasizes dreamily.

Besides, when there's snow on the ground it crackles underfoot. The waves make a crashing sound like they're after you when you're running, and run you must so as not to freeze. When I'm running alongside the wide open sea, it seems like those angry, stormy waves are after me. My heart beats harder and harder like a storm and the whole world becomes a tempest.

Edit *Attracted to her enthusiasm, he stares at her in amazement as she's speaking. When she's finished he exclaims.*
You yourself are a tempest!
Grabs her in his arms and pulls her toward him. Kisses her passionately.

Sonia *pulls away from him and looks at him good-naturedly.*

Edit *stands there looking lost.*

Sonia And have you vanquished the storm?
Removes her hat.
We're not going today. It's a surefire way to catch cold.
Sits down.

Edit *Sits down across from her.*
What a remarkable person you are. When you're affected by something bad there's no end to how bad it appears to you, and you're able to convince others of it as well. When you like something, your enthusiasm is without boundary. You are so extreme, Sonia, I must say that you not only derail yourself with your intensity but you drag others along with you to God knows where.

Sonia Ha, ha ha. Make sure you don't get carried away somewhere.

Edit I'm not in the least bit afraid of that.

Sonia You should be afraid.

Edit   Why?

Sonia   Because you're a boy, my friend. Yes, a young man your age is still a boy.

Edit   *Insulted.*
Don't talk that way. Please. You have no right to speak to me in that tone.
Growing angrier.
It's not true. Not true. You know it. No one treats me like a boy and neither will you. You don't love me.

Sonia   *Tries to interrupt him.*
Why so upset?

Edit   *With previous tone.*
Why so upset? After you make me out to be such a nothing? You not only had a good laugh at my marriage proposal but you're also laughing at my love for you!

Sonia   *Stands up and takes his hand.*
Relax. If I insulted you …

Edit   *Doesn't let her speak.*
If I insulted you!
Frees his hand.
You treat me like a child! … Taking me by the hand to try to quiet me …

Sonia   *Getting upset herself.*
Yes, a child! That's exactly what you are!
Sits back down.
If you weren't you'd understand that I not only love you, I worship you.

Edit   *In joyous ecstasy.*
Sonia—oh, how happy I am to hear that.
Takes her hands.
My love, you rare, outstanding girl.
You will be mine!

Sonia   *Her countenance expresses a difficult inner battle.*
No, never! It will never happen.

Edit   *Sadly.*
Why?! *Presses her arm.*
Tell me, why?

Sonia   *Suffering.*
Calm yourself.

Edit   *Lets go of her. Reclines on the couch slouching.*

Sonia   Sits *down next to him. Tenderly takes his hand.*
Leo, listen to me.

Edit   *Sits up and yells out with childish capriciousness.*
I'm not listening. I don't want to hear anything. You must be mine! You love me. You just said so yourself, that you worship me. And I can't live without you!
Throws his head on her bosom and cries.

Sonia   *Pats his hair, kisses it. Pulls him tightly to her.*
Yes, I must be yours ... but it's not going to happen.

Edit   What do you mean?

Sonia   Not now! Now is not the time to talk about it.
Kisses him sorrowfully.

Dr. Dave   *Itelson enters.*

Edit   *jumps up.*

Sonia   *looks down ashamed.*

Dave   *Embarrassed.*
Pardon me.

Sonia   *Stands. Speaks apologetically.*
Please excuse me, Dave, for neglecting to introduce you to my friend, Leo Edit.
To EDIT.
This is my brother, Dave Itelson.

Dave   *Shakes* EDIT's *hand.*
   Needless to say, Mr. Edit, it's a pleasure to meet you.

Edit   The pleasure is all mine, Dr. Itelson. I've been asking Sonia to introduce us for a while now, but she's horrid.

Dave   Yes, Sonia, you're awful.
   Squeezes her hand.
   But as a result, I'm pleasantly surprised.

Edit   *Smiles.*

Dave   *Sits down.*
   Where are the hosts?

Sonia   At the theatre.

Dave   *Checks his watch.*
   It's after six. They should be home soon.

Edit   It's already past six? I had to call a friend at six. Sonia, is there a phone in the house?

Sonia   No.

Edit   I've got to go make a phone call.
   Puts on his coat to exit.

Sonia   Wait for me. I want to go for a walk.

Dave   He's in a hurry and you're not even dressed.

Sonia   *Quickly puts her hat and coat on.*
   I'm ready.

Dave   Not for this weather you're not.
   Don't wait for her, Mr. Edit; she's got to dress better.

Edit   I'll be right back.
   Exits.

Sonia   Fanny doesn't feel well again.

Dave   I know. She came to see me yesterday.

Sonia   Earlier Simon said he wanted to hire a housekeeper.

Dave   That would be helpful. Fanny not only must not exert herself, she needs to rest.

Sonia   But Simon's plan also entails bringing the baby home.

Dave   You can't blame him. He probably can't afford both a housekeeper and a wet nurse.

Sonia   *Upset.*
You agree we should take the baby away from the wet nurse?!
That's impossible. It would mean killing the frail, little innocent thing. You said so yourself! If we had given her twin brother over to a wet nurse he'd be alive today. They should never have been brought into this world. But if they're already here it's criminal not to protect them by any means possible.

Dave   Yes. She should be with the wet nurse until she's at least four months old. But what do they know about it? His only concern is that his wife be a lady. And hers is that she is sick, weak, and heartbroken. I didn't mean that the baby should be taken from the wet nurse. Fanny must go away to rest. She shouldn't be at home. I've actually come here to discuss that with Simon.

Sonia   Where do you think she should go?

Dave   Didn't Fanny tell you? I want to send her to Los Angeles to a friend of mine. He'll see to her and make sure she's comfortable for as long as she wants to be there.

Sonia   *In a panic.*
Why does she have to go to Los Angeles?

Dave   *Smiles.*

Don't be frightened. It's not her lungs. I only chose California because it's far from New York and … but let's not talk about that.

Sonia   Are you going to wait for them? I think they're going to see the baby after the theatre.

Dave   Hopefully they won't be much longer. I only have another half hour.

Sonia   Then I won't be seeing you again tonight. Good night to you.

Dave   Going already?

Sonia   I said I want to go for a walk. I've been indoors all day.

Dave   Yes, but you can wait a few minutes until he returns. You're a dear. Are you sure there's nothing you want to tell me?

Sonia   Maybe I'd feel like sharing if I had something to tell you.

Dave   *Disappointed. After a short pause.*
   I don't get it! It's obvious at first sight that he's a splendid young man and that he's undoubtedly in love with you. And you with him.

Sonia   *Cuts him off.*
   Oh I see you're convinced. Yes Brother, I love him.

Dave   *Nu*, so?

Sonia   *Nu*—there are problems.

Dave   Like what?

Sonia   You noticed that he's a stunning young man, and that he's in love, but you failed to notice that the young man is too young. He is twenty-one years old.

Dave   A twenty-one-year-old is not as young as you're making him out to be.

Sonia   Maybe for an eighteen-year-old girl.

Dave   And you consider yourself an old maid already?

Sonia   *Kholile*, God forbid.
Shows him the ring on her finger.
You gave me this ring for my twenty-eighth birthday.

Dave   So what. A few years younger or older is no big deal. I'm older than you and if I fell in love with a twenty-year-old girl I wouldn't view it as a tragedy.

Sonia   I don't know if it would be a joy for you but for me, it definitely is not.

Dave   What's the difference if it's me or you? As long as it comes to something.

Sonia   *Cuts him off.*
Easy for you to say, how would you feel if you fell in love and then found out she was 7 years older than you?

Dave   When a man is truly in love, nothing gets in the way.

Sonia   Maybe a man can forgive his wife everything except a few unclaimed years.

Dave   Who's asking you to deny it?

Sonia   It's useless talking to you about this. Oh, how I love him. I only want to make him happy. As long as I'm in this circumstance Dave, if you only knew what kind of person he is—intelligent, passionate, good! And as pure as a babe.

Dave   You sound like someone who's head over heels my sister.
Lowers his voice.
And what's your plan for making him happy—free love?

Sonia   Leave that to me.

Dave   Don't get mad at me for pressing you about this. You know how much you two sisters mean to me.

Sonia   You are precious to me too, but I would never mix into your private life.

Dave   I am a man.

Sonia   Ha, ha. You just said we were equal!
   A knock at the door.

Dave   Come in.

Edit   *Enters.*
   Pardon me.

Dave   For what?

Edit   For not knocking sooner.

Sonia   What do you mean?

Edit   I've transgressed Sonia, and it's no doubt your fault. I overheard you telling your brother how much you love me. I probably shouldn't have been listening in but I was frozen in place hearing your fears.

Dave   *Smiling.*
   It's definitely Sonia's fault.

Edit   It's good she didn't respond, I mean to your question. She's always overestimating me—but what she said about purity—it's practically a religion to me.
   Pleadingly.
   Tell me doctor, what's making her so upset. Making me happy? As long as she is in the position to, why shouldn't she? Why is it so hard for her to commit to marrying me?

Dave   Let me be frank with you my friend—Sonia is older than you and she's afraid that might make you unhappy.

Edit   Why would that disturb our happiness? How funny. Are you joking Sonia?

Sonia   It's no joke. I'm five years older than you.

Edit   What's it to me how much older you are? Who's counting?

Dave   So there's nothing to tally up now, my friends.

Edit   What's the difference—now, later, always, I will always love her!
FANNY *and* SIMON *enter.*

Sonia   Hugs FANNY.
Give me away, Fanny, I've been overcome.

CURTAIN

ACT II

Seven years later.

Beautifully decorated room in EDIT's home. Two windows, vases with flowers on sills, a door leading to bedroom, another door to other rooms.

Evening

Edit *sits at a table absorbed in a book.* SONIA *is standing by an open window looking out onto the street. Turns to* EDIT *about to say something but doesn't say it. Looks out the window again. Turns back as if talking to herself.*

Sonia   It's so nice outside now.
Goes over to EDIT *and looks into the book he's reading.*

Edit   Looks *at her reproachfully. Goes back to reading.*

Sonia   *Insulted. Sits on couch leaning her head on her hand.*

Edit   After *a short pause closes his book and turns to her.*
Don't you feel well?

Sonia   *Sadly.*
You expect me to feel good after such a look?

Edit   It's not my fault Sonia.

Sonia   Do you think it's my fault then?

Edit   *Getting upset.*
You asked for it. I'm reading. I've asked you countless times
not to disturb me when I'm reading.

Sonia   In *her previous sad tone.*
Why would my looking into your book disturb you?

Edit   *More upset.*
You know what I mean. Do you think I didn't get your
look?
You were about to drag me somewhere.

Sonia   Drag you? What kind of expression is that?

Edit   There's no other way to say it. Whenever I'm in the
mood to stay home and read, or something like it, you start
with: Leo let's go somewhere. That's being dragged.

Sonia   Wipes *away tears.*

Edit   *Notices. Stands up hastily. Nervously waves his hand.*
Oh, I can't take this anymore. You know that tears are the
worst for me! I don't want to see them!

Sonia   Collects *herself.*
I can't help it, Leo.

Edit   You always have the same excuse. If you can't help it,
then do something about it!

Sonia   Stands *in great distress.*
What do you want! What do you want from me?

Edit   Now you're getting worked up?

Sonia   Still *upset.*
Oh God help me—how can I not? You're driving me crazy. You won't stop picking on me lately. It is literally impossible to tolerate! Why don't you think about what makes you so upset. So what if I was going to ask you to go for a walk. Is that such a sin? It's such a lovely evening.
Looks toward the window.
Look how lovely the stars are.

Edit   *Impatiently.*
So, it's beautiful out, look at the stars, who's stopping you?

Sonia   *Bitterly.*
Thanks for the permission!
EDIT *Calmer.*
Why does it make a difference to you whether I'm looking at the sky or my book. Do I dictate to you what to do or where to go? You're free to do what you want. Do whatever your heart desires. You don't take advantage of your freedom or even value it. You so want to go for a walk, but you don't. And now you're blaming me, as if I were holding you back.

Sonia   I can't go by myself.
Sadly sits down in a corner chair.

Edit   Pretend it's daytime and I'm at the office. Go alone. Why do you need me when I'm home?

Sonia   I'm alone all day so at night I can't bear the loneliness.

Edit   *Holds back a sigh.*
I understand.
Sits down opposite her.
But whose fault is that? If you had a child or two you wouldn't be feeling lonely now.

Sonia   *Astonished.*
Two?

Edit   Why are you so taken aback? We've already been married seven years. We could've had two or three children by now.

Sonia   It doesn't bother me that we don't.

Edit   What do you mean it doesn't bother you? Are you trying to convince me you don't want children? What are you lacking then? What's making you feel so lonely? You know I know how much you love children?

Sonia   That's exactly why I don't want to bring them into this world, because I love them so much.

Edit   You mean you don't want them to be born for lack of love. Who will you love then?

Sonia   Oh—there are enough already. If they were only well loved, properly raised and cared for so many of them wouldn't die! The less born the better.

Edit   *Impatiently.*
I'm not in a position to philosophize. I'm at a loss as to what to call this foolish idea you've cooked up in your head, Sonia. Let's say it's justifiable to devote yourself to those who are already here rather than bringing more into the world. What do we do with our instinct then? What do we do with the urge to have children? Does it satisfy either you or me that there are already so many? We don't have any! To have them you have no other choice but to bring them.

Sonia   *After a slight pause.*
First in a moved tone and then strongly convinced.
There are plenty of lonely children out there. They're either orphans or they've been abandoned by their parents. I feel so sorry for those babes—being raised by total strangers, severe people. Imagine what it would be like to adopt one like that, to teach it to call us Mommy and Daddy. And we ourselves would lovingly call it our baby. After a few nights of rocking and nurturing it, wouldn't we feel like it were our own?

Edit   Impossible! I admit it would awake certain feelings
but to call it our own? Never! And do you really think that
we'd even feel some happiness or pleasure from it? The more
beautiful the child the more we'd resent it. You'd look at it
and deep in your heart you'd say it wasn't ours. It would be
someone else's, the pleasure would be someone else's.

Sonia   Why worry about that. They wouldn't reap any of
the pleasure. Having freed themselves of the burden they
certainly wouldn't garner any of the tenderness! The child
would belong more to those who raised it then to those who
brought it into the world.

Edit   Are you saying that children who've been raised by
nannies and/or teachers belong more to them than to their
parents?

Sonia   That's different. It's definitely criminal of parents
to totally depend on hired help and not make the effort to
properly raise their children. But you can't say they don't
have the right to them. Hired help only do it for the money.
There's nothing else coming to them. But those who don't
sleep nights caring for newborns they've taken in out of
compassion, love them like their own life. Who else takes
more pleasure in a child's abilities and beauty than those
noble people?

Edit   It's not a question of what's right; it depends on
whether you feel it or not.

Sonia   Even if you don't, you know that you've given all
you've got.

Edit   What do you mean all you've got?

Sonia   I mean that no matter how much parents do for their
children, it's not enough. Even when they give themselves
entirely, the pain of bringing them into this world is great.

Edit   *In a tone.*

Again with that same philosophy of bringing them into this world. I beg you Sonia, once and for all, stop it. I've heard enough of your sermons. I don't want children anymore … you hear me? Oh, a child … without one we're doomed to never be happy.

Sonia   *Sighs.*

Edit   You're sighing. That's consoling.

Sonia   Would you like me to console you?

Edit   Oh no! Woe to those who need to be consoled. It's not about me.
Answer me! Give me a direct honest answer.
If you could … would you want to have a child?

Sonia   *Waffling.*
I wish I could.. I … I … would like to …

Edit   *Happily but unsure.*
Really? You promise?
Hugs her.
Sonia! Darling! How happy we'll be when we have a child … just one little baby … but … but … why did you say if you could? You seemed doubtful.

Sonia   Professor Platt assured me he had no doubt I would have children if I had the operation …

Edit   *Frightened. Steps away from her.*
When did you see him?

Sonia   A few months ago.

Edit   And you didn't say anything to me about it? I can see why you wouldn't be in a hurry with such news …
Paces floor worried. Stands still and speaks reproachfully.
You need to be operated on. I sensed this; your behavior couldn't have led to anything else!

Brushes her away very disturbed. Takes his hat and begins to exit.

Sonia   Holding *back tears.*
Where are you going?

Edit   *Doesn't answer but remains frozen.*

Sonia   Where are you going Leo?
I feel so wretched—please don't go.

Edit   *Painfully.*
I can't help it, Sonia. I'm also miserable.
Puts on his hat and proceeds to leave.

Sonia   *Anxiously.*
Leo! Oh Leo, don't go!
Don't leave me alone now ...

Edit   *Turns back enraged.*
You can't be alone and I can't be with you!

Sonia   *Bursts into hysteria.*

Edit   My God! This is intolerable.
Doorbell rings.
Someone's here. Oh God, calm yourself.

Sonia   *Composes herself.*
Don't let anyone in.
Rings get louder.

Edit   How cannot I not open the door. We're so loud there's no doubt we're home.

Sonia   We're in no condition to entertain guests.

Edit   Go into another room. At least I haven't been crying hysterically.
Ringing intensifies.

Sonia   *Exits to bedroom.*

Edit   *Opens the door.*

Dr. DAVE *Itelson enters.*

Dave   Good evening!

Edit   *Quietly.*
Good evening, Dave.

Dave   *Looks around the room.*
You're alone?

Edit   Can't you see?

Dave   *Smiling.*
I see but I heard someone else.

Edit   And I don't doubt you know who it was.

Dave   Yes, but why did she run off?

Edit   She probably wouldn't have if she knew it was you.
Why are you standing there in your hat and coat? Are you
waiting for me to take them?
    Tries to take his things but DAVE *doesn't let him.*

Dave   Thank you, but perhaps you should let me take your
hat.
    Takes it off him and hangs it up with his.
    Turns to EDIT *in a joking tone.*
    Now dear sir, have a seat.
    Points to a chair.

Edit   *Sits down smiling sadly.*

Dave   *Sits opposite him.*
    Thoughtfulness turns to a smile.
    I obviously disturbed a feisty little scene.

Edit   You disturbed a huge scene that will most likely be
staged again.

Dave   Oh no Brother—I don't care what you call what just happened here, but to repeat it? That would be very foolish.

Sonia   *Enters from bedroom.*

Dave   *Stands to greet her.*
    Here she is!
    Considers her crying face. Makes a funny face.
    What a face!
    Takes her arm and leads her to a door.
    Go crybaby, wash away your tears.
    Lets her go and returns to his seat opposite EDIT.
    And you, you angry mess, straighten yourself out and don't get so puffed up.

Sonia   *Sighs quietly. Exits.*

Dave   *Yells after her.*
    Make it quick Sonia, and come back like a good girl.

Edit   What did the specialist tell Sonia?

Dave   *Gets serious but makes an effort not to show his concern.*
    Sonia must have told you.

Edit   But I'm asking you. I want you to tell me?

Dave   Okay, but … let's put it off to another time. Sonia's about to come back …

Edit   *Interrupts him.*
    It doesn't matter. We were just talking about it and I really can't talk about anything else right now.

Dave   If you like I'll explain everything to you.

Edit   Please, but everything—and the truth.

Dave   I never would have believed Leo, that you would doubt my honesty. But I'll excuse you. You then must not take offence at my keeping the doctor's diagnosis from you?

Edit   You didn't even say a word to me about going to the doctor's.

Dave   *Mournfully.*
  What was there to say?

Edit   *Frightened.*
  What do you mean? Did the doctor refuse the case?

Dave   Oh no, but …

Edit   Getting *upset.*
  But what—speak clearly!

Dave   *In the same tone.*
  To have children there must be an operation.

Edit   Sonia told me that. I must know what kind of operation. Will it put her in danger?

Dave   *Sighs.*
  Every operation is dangerous. You can never be sure—even the simplest procedure is not 100 percent.

Edit   *Despairing.*
  That means there's no hope here. We are destined to be childless, or to put it more accurately, to be unhappy.

Dave   You don't have to be childless and you can still be happy.

Edit   Do you think she should have the operation? You just said it was dangerous.

Dave   *Suffering.*
  I didn't mean she should have the operation. We can't let it get to that. I mean you should adopt a child. It will naturally

be difficult at first but later when you get used to it it'll feel like your own.

Edit *Sarcastically.*
You're making a big mistake if you think that's going to make us happy. Even better—let me assure you—that will never happen!
I never would've expected to get such advice from you Dave.

Dave I can't tell you how hard it is for me to give you such advice but unfortunately I don't see any other way than no child at all.

Edit *Interrupts him.*
So it's done—we're doomed to be unhappy.

Dave You must not allow that Leo. Why should you be miserable when you could do something to help yourselves. You wouldn't be the first to adopt because of not being able to have children. You could be very happy.

Edit Woe onto me to be anointed father of an adopted child for my twenty-eighth birthday! What will my family, my friends, say? Most of them aren't even married yet. Not bound—free, as is customary at my age. Maybe for her, for Sonia, it's suitable. A woman in her years that can't have children would naturally want to give it a go with strangers.

Dave *Angry.*
Oh, now you're going to get rid of her on account of the few years between you.

Edit I'm not getting rid of her. She didn't know it would come to this. She was always so honorable, so proud.
Sighs.
But all that is in the past. She is very different now. The independent Sonia Itelson has transformed into a helpless woman.

Dave *Smiles.*

Edit   You don't believe it?

Dave   *Still smiling.*
   If that's true, it's to your credit.

Edit   Oh, you think it's my fault? I assure you that it's not.
Under my influence she'd be progressing, constantly moving
forward. I've offered her every possibility for advancement.
But she's used it to her detriment. She's become what I said
she was. And do you know what brought her to this? Her
crazy ideas about going against nature. Railing against
having children when her heart melted at the sight of them.
It's no wonder she's become so fragile and brittle. If she
sees a blemish on my face she gets scared. If she doesn't like
something I do or say—right away she cries.
   Sighs.
   A day doesn't go by without her crying, without whining
or tears.

Dave   *Worried.*
   I had no idea my poor sister was so unhappy.

Edit   And whose fault is that, her unhappiness, our troubled
lives, if not hers?

Dave   It's not entirely her fault Leo.

Edit   *Bitterly.*
   No? Didn't she bring this situation on herself?

Dave   You mean the fact that you're childless? First of all,
I would like to draw to your attention to that she is not as
guilty in this as you would like to believe. And second, I
heard you say that the child thing is not the only problem
that's spoiling your lives. You're unhappy about many more
things.

Edit   That is true—but if we only had a child all these other
troubles would not exist. For example, I earlier made a
reference to her age. If I suffer from it, it is not only because

we don't have children. When you gaze at a woman, and see her as the mother of your children, you don't need her to be so charming. And besides that, you don't pay that much attention to her looks, because your free time is taken up with your children. Those little innocent ones, who demand most of your attention, satisfy everything.

Sighs.

What's the point of talking about it?

Pause.

What did you mean when you said it wasn't her fault that we are childless?

Dave   I meant she wasn't guilty. Circumstances led her to do what she did ... not only her crazy ideas, as you call them. It's true that it's also that, but more pivotal is her fear of losing her youth, the beauty of her figure. She won't admit to it and she may not even know it herself, but that's what I realized when several months ago I remarked that going against nature aged her. She got scared and asked me to go to a specialist with her. Unfortunately it was already too late. The doctor said he couldn't help her. But he kept the dangers that are connected to it from her.

Edit   It's like you say—our tragedy stems from the fact that she wanted to stubbornly hold on to her youth. Yes, that would surely be a woman's downfall. You might be able to prolong your youth but to clutch to it in fear of it disappearing—that is destructive. The more you run from your aging the faster it approaches.

Dave   What are you talking about aging? She's only thirty-five.

Edit   But she looks like a forty-year-old woman.
Loud knock at the door.
Come in.

Simon   *enters.*

Simon   Good evening.

Edit & Dave *Together.*
Good evening.

Edit *Turns around.*
A guest. Sit down Simon.

Simon   Thank you but I'm too busy to take a seat.

Dave *Laughs.*
You're not being asked to take a seat but to sit down.

Simon *Insulted.*
Isn't it the same thing?

Dave *More serious.*
Let it be the same but what's the rush? What are you so busy with?

Simon   Fanny's not well. She told me not to dawdle but to get you and return quickly.

Dave *Amazed.*
Fanny doesn't feel well? What's wrong with her? I was just over there a few hours ago and she wasn't complaining about anything. She looked quite well.

Simon   She went to the doctor and as soon as she got home she started feeling badly.

Dave *Very upset.*
She was at the doctor's? Is that so? So what do you want from me?

Simon *Guiltily.*
You can probably give her something to make her feel better.

Dave   I can't give her anything.
Stands up angrily.
Go to him—that colleague of mine.

Simon   He said he couldn't come.

Dave *Angrier.*

Can't come. That good for nothing! He's probably afraid he's brought on a disaster so it wouldn't be in his best interest to come. Go tell him she's unwell and that he must come at once. Tell him I'm not going to. I will no longer be a party to him and his noble work. Maybe when he develops some character and becomes more responsible he'll restrain himself from doing such things. And also—it shouldn't be so easy for you. When a brother warns not to do it and then you summon him expecting him to come right over ... saving yourself from going to unfamiliar doctors ... know that I won't always be there for you. Go find another doctor to help you.

Simon   *Worried.*
But what should we do?

Dave   What do you mean what should you do? Why didn't you have another child or even a few more. You only have one and she's already of school age. The burden will fall on her if you don't have any more.

Simon   We don't want to be bothered. We've already had plenty of trouble with just this one. Now that she's grown ...
Smiles.
she's almost a lady and her mother can also be a lady now. We can go out, she can dress stylishly.

Dave   *Interrupts him.*
Shut up! It would be better if you shut-up!

Simon   *Shamed.*
It's not only that. Fanny says she would rather die than have another set of twins.

Dave   She's afraid of having twins ... and you're afraid she won't be able to be a lady.

Edit   Fanny is more afraid of losing her youth than having twins. And yes, it's much easier for a woman to put herself down than bring herself up.

Pats SIMON *on the back.*
Simon you're all right. You've turned FANNY into a complete woman.

Dave   You're right. She's not so dumb to believe she's doomed to always give birth to twins. She just wants to have fun. And because of that she puts her life in danger.

Mrs. Golden   *Rushes in leading* LILLY *by the hand.*
LILLY *clings to her.*
Is Mr. Rabinov here?

Edit   Yes.

Mrs. Golden   What kind of man goes out to get a doctor and disappears himself?

Dave   She's not feeling better yet?

Mrs. Golden   Not yet. She asked me to go to your office, to see what's taking you so long. But I've wasted my time, seeing that you're here.

Dave   I'll write her a prescription.
Writes a script and gives it to SIMON.
Go right to the drugstore and fill this prescription. It's pills. Give her two every hour and when she feels better one an hour. I'll come over. Yes, tell her I'll be there as soon as I can.

Edit   You should probably go now.

Dave   The pills will give her relief. There's nothing more that can be done for her right now anyway.
To Simon.
Go already. Why are you standing there?

Simon   I'm on my way. Good night. Thank-you Doctor!

Dave   *With a tone.*
Don't thank me and don't call me Doctor. How many times have I told you?

Simon   I beg your pardon Doctor! I know you don't like it but whenever I try to call you by your first name Doctor comes out.

Edit   Good night.

Dave   I'll see you soon Simon.

Simon   All right.
Turns to the wet nurse.
Are you coming back to us, Mrs. Golden?

Mrs. Golden   Certainly, if she's home alone I'll be right there.

Simon   *exits.*

Mrs. Golden   Where is Mrs. Edit? Since I'm already here I'd love to see her.

Edit   I believe she'll be right out. Have a seat.

Mrs. Golden   I've no time to sit.

Edit   *Takes* LILLY's *hand.*
Why are you standing there like that?

Lilly
Pulls away and clings to the wet nurse even more.

Edit   You're clinging to Mrs. Golden's apron like a baby. Aren't you embarrassed?
Picks her up and sits down on the sofa with her.
If you're such a baby we'll have to hold you like one.
LILLY Pulls *away from him, embarrassed.*
I'm not a baby.

Mrs. Golden   Don't be embarrassed my little one.
She hasn't seen me for a few days, so she doesn't want to leave me. And her mother isn't well today. I found her crying when I got there.

Dave   Why were you crying, Lilly?

Lilly   I get so sad when my mother is sick. I don't have anyone to play with, like other children, who have sisters and brothers.
Cries.
She's always getting sick and I'm left all alone.

Dave   Sadly *shakes his head.*

Edit   *Pats* LILLY's *hair.*
Don't cry little one—your mother will get well.
You know what? Why don't you sleep over here? Aunt Sonia will be home soon and we'll all go out for a walk. If you want we'll go to the ice cream parlor.

Lilly   I want to go to the movies.

Edit   All right. The movies it is then.

Mrs. Golden   Are you going to spend the night here, Lillinke?
I'm going home.

Lilly   Back to our house?

Mrs. Golden   Yes.

Lilly   Then I'm going with you.

Edit   Why don't you want to stay over here Lilly?

Dave   If Mrs. Golden is at her house, she won't stay here.

Lilly   *Kisses* EDIT.
Good night, Uncle Leo.

Edit   *Hugs her. Kisses her.*
Good night, Kidele. Will you come over tomorrow?

Lilly   Yes.
Kisses DAVE
Good night, Uncle Dave.

Dave　Kisses *her*.
I'll be over soon my sweet little girl.

Mrs. Golden　*Takes* LILLY*'s hand.*
Good night. Regards to Mrs. Edit.

Edit　Thanks. Good night.
Exit wet nurse and LILLY.

Edit　She is so attached to that wet-nurse. She was about to stay over but as soon as she heard Mrs. Golden was going back to their house she changed her mind.

Dave　They are very attached to each other. Mrs. Golden loves Lillitchken like her own. She feels very close to our whole family because of her.

Edit　*After a short pause.*
Simon just caught a lesson from you he never expected.

Dave　It's a good thing they listened to me seven years ago. Fanny would not be alive today if they hadn't. She didn't get as sick as she would have with all those parties they're always going to. Sonia knew it and clued me in. And as you know, I arranged for Fanny to go to Los Angeles, where she was able to spend ten months in total rest. If she had stayed home she probably would have occupied herself with stylish dresses and running to doctors. She was so nervous, too weak to have a child. And the means she employed to not have the child would certainly have killed her if she had not gone away. The only way to handle it was how I advised them then, and how I would advise anyone in the same situation.

Edit　I thought that Fanny went to California then because of the air and I don't doubt that Simon thought the same. If not, he definitely wouldn't have let her go.

Dave　Yes, that's what I led him to believe. Most men in such cases would have to be deceived in the same manner, not only him.

Edit   I'm going to see what happened to Sonia. As usual she's waiting for me to make up with her. Oh, this fighting and making up, Dave, I must hand it to you for not being married.
  Exits.

Dave   *Sighs.*
  He's making her miserable.

Edit   *Comes back in looking distressed.*

Dave   What is she doing?

Edit   She's not here. I wonder where she went.

Dave   She probably went for a walk or to buy something.

Edit   I don't think either.
  Someone is heard approaching the door.

Edit   *Listens.*

Sonia   *Comes in wearing a dark coat and a hat of the same color.*

Dave   Where are you coming from?
  Checks out her outfit.
  You're dressed as if you've been in the car.
  Smiles.
  Did you go for a ride?

Sonia   I didn't go that far that I needed a ride. Just walked over to the drugstore.

Dave   What were you doing at the drugstore?

Sonia   I called Dr. White, Professor Platt's assistant.

Dave   *Perturbed.*
  What did you need from them?

Sonia   I made an appointment for Monday to meet with the professor in his private hospital.

Dave   *Frightened.*
What do you mean? You want to have the operation?

Sonia   Yes, I've decided to.

Dave   No Sonia—you will not be operated on. I will not allow it.

Edit   Neither will I. I now have no doubt that the operation is dangerous.

Sonia   I will have the operation and not think about the danger. What's the worst that can happen—I'll die? Well, I can't live like this anyway. My life is worthless without a child.

Edit   It's a little late for you to come to this conclusion. I've been waiting for this. I've been telling you this, but you wouldn't listen. And when you did finally listen, you answered with a philosophical lecture. But I knew all along that your foolish convictions had no chance against nature's pull.

Sonia   If you weren't so against adopting a child, things would be different.
Begging.
Let's try it Leo, it would mean an end to our pain.

Edit   You probably doubt that yourself, but I assure you Sonia that an alien child won't make you happy. Your heart wants to be a mother—not just raise a child. But you can try it.

Sonia   *Suppressing her joy.*
Do you really mean it? Are you serious?

Edit   Yes, go ahead—get a child.

Dave   You don't have to do this, Leo. After our earlier conversation I know how you feel. Sonia cannot be held accountable for that.

Edit   It's the only thing left.
Turns to SONIA.
Sonia, ask Dave to find a child.

Sonia   We don't have to, I know of an orphan we can adopt. We can go now; it's not far—only twenty minutes by car.

Dave   What's the rush—we can do it another time.

Sonia   Why put it off? It doesn't make a difference.

Edit   True, it doesn't make a difference. Go take her over there Dave, if you want.

Dave   If you want I will, but first I must go look in on Fanny.

Sonia   Why is that so important? Is she sick?

Dave   Fanny doesn't feel good.

Sonia   *Frightened.*
What's wrong with her?

Dave   I don't know—I haven't seen her yet.

Sonia   Let's go. We'll go to her place first.

Dave   All right.
Puts on his coat and hat and asks Sonia's arm.

Sonia   Will you be home, Leo?

Edit   I believe so.

Sonia   *Imploring.*
Wait for me. I beg you. Don't go anywhere.
Exit DAVE *and* SONIA.
EDIT *remains, distressed.*
He sits. Gets up again.

Edit   I can't be in this house right now. They may be back soon. And on top of it bring ... oh I can't take it.

Puts on his hat and coat. Turns lights out.

She'll come and not find ...

Throws his hat on the table. Sits down exhausted. Breaks down.

CURTAIN

ACT III

EDIT's *house*
Same as Act II but more vases with flowers
A spring morning

Edit   *Pacing the room distressed. Looks at his watch.*

Half past eight. If he's not here soon, he won't be here before ten when office hours are over.

Doorbell rings quietly.

Come in.

Dave   *Enters.*

Good morning, I was worried you'd be delayed until after office hours.

Dave   I almost had to stay.

Edit   *Distressed.*

For God's sake how could you? You know I have to leave and we mustn't leave her alone.

Puts on his hat. Tiptoes over to the bedroom. Cracks the door slightly. Listens.

Dave   *To himself.*

We mustn't leave her alone? Will watching over her do any good?

Edit   Turns *back from bedroom with similar caution.*

She's still asleep. I'm leaving Dave. I'll most likely be back by one. At least you'll be able to attend your afternoon office hours. I'll just get the tea ready.

Dave   No need to rush. It's not essential for me to be in the office during the day. Very few patients come in then. But I want to tell you Leo that patrolling her will not help. This time her decision to have the operation will not change. The first time she decided to do it, a few months ago, she maintained her stance, but when you agreed to take in a child …

Edit   You didn't believe it would help then, did you?
Sighs.
But I let you try, I knew that a strange child would not only fail to fulfill maternal instincts but could possibly make the situation a lot worse.

Dave   Yes, you were right. The foreign child exasperated her maternal instincts to the point of wanting her own child even more. If the doctor had assured her it was impossible to have her own children she might have gotten used to it, and with time been happy.

Edit   *Sadly.*
I don't understand the doctor persuading her to have the operation knowing it could endanger her life.

Dave   *Embittered.*
Yes, her life is endangered, but it gives him the opportunity of being recognized.
Angrily motions with his hand.
Oh, those colleagues of mine. And why does it have to be my sister that he has to try it out on? No, I will not allow it.
In a calm tone.
You can go, Leo. She will not go have the operation.

Edit   Only you have the power to stop her. There is nothing I can do about it. I've already tried everything I could think of. I not only agreed to take in the baby but also helped tend to it. I spent plenty of nights staying up with that baby because I knew the new mother who so pitied the little orphan had no patience to devote herself to it. At the first she was ashamed to admit her impatience, but when she could no longer hide that the baby was a burden to her, we had to give it back to our friends. I thought it would create the space for me to devote myself to her—to go out more often, and generally spend more time together to her liking. I thought that would make her feel better and that she would stop fretting about a child. If that had been the case, I'm sure I too would have gotten used to the idea and we would have made do with the way things were.

Dave   You have without a doubt done enough my friend.

Edit   *Mildly angry.*
Don't flatter me, please; I hate to be thought of as good person.

Dave   *Smiling.*
You are a bad person, a very bad one. Now don't be mad.

Edit   I'm not mad but your tone irritates me. I've done enough.
Looks at his watch.
It's already after nine. I must go.

Dave   Go and stay calm. Your work requires an even temper.

Edit   My boss has already drawn that to my attention. He also added that a bookkeeper earning such a high salary should not make any mistakes.

Dave   *Jokingly.*
You can't say he's wrong.

Edit   Certainly not. Good bye.

Dave   Bye Leo.

Edit   *Exits.*

Dave   *Sits down. Picks up a newspaper.*
   After a short pause, a loud knock at the door.
   Come in.
   A very discomposed woman rushes in. Speaks in one breath.
   Oh you're here. Thank God I've found you. I made the girl
in the office tell me where you were.

Dave   What is it? What's happened?

Woman   *In the same tone.*
   You don't know? My baby is very sick and you're not at
the office.

Dave   My dear woman, I cannot come today. You must call
on another doctor.

Woman   *In a panic.*
   For God's sake! What do you mean? How can I go to
another doctor now? You've been treating him this whole
time. What would another doctor know about it?
   Cries.
   He may die before another doctor figures out what's wrong
with him.
   Cries harder.

Dave   *Goes over to her and takes her hand.*
   Calm down. Your child is not as ill as you think, and I'll
refer you to a doctor you can trust.

Woman   *Angrily.*
   I don't need your referrals. If I wanted another doctor I
would know where to go myself.

Dave   *Agitated.*
   But I can't help you. I can't come now.

Woman   *Begging.*
   Have pity, Doctor, please come, my child is dying.
   Cries horribly.

Sonia   *Rushes in from the bedroom. She is in a robe and slippers. Her hair is in disarray.*
Dave, why aren't you going—go, run.

Dave   Puts *on his coat. Looks at* SONIA *pleadingly.*

Sonia   I give you my word I won't go anywhere until you come back.

Dave   *Despairing.*

Until   I come back ...
Exits with the woman at his heels.

Sonia   My poor brother, how he suffers.
Sighs.
I cause him only suffering. And Leo, my darling, loving Leo, he does not deserve to suffer so either. He is such a good one. Oh how good he is. I take it he didn't leave until Dave arrived. How will he bear it when he comes home and finds me gone?
Wipes her tears.
And most likely I won't be back. I'll probably never lay eyes on this place again.
Weeps. Stops crying. Reflects for a moment.
What if I don't come back? Is that so frightening?
Brushes the thought away with her hand.
What foolishness.
Exits through door leading to bedrooms.
Stage is empty for a while.
Doorbell rings.

Sonia   *Comes back in. Her hair is done. She is hurriedly buttoning her simple dress. Goes to door and nervously asks:*
Who is it please?
A voice from the other side:
Open up and you'll see.

Sonia   Is that you, Fanny?
Opens the door.

FANNY *enters looking well and full of life. She is dressed in the latest fashion. She notices* SONIA *buttoning her dress.*

Fanny   Oh, you're in the middle of dressing.

Sonia   I'm not in the middle. As you can see I'm done.

Fanny   *Evaluates her.*
What kind of dress have you put on? You could have worn a nicer dress on such a beautiful morning.

Sonia   *Sighs.*
Yes, it is a beautiful day today but for where I'm going this dress will do.

Fanny   *Unnerved.*
Where then are you going and why are you so perturbed?

Sonia   Perturbed? That's silly. When something has to be done it should be done without trepidation.

Fanny   *Suppresses a sigh.*
I know where you're going.
Turns away to wipe some tears.

Sonia   *Notices and takes her hand. Forces a smile.*
I am foolhardy but you are even more dimwitted. What is there to cry about?

Fanny   *cries.*

Sonia   *leads her to a sofa and sits down next to her.*
I beg you, Fanny, stop crying. You're making it harder for me!

Fanny   *Makes an effort to stop. Wipes her tears.*
Leo is letting you go?

Sonia   Would not letting help then? I am a grown woman. I know and feel I have to do this. There is no other way.

Fanny   And Dave, what does Dave say?

Sonia   *Stands up upset.*

You're being childish, Fanny. What difference does it make what he says? I'm telling you I've decided and there's nothing more to say about it. And on top of that you can find out what he thinks from him, he'll be here shortly. I'm going out for a while. I must go over to the drugstore to phone the hospital.
Exits.

Fanny   *Takes off her hat and sets it beside her.*

Simon   *enters.*

Simon   I just saw Sonia. She told me you were here alone.
Contemplates her faraway mien.
Are you ashamed to admit the condition you're in?

Fanny   *Doesn't answer.*
Removes a compact from her purse, wipes her face, and powders. Puts compact back in purse.

Simon   *Continues to evaluate her.*
Now you look like a lady again. It is still apparent that you've been crying but it doesn't matter.

Fanny   *Ironically.*
Thank God, it doesn't matter.

Simon   *Sits down by* FANNY *and takes her hand.*
Now darling, tell me the truth about what's really going on here.

Fanny   *Sighs.*
Sonia's going to have the operation.

Simon   So what else is new? I've been hearing about this operation for ages. Is that why you've been crying?

Fanny   We're not just talking about it anymore. She's about to go to the hospital.

Simon   *A bit flustered.*
Really? It's been decided?
Lets go of FANNY's *hand.*

Fanny   For sure. She's all ready to go …

Simon   It's probably for the best. Let her once and for all do it already and settle the matter. If it works then great … and if not, she'll know once and for all not to bother about it anymore.

Fanny   *Distraught.*
This is not only about her getting help. From what I understand, per Dave's opposition to the operation, she is putting her life on the line.

Simon   *Alarmed.*
Why is she doing it? Is someone forcing her, demanding she have children, like in other instances I've heard about? Leo wouldn't do that. He's exemplary, blameless.
Dumbfounded.
He's a diamond and an angel, a regular angel.

Fanny   *With a tone.*
Yes, a diamond, an angel, but still a child. I don't doubt that Sonia is putting her life on the line more for him than for herself.

Simon   She shouldn't do it then. It's ridiculous. If there are children, fine. If there aren't, it's no reason to kill yourself.

Fanny   That's easy for you to say when you know we could have more.

Simon   But you see, we don't want anymore.
Oh yes, I almost forgot, did Sonia lend you the money?

Fanny   No, I didn't even ask. How could I burden her at such a moment?

Simon   We'll manage without her help. We'll have plenty of money next week.

Fanny   But I need it tomorrow …

Simon   You mean for the doctor?

Fanny   Absolutely. He's leaving tomorrow for a month's vacation.

Simon   And will it be too late when he returns?

Fanny   *Angry.*
What are you talking about; don't you know that the sooner you attend to these things the better? You don't want what happened to Stella to happen to me. She neglected to deal with it until it was too late.

Simon   *Pondering further.*
Nu, so what would be the great tragedy if we left things as they are?
The Bermans also have only one child. They only have a son and for her to have a little daughter would ...
Caresses her fondly.
We could have a little boy.

Fanny   *Capriciously*
And you know that's what it would be?

Simon   *With the same sweetness*
Even if it were a girl ...

Fanny   *Moves away from him.*
Whatever it might be, I don't want to be bothered with any babies. If we don't have the money, I'll ask Dave to lend it to us. He'll be here shortly.

Simon   *Insulted.*
Are you a fool! Do you think I'm saying this because of the money?

Fanny   In *the same tone.*
I don't care why you're saying it. I don't want to talk about it anymore. Do you hear me?
Cries.

Simon   *Takes her in his arms.*

It's okay, darling, it's alright. If you don't want it, we don't need it. There's no need to cry. I'll get what we need for the doctor today. But don't ask Dave, I hate to borrow from him. First of all, he'll figure out why we need the money. And second, I don't want to hear his admonitions. He'll come right back with why can't we get along on my wages and how it's time to live responsibly.

Fanny   *Cuts him off.*
Is he wrong then? It's embarrassing to always have to borrow. What would we do if we had a big family?

Simon   We would be richer than we are now.

Fanny   *Looks at him bewildered.*

Simon   Don't you know what I mean darling? We would lead different lives if there were little ones in the house. We would stay home. And if we didn't go anywhere, money wouldn't be spent.

Fanny   *Upset.*
Who is stopping you from conducting yourself differently? Is it my fault?
Stands up.
I'm always asking you to live more prudently. Did we have to go to that wedding yesterday? It cost us way too much. My dress alone was over $100. Was it really necessary? If I had that money now, I would have saved myself all this fretting.

Simon   You're a fool. Who is making you feel guilty or asking you to fret? You've never lacked for anything up till now and you won't be lacking for anything now either. We had to go to the wedding just like we have to go wherever it is we go. Why not? Our daughter is not a baby anymore so there's nothing to keep us at home.
Livens up.
And you! You're a free bird. So why shouldn't I take my little bird out and fly around with her.
Takes her hands and dances her around.

Fanny   Let go of me. Let go of me. I beg you.

Simon   *Sits her down with him in their previous place.*
Give me a kiss and I'll let you go.

Fanny   *Kisses him.*

Simon   I'll give you ten for that one.
Kisses her.

Dave   *Comes in. Laughs.*
Are you just now falling in love?

Fanny   He's crazy.

Dave   *Still laughing.*
I wouldn't say he's crazy.

Simon   Is it my fault then? Such a darling draws me in like a magnet.

Dave   You don't need to make excuses. Any couple married ten years shouldn't experience anything worse. But what are you both doing here? Don't you have to be at work today, Simon?

Simon   We went to a wedding yesterday and since it's slow at my place, only top management is at work, I asked my assistant to open the shop so I could go in late and Fanny needed something here so we came over.

Dave   Now I understand. And where is Lillitshke?

Fanny   She's in school.

Dave   *Reproachfully.*
As I understand, she got to bed when it was almost time to wake up, and you woke her up to go to school?

Simon   We didn't need to wake her; she woke us up crying that she didn't want to be late.

Dave   *Happy.*
   If that's so, then she's all right. What do you say, Simon, is she growing up to be a lady?

Simon   And you think she isn't?

Dave   No, I think she's growing into a good person.
   Doorbell rings.

Simon   *Opens door.*

Mrs. Golden *Enters.*
   You're actually here? Good morning.

Simon   Good morning. Good morning.

Mrs. Golden   I waited an hour outside your house.
   Gives FANNY *a nicely bundled package.*
   I baked yesterday. So I baked a little cake for the baby.

Simon   So where's mine?

Fanny   *Unwraps a good-sized cake.*
   There's enough here for you too. It'll suffice for everyone.

Simon   *Takes the cake.*
   Take a look at this. This is what Mrs. Golden calls a *cakeele.*

Mrs. Golden   I know you're a *nasher.*

Simon   *Takes out his penknife.*
   If you're going to call me a *nasher*, then I must have a taste of this cake.

Mrs. Goldin   *Grabs the knife away from him.*
   It's for Lillinke to cut.
   With a pleasurable smile.
   She'll get a kick out of it.

Simon   I knew it was just for Lillian.

Mrs. Golden   That's not true. I had everyone in mind. The doctor too.

Dave *With a smile.*
Thank you so much Mrs. Golden.
Turns to FANNY.
Where's Sonia?

Fanny She went over to the drugstore to phone the hospital.

Dave Most likely to let them know she's on her way.
Sighs.
I see there's nothing we can do to change her mind.

Simon I'm going to the shop. Good bye.

Fanny Will you be late coming home?

Simon No. I don't have much to do there.
Goes toward door.

Dave Wait, Simon, I'm going too.
Fanny, tell Sonia I'll be right back, I have to make an important visit.
DAVE *&* SIMON *exit.*

Fanny How upset he is, poor Dave. It's a good thing he doesn't know about me yet. You know, Mrs. Golden, he would so want me to have another child.

Mrs. Golden That's no surprise. One sister has none and the other one only has *eyn shtikl kind*. I really don't know what you're thinking, Mrs. Rabinov. If you think your husband doesn't want any more children, you're mistaken. He would be very happy to help tend to a *beybele*.

Fanny I know but I can't be bothered with it.
I won't be able to get used to being tied down again, going around with a carriage. Oh, it's so good to be free now.

Mrs. Golden May she be protected against the evil eye. In a few years she'll look like a young lady.

Fanny And everyone says I look like a girl.

With renewed spirit.

When we're out together we'll look like two friends. Oh how beautiful it will be. I'm so happy.

Suddenly gets gloomy.

I'll only be happy if Sonia has a child.

Wipes her tears.

SONIA *enters. Sees this.*

Sonia   *With reproach.*

Feh, it's nothing. Great, instead of buoying me up, Fanny, you're crying.

Fanny   *Stands. Looks down.*

I'm not crying. I was just thinking how nice it would be when you have a child. That's why my eyes welled up, just thinking about it.

Wipes her eyes again.

Sonia   *Moved*

Is that what you've been thinking about?

Hugs her.

Fanele, sister mine.

Lets her go.

Do you really think it? I mean are you actually hoping it may still be possible?

Cries.

It's so nice to have hope but I can't even allow myself it. I know the only way I could possibly have a child is to have this operation. But when I think of everyone ranting about how dangerous it is, and how I shouldn't do it unless I want to die …

Hides her face in her hands and sobs bitterly.

Fanny   *Pleadingly.*

Calm yourself Sonia. Why imagine the worst? Hope for the best. Many women have these operations. They recover and even have children afterward.

Sonia   *Stops crying. Gives* FANNY *a kiss.*

Thank you, Feygele, for encouraging me at this final hour, but it's more likely I'm marching to my end.

Sees MRS. GOLDEN *wiping away tears with her apron,*

Oh, Mrs. Golden, you're here too? I'm so happy to get the chance to see you before my departure.

Mrs. Golden   *Cries loudly.*

Sonia   *Pats her.*

My poor one, I'm causing you to suffer as well. *Nu,* don't cry, don't cry, my dear one. I'm sure you're praying for everything to be fine.

Mrs. Golden   *Quietly crying.*
I am praying to God.

Sonia   *Kisses her.*

Mrs. Golden   *Kisses* SONIA *on each cheek.*
May God help you and give you what you want.
Exits wiping her tears.

Sonia   *Exits to bedroom.*
Comes back with a small suitcase. Puts it down.
I wish Dave would get here already. What's taking him so long?

Fanny   He was here before but since you weren't here, he left to make an important visit. He'll be back soon.

Sonia   In the meantime, I need to occupy myself with something.
Thinks.
What important thing was I supposed to take care of?
Has a realization.
Oh, water the plants.
Exits to kitchen. Brings back two watering cans. Gives one to FANNY.
Can you be so kind as to help me?
If we both do it, it won't take as long.

Fanny   Certainly. It's my favorite task.
They both sprinkle the flowers.

Fanny   Oh, what a refreshing aroma. There is no greater pleasure than to be around flowers.

Sonia   Do you really think so?

Fanny   *Enthusiastically.*
You have a veritable flower garden here.

Sonia   *Sighs.*
Yes, it is a great pleasure to be around, to have a flower garden in my own home, as you say.
Puts away the watering can.
Watering the flowers that I myself planted, nurtured, and love so much, I often think I would rather be washing diapers.
Wipes tears.

Fanny   Washing diapers is really something to long for. And on top of that you had the job and didn't enjoy it at all.

Sonia   *Annoyed.*
I think that you, Fanny, can well understand the difference between washing diapers for your own rather than for another. I may have made a mistake but don't think I didn't love that child. She is baked into my heart. I couldn't devote myself to her because my heart longed to have my own child. You see, if there were absolutely no hope of having one, I am sure I would have been able to be a mother to that little orphan.

Dave   *enters.*

Fanny   *carries out the cans. Comes right back.*

Sonia   *To* DAVE
You're finally here.
She puts on a sensible black hat.

Dave   Leo isn't here yet?

Sonia   *Upset.*
Was he just going to work for a couple of hours then?

Dave   He said he was just going to finish up the payroll.
I suggested he work the whole day, but I don't believe he'll do that.

Sonia   It's time for me to go.
Takes her suitcase.

Dave   Takes *it from her and puts it back down on the floor.*
You're not going until Leo comes.

Sonia   *Unnerved.*
Are you planning to hold me back with force?

Dave   *Gently.*
Don't be silly. Let me just call him and tell him to come home. And until he comes, please be so kind as to wait.

Sonia   *With a pained smile.*
I should be so kind as to wait. No, Brother, I will not be so kind. Why don't you be so kind and escort me to the hospital.

Dave   *Discomposed.*
No, Ma'am, I will not take you to your death.

Sonia   *Covers her ears with her hands.*
Shut up! Here you go again with your death.

Dave   *In previous tone.*
I have not brought death into it. You're the one who wants to go toward it.

Sonia   *Even more shaken.*
Nu, let's say it's to my death, but I'm going anyway. I don't understand what you want from me. Why are you only interested in breaking my courage?

Dave   You don't have any courage. If you were a courageous person, you would accept your situation. It's ridiculous to risk your life at this point. If you die under the knife no one will even pity you.

Sonia   I don't want pity. I cannot tolerate it and that is why I'm doing this.

Dave   What do you mean? Explain it to me.

Sonia   Oh, that is a wound not to be touched.

Dave   I am a doctor, Sonia, and you're telling me I must not touch wounds.

Sonia   *Pained.*
It's a spiritual wound.

Fanny   *Crying quietly.*
Why are you badgering her? Don't you see she's made up her mind? Why are you making it harder for her?

Dave   *Angrily.*
Shut up you weakling.
In a tone.
I shouldn't make it harder for her, she says through a river of tears. Is that all you can do?

Fanny   *Cries aloud.*
What would you like me to do?

Dave   I want you to go home. That will make it easier for both of you.
Takes her by the hand and opens the door.
You're better off going home and making dinner for Lilletshke.

Fanny   *Still crying.*
Let me say good bye.

Dave   *Angry.*
Go, go.
Pushes her out and closes the door.

Sonia   Why must you pick on the poor soul? You didn't even let her say good bye.

Dave   *Regretfully.*
So, you think it's necessary too?Please allow me to talk to you about something more important.

Sonia   Talk, but please, make it short. You must understand it's better for me to leave before Leo gets back.

Dave   It's actually Leo I want to talk to you about.
Pleadingly.
I don't understand how you don't have any compassion for him.

Sonia   If I didn't have compassion for him, I wouldn't be risking my life.

Dave   *Stunned.*
What?! You're doing this for him?
Don't you know he's against this operation?

Sonia   I know. But I also know how unhappy he is being childless. And that won't let me to rest.

Dave   He wouldn't be so unhappy if you were different, if you didn't go around so sad all the time, perpetually distraught. If you were happy and gay instead, you would see the effect that would have on him.

Sonia   In *a tone.*
Happy, gay, light-hearted, I should feel all those things? Will my greatest desire for happiness give me happiness?

Dave   There is no reason for you not to be happy. You are married to an honorable man that you worship and who loves you. You've never wanted for material things. You have an ideal home in excellent taste. The slightest thing, including every book on these shelves, is not bought without your consent.

Looks at the flowers.

You love flowers so you don't lack for them. You should feel as if you're in paradise. You love music so no one stops you from going to operas, concerts.

Sonia   *Impatient.*

Yes, everything is fine but my heart longs and gnaws for what I'm missing.

A child's cry is heard from outside.

Mommy, Mommy, Benny's hitting me Mommy.

Hears the child's cries. Listens intensely.

To DAVE

You hear that? When I hear that hallowed call—Mommy …

Cries.

Dave   *Looks sorrowfully upon her.*

Sonia   *Stops crying. Wipes her tears.*

I believe, Brother, you have nothing left to say to me.

Dave   I just want to ask you something, Sonia. What you said earlier leads me to believe there is something else I am not aware of. I beg you, tell me about it before you go.

Sonia   I told you it's hard for me to talk about it, but if you insist …

Pause.

Leo agreed to the child because he pitied us both. That's also why he's being so nice to me now. If I weren't so distraught I would proudly return his kindness.

Weeps.

But my pride has ruined this unequal marriage. The only thing I'm good for now is suffering. Oh, how deeply the childless man suffers. Oh, how he suffers.

Covers her face crying. Wipes her tears.

A child would be his only salvation.

Hugs DAVE *and kisses him.*

Dave   *Kisses her movingly. Bows his head in grief.*

Sonia   *Exits carrying her travel bag.*

Dave   *Yells out heart-wrenchingly.*
   Sonia!

CURTAIN

ACT IV

Same room at the EDITS—*dimly lit—neat but no flowers,
only a few withered ones in their vases. Autumn evening.
No one on stage. Silence for a little while—then someone is
heard entering the front room.*

Sonia   *Comes in. She has aged and looks weary. She is
shabbily dressed. Locking the door she feels the emptiness
... throws her keys on the table, then her purse, handkerchief
and hat, drapes her coat haphazardly over a chair–part of it
touches the floor. She contemplates the room.*
   Oh how lonely it is in here!
   Turns nervously toward the kitchen.
   Why is the clock ticking so loudly in there!
   *Exits to kitchen. Comes back in. Stands by door listening.
Emerges into loneliness tuning into the monotone tick-tock
that makes her feel even more alone. Goes back out. Comes
back unwinding the clock.*
   There. I've stopped it!
   *Puts it on the table next to the pile of her things. Sits down
in a chair exhausted. After a slight pause.*
   Ach it's so quiet—not a sound to be heard.
   Glances at the table.
   It's even worse with the clock off.
   Winds the clock back up to tick. Puts it back on the table.
   Nu, let it tick. It's better than silence.
   She is quiet for a moment.
   What am I sitting in the dark for?

Gets up and turns on a light.

That's more cheerful. I should turn the lights on in there too!

Turns on lights in the other rooms.

Coming back she remains standing in the middle of the room looking around.

When there's company all the rooms are lit, people's voices resound, there's laughter, noise … but here—nothing but loneliness!

Turns off all the lights except for the first one that was originally lighting the room.

Sighs.

Darkness is more fitting here.

Doorbell rings.

Jumps in fright and grabs her heart.

How nervous I am!

Opens the door and screams out in surprise.

Ida!

Ida   *A beautiful woman, over thirty-five but looking a lot younger, enters.*

Sonitshke!

They hug and kiss.

Sonia   *Takes IDA's hand.*

How are you, Idale? Ach, what a guest! I never dreamed of ever seeing you again.

Ida   *Smiles.*

Why? Did you think it impossible to come to New York from Kansas City? Or to go from here to there? You always said, if you knew what you wanted anything was possible.

Sonia   *In a sad tone.*

True. But one needs to know how to want.

Ida   *Looks at her.*

What do you mean?

Sonia   *Sighs.*
There are times my dear when one doesn't know how to do anything, even how to want something.

Ida   *Studies her.*
You look disturbed, pained. What's the matter with you?

Sonia   *Embarrassed.*
Oh, let's better talk about you.
But why are you standing?
Takes her hat.
I was so taken aback I neglected to ask you to sit down.
Points to a chair. Sits near her.

Ida   Did you also forget to turn on the lights?
Turns on a light.

Sonia   *As if to herself.*
That's because I just did.

Ida   *Studies the room. Throws distressed glances at* SONIA.

Sonia   *Notices.*
Are you looking at how well ordered everything is in here?
Forces a smile.
It's lovely in my house, isn't it?

Ida   *Uneasy.*
What's going on here?

Sonia   *Pained.*
Don't ask dear one. Didn't I ask you to tell me about yourself?

Ida   No.
Takes SONIA's *hand.*
First you must tell me everything. I see that you're very unhappy.

Sonia   *Smiles mournfully.*
If you see it, it saves me having to tell you.

Ida   Hides *tears wiping them discreetly.*
   How is Fanny?

Sonia   *Sighs heavily. Bows her head.*

Ida   *Frightened.*
   Why are you silent? Tell me, how is Fanny?

Sonia   There is nothing more to say about her.

Ida   *Cries out.*
   When did she die?

Sonia   *Crying.*
   It's been almost a year since I've lost my poor sister, along with any hope of ever having a child.

Ida   *Wipes tears.*
   I don't understand what you mean? Do you mean you lost her along with any hope?

Sonia   I'll explain it to you, but first I want to tell you that my unhappiness is only due to my childlessness.

Ida   I understood that but what does it have to do with Fanny's death?

Sonia   It has a lot to do with it. Both of us suffered because we sinned against nature. Both of us! We both sought measures against becoming mothers. The only difference is that I regret it and she spared herself the trouble.

Ida   *Interrupting.*
   But didn't she have children?

Sonia   Yes, she had twins of whom only a girl remains; she'll be eleven next month, the poor orphan.
   Cries.
   Her birthday will be a sad one.
   Wipes her tears.

She was her only child and she didn't want to have any more.

Becomes pensive.

And me? I felt the same way she did. And that's why I wound up with nothing!

Ida   Why?

Sonia   I was mistaken. I thought more of myself than I actually was. I thought my mind could overcome my feelings.

Ida   You shouldn't have gotten married just to be taken care of.

Sonia   If only I hadn't lived that way!
Pause.

Ida   You still haven't explained the connection of Fanny's death to you losing hope.

Sonia   Oh well, when I finally caught on to my mistake it was already too late. The famous doctor I turned to upon Dave's recommendation said that if I wanted a child I would have to undergo a dangerous operation. There was no doubt the operation was going to be horrible. Dave, as doctor, naturally knew that and tried to talk me out of it. My husband was no less against it. But I didn't listen to them and went to have the operation.

Sighs.

When I was already on the operating table Fanny was brought in, in critical condition. At the very moment I was about to put my life in danger in order to have a child, she was trying to get rid of one. She was losing blood and needed emergency surgery as soon as possible. There was no other doctor at the hospital to do the operation but the one who was about to operate on me. So not wanting to, he had to put her on the table first. And that is where she died.

Cries.

Ida   *Wipes her tears.*
   Now I understand—he then had no courage left to operate on you?

Sonia   Yes—he declined to do it.

Ida   *After a short pause continues angrily.*
   How's Dave?

Sonia   If it weren't for all this, he'd be fine. He has a large practice and a stellar reputation. But we have ruined his life.

Ida   *With the same anger.*
   Has he not married yet?

Sonia   I don't think he ever even thinks about marriage.

Ida   Why?

Sonia   *Smiles.*
   Maybe because of you.

Ida   Oh no, he never loved me.

Sonia   There's nothing to say about that now, but I have no doubt that he loved you.

Ida   *Nu*, then why didn't he say something then?

Sonia   Maybe he was shy. You know—a former yeshiva boy. And you were so vain.

Ida   *Interrupting.*
   Vain? But you yourself said there's no use talking about it now. I called his office earlier. His nurse gave me your address. He wasn't in.

Sonia   You had Dave's address?

Ida   No, but I found it in the directory. I knew he had a practice in New York.
   Pause.

Sonia   *Nu*, how have you been all this time? You've already heard all our news. I hope your story is happier.

Ida   I can't complain. I have a good husband.
  Hiding joy.
  Lovely children.

Sonia   *Curiously.*
  Really, how many?

Ida   Three. A daughter and two sons.

Sonia   *Impressed.*
  Two boys! And a girl! Marvelous! Are they all grown up?

Ida   My daughter is eight, the older boy is five, and the baby is two.

Sonia   *In the same tone.*
  That is truly lovely. They're all three years apart. Have you brought them with you?

Ida   Only the baby.

Sonia   Where have you left him?

Ida   At my friends'. They picked me up early this morning at Grand Central and took him home with them.
  Knock at door.

Sonia   Come in.

Mrs. Golden   *Enters.*
  Good evening!

Sonia   A guest, good evening, how's Lilletchke?

Mrs. Golden   She's all right, may no evil eye befall her, she's developing quite nicely.

Sonia   Why didn't you bring her with?

Mrs. Golden *Self-conscious.*

I don't know, she said she had to study.

Sonia   Sit down.
Points to a chair.

Mrs. Golden   Thanks, but here's work to be done around here, no time for sitting.
Looks around the room contritely.
I couldn't find the time to come over all week. It's a sin how much there is to do here. I still have plenty to do at home, but I figured I better get over here today! I rushed through making supper and washing the dishes and came right over.

Sonia   If it's too hard for you, there's no need. It would be better if you could find us someone who could be here a few times a week.

Mrs. Golden   I'll have to do that but in the meantime, I'd better get to work.
Exits to kitchen.

Sonia   Aren't you going to start here, Mrs. Golden?

Mrs. Golden   No, I'll clean the kitchen first.
Exits.

Ida   Who is this Lilletshke you asked about?

Sonia   *Sighs.*
She's Fanny's girl. She's been staying with this woman the past few weeks. She was Lilletshke's wet nurse and took care of her when she was a baby as if she were her own. She tended to her then and now doesn't know what to do with her—she takes better care of her than of her own children.

Ida   *Suppresses a sigh.*
Really, she takes care of the child? And where is the father?

Sonia He's in Cleveland. Just until a few months ago he bummed around here. After Fanny died he got sick, probably from grief. He was unable to work. And when he got well enough, he had already been replaced. He spent a long time looking for a job but never found one, which forced him to go back on the machine. That made him very depressed. He became demoralized. We didn't think he could go on that way much longer. Dave got him to give up his job and took him to the country for a few weeks when he went on vacation. Then Simon went to Cleveland to visit a compatriot, a cloak manufacturer. What he's doing now, I don't know. He doesn't write to us.

Mrs. Golden *Enters wearing an apron. Her hands are smeared.*
Do you have any soap around here, Mrs. Edit? I have to do the dishes. I just cleaned the oven and now I must wash the floor and can't find a speck of soap.

Sonia *Stands.*
I'll go get some.
Puts on a shawl. Exits.

Mrs. Golden *exits to kitchen.*

Ida He never married ...
Pensively.
I must see him one more time.

Mrs. Golden *Enters.*
I'll straighten up in here in the meantime.
Looks at her hands.
But I would get this all over everything. Without soap I'll never get my hands clean.

Ida Of course, you won't. Have a seat in the meantime.

Mrs. Golden *Sits.*

Do you think I have time to sit? I want to get done as soon as possible.

Looks at the table and everything around it.

What a mess. You can't blame the little one for not wanting to come here.

Ida   You mean Mrs. Edit's niece?

Mrs. Golden   Yea, Lillenke. Whenever I ask her to come here with me she always says next time. I got really mad at her today and she burst into tears. She doesn't want to be at her aunt's because she gets so sad here.

Ida   I figured when you spoke of her earlier; the child didn't want to come here. You did well not to have said as much.

Mrs. Golden   You think she doesn't get it? If Mrs. Edit thought the little orphan wanted to be here with her she wouldn't have sent her to strangers.

Ida   Oh, Mrs. Golden, you shouldn't say she's with strangers. I heard how devoted you are to her. You love her and treat her as your own.

Mrs. Golden   My darling little one, she's always been baked into my heart; from the minute I first laid her to my breast. But since her mother died … I feel like I'm her mother, but I'm nothing more than her nursemaid. I consider myself a stranger. Mr. Edit often throws it in Mrs. Edit's face—why did she give Lilly away to strangers. Why doesn't she keep her here with them?

Ida   *Surprised.*

Really, he must be a really good person?

Mrs. Golden   *Impressed.*

Good? Now there's a person without gall. An evening doesn't go by without him coming over to see Lilly. And how gently he treats her. He often brings her presents and always assures me I'm treating her well. But to her ... to her, he's heartbreakingly awful.

Ida   You mean his wife?

Mrs. Golden   *Sighs.*
Yes, Mrs. Edit, she puts up with so much from him that I don't even know how she bears it. All he does is call her dead. Have you ever heard of a living person being called dead?

Ida   That's horrible.

Mrs. Golden   It really could drive someone to their death.

Ida   Has he always been so awful to her?

Mrs. Golden   God forbid! He would have laid his life down for her up until she went to have that operation.

Sonia   *Enters.* MRS. GOLDEN *becomes self-conscious. Stands.*
Here's soap and detergent.
Gives MRS. GOLDEN *a package.*

Mrs. Golden   Now I can begin my work.
Exits.

Sonia   *Watches her exit.*
What a dear soul. If it weren't for her I'd probably be dead already.
Emphasizing.
If I'm not dead already, if you can call this living.

Ida   What do you mean?

Sonia   Don't you understand?
Sighs.
I mean that I am dead—dead like the dead.

Ida   *Protests.*
That's foolishness!

Sonia   *With a sad smile.*

Do   you really think so? My husband …

Ida   *Interrupts her.*
   Keeps repeating it to you and you believe him!

Sonia   Ah—Mrs. Golden told you.

Ida   *Shamed.*
   Oh no.

Sonia   It's okay—I hold nothing against her. She told the truth … and you dear, please don't be angry with my husband for speaking the truth.

Ida   *Looks at her trying to hide her distress.*

Sonia   Perceives *it; speaks painfully.*
   Nu, don't you see it in me?
   Looks around.
   Doesn't the way the house looks confirm it? If I still had a little life left in me …

Ida   *Doesn't let her finish.*
   You are deluded—those are only signs of sloth, of weakness.

Sonia   Laughs *bitterly.*
   Ha, ha, is that not death? Isn't a weak, slovenly person the same as a dead one?

Ida   Feels *she is being unjust.*
   It's natural after everything you've been through to be weakened and being in such a weak state you can't help but neglect things. But there is no reason to be in such despair. Why don't you instead try to strengthen yourself, get back to yourself.

Sonia   That I can't do.
   Sighs.
   And have no reason to.

Ida   That is precisely why you can't—you think you have nothing to live for. But you may be mistaken. As I see it, you think your husband doesn't love you ...

Sonia   Interrupts *her.*
I'm convinced he doesn't.

Ida   And do you love him?

Sonia   My love for him is the only sign of life in me.

Ida   *Triumphantly.*
That's a good sign! Dead people, as you are calling yourself, do not love.
Thinks.
So, we've decided that you love.
Smiles.
Isn't that right, you're alive? You can no longer deny it.

Sonia   *Smiles sadly.*
If you say so.

Ida   Of course—I want you to live!
Now listen to the plan I've just come up with ... oh, if you would only agree to it.
Enthusiastically.
Oh if only you would agree to it Sonia!
Takes SONIA'*s hand.*
Yes, you'll do it—you'll have to!

Sonia   *Laughs.*
But tell me, what is it?

Ida   I want you to come to Kansas City with me.

Sonia   Now that's a wild idea. And what do you think I'll do there?

Ida   What will you do? Heal. I'm betting you'll get completely back to yourself there. I have a great woman who takes care of the children and a girl who does the cleaning; we'll be able to have fun together; we'll have a great time.

Dave   *Rushes in. Cries out in amazement.*
You really are here!
Squeezes IDA*'s hand.*
I cannot tell you how surprised I was Ida when I got the message that you were here in New York. When did you arrive?

Ida   Early this morning—half past eight.

Dave   In *the same tone.*
It's so nice of you to remember your old New York friends. But why didn't you let us know you were coming?
Sits.

Ida   *Lightly blows it off.*
How could I have? Had you sent me your address?
Casts a glance at SONIA.
And Sonia also hasn't found it necessary to contact me.

Dave   You're right.
Sighs.
Sonia's probably told you everything already, so please don't be offended.

Ida   Yes, but it's no excuse, friends must always confide in each other, no matter what it is. But that's not something we need to talk about right now. I want to propose a plan ...
Turns to SONIA,
... that we just discussed.

Sonia   Oh—you mean about me going to Kansas City for a visit?

Ida   Yes—let's hear what Dave has to say about it. I proposed Sonia come back to Kansas City with me. I think it would be very good for her to be away from home for a few months. As far as I can see her condition will not improve

here. She devotes herself entirely to her suffering. It just
makes her weaker and more miserable.

Dave   You're right. She will not get better here. She must
have something to occupy her! And she needs to be with
someone who will not allow her to go to seed. And you,
Ida, are the right person to do it. Ach, if you would only
undertake it.

Ida   It would be my pleasure. If she would only want to go.
But she will have to.
    To SONIA
    Sonia, don't you want to go with me?

Dave   That's good, that's how we must talk to her now.

Sonia   I won't deny it.
    Smiles bitterly.
    And Leo will go along with it too. He'll be very happy with
your plan.

Dave   Definitely. He'll be happy because this is the best thing
for you.

Ida   Then that's how we'll leave it.
    Stands.
    I have to go to my baby. I'll see you again tomorrow Sonia.
    Kisses her.

Dave   *Stands.*
    I'll take you Ida.
    Smiles.
    It'll give me a chance to find out how you are. But I see that
you're all right.
    Upset.
    You've hardly changed in the nine years we haven't seen
each other.

Ida   *Also upset.*

You call that a compliment. Yes, it would be a pleasure if you escorted me to my friends' house. I've grown unaccustomed to New York. Ha, ha I got a little lost earlier. But Sonia will be left alone. Maybe you should stay with her.

Sonia   It doesn't matter—I'm used to being alone.

Dave   I'll be back later Sonia. Best to Leo.

Ida   Regards from me as well.

Sonia   Thank you.

IDA *Kisses* SONIA.

DAVE *and* IDA *exit.*

Mrs. Golden *Enters.*
   Has your guest left already?

Sonia   Yes.

Mrs. Golden   What a nice woman she is.

Sonia   Of course she is, she's my best friend.

Mrs. Golden   She's so beautiful; she must still be quite young.

Sonia   Young? She is not. She's a few years older than me. But she looks young. Dave hasn't seen her in nine years and says she hasn't changed a bit.
   Sighs and mutters to herself.
   Not only hasn't she gotten older but she looks younger. That's because she married someone older than her. When you're younger than your husband you think you're a youngster and that makes you feel young. But when the woman is older she must unwillingly consider herself old and therefore actually feels that way.
   Sighs.
   And that makes her look older as well.

Mrs. Golden   *Exits.*

Sonia   *Begins straightening up the room, moving things from one place to another. Objects slip out of her hands. She presently gets tired and lies down on the sofa.*
She has three children—two boys and a girl.

Mrs. Golden   *Enters with a dust cloth and proceeds to clean the furniture. SONIA doesn't notice her.*

Three children ...

Mrs. Golden   *Cuts in.*
What did you say?

Sonia   Ahh,
After a slight pause.
You're already working in here? I started to straighten up but couldn't get anything done. Everything was slipping from my hands. I felt weak and as you can see I needed to lie down.

Mrs. Golden   Why should you strain yourself? Rest. I'll do it.

Sonia   *Enunciates.*
You'll finish it for me, right? Ach, how helpless I am. Is my husband wrong then?

Mrs. Golden   *Sighs.*
Continues working.

Sonia   *After a pause.*
Three children—two boys and a girl.
Dozes off.

Mrs. Golden *Contemplates her fearfully.*
She's sleeping but it didn't sound like sleep-talking.
Puts her hand on SONIA's forehead.
Hot as fire. She has a fever. I must run and get Edit.
EDIT *and* DAVE *enter.*
Look at that, you're both here.
They look at her perplexed.

I was just on my way to get you, Mr. Edit, but since you're both here now—all the better.

Edit   What's wrong then?

Mrs. Golden   Mrs. Edit doesn't feel well.

Edit   That's nothing new, when does she ever feel well?

Mrs. Golden   But she's really very sick now—she has a fever.

Dave   *Contemplates* SONIA *and speaks quietly.*
It doesn't look like she has a fever. What was she complaining about, Mrs. Golden?

Mrs. Golden   She didn't say that anything hurt her, but she was talking to herself as if she were delirious.

Dave   What did she say?

Edit   Ach, Mrs. Golden imagined it—there's no fever, she's as pale as a corpse.

Mrs. Golden   You mustn't speak that way, Mr. Edit. Pale as a corpse—you must know how ill that makes her. That she was speaking in delirium was not imagined. She kept on mentioning children, three children, two boys and a girl, to the point of frightening me.

Dave   Oh that's nothing. Ida probably told her about her children so she was repeating it.

Edit   So why talk about it? And especially to herself? No, Dave, this is not nothing. It points to how debased she is.

Sonia   *Sighs.*

Mrs. Golden   *Notices. Looks at* SONIA *upset.*

Dave   Don't diagnose her yet, Leo.

Sonia   *Sighs again.*

Mrs. Golden   *Winks at them.*

Dave   *Takes* SONIA*'s hand.*
How do you feel Sonia?

Sonia   *Quietly begins weeping.*

Edit   Oh no, she's crying again. *Nu*, I'd better go.
I can't even be in this house for a minute.
SONIA*'s weeping increases, choking her.*

Edit   Oh my God, I can't take it anymore.

Mrs. Golden   You can't take her crying? You're the one that
makes her cry.

Edit   If I'm the one who makes her cry, then it's better I
leave.

Sonia   Leo, Leo, oh Leo.
Gets hysterical.

Edit   *Frightened. Hatefully goes over to her and takes her
hand.*
Sonia, calm down.
Pats her hair.
I beg you, please, calm yourself; you know how these
hysterics affect me.
SONIA*'s sobs quiet down a bit.*

Edit Pats   *her hair. Gently addresses her.*
That's good. You're such a good one. Restrain yourself dear.

Dave Puts   *on his coat.*
Motions to MRS. GOLDEN *to follow him and both exit.*

Sonia   *Grabs* EDIT*'s hand, kisses it, and presses it to her
heart.*

Edit   Stay calm, darling.

Sonia　I am the cause of your suffering. If only I had control over these hysterical outbursts.
Wipes her tears.

Edit　Don't get upset, Sonia. It's my fault— I'm the one that provokes you.

Sonia　Don't blame yourself darling. Ach, how good you are.

Edit　Gets *mad. Immediately tries to control himself.*
Now you're singing my praises. You know I hate it when you do that.

Sonia　*Submissively.*
Nu, I'm sorry …

Edit　I forgive you, I'm sorry.
Forces a smile. This frightens her. He steps away from her.
I met your girlfriend earlier. I ran into her on the street with Dave. She isn't at all timid or provincial. She is self-assured and very interesting.

Sonia　I'm pleased you like her so much.

Edit　Oh very— mostly I like her looks. I don't mean her beauty, but that she keeps herself looking so young. Dave told me she's older than you.

Sonia　Yes, by a few years.

Edit　She truly deserves credit. A middle-aged woman who looks like a young lady and is full of life. She's still in love with Dave, isn't she? You can tell by the way she looks at him.

Sonia　I noticed that too.

Edit　A mother of three children.

Sonia　*Suppresses a sigh.*
And is still young. She has time for leisure—others take care of her children so her mind wanders unwittingly to her lover.

Edit *Smiles sadly.*
And where does your mind wander? You also have time on your hands.

Sonia I think about nothing.

Edit *Sighs.*
That's touching. You're not even capable of thinking about anything. How you've lost your way ... Dead—you're dead, my friend.

Sonia Horribly *anguished. Trying not to lose control.*
Listen! Don't you dare say that again. If I hear it from you one more I will die.

Edit Grabs *her hands in fright.*
Sonia, oh how horrible I am. I'll never say it again. Oh, how I suffer—but I'm also tortured. Oh, I feel so terrible Sonia.
Covers his face with his hands. Cries.

Sonia Pulls *him toward her.*
Leo—stop it—oh I can't take it.

Edit *Sits down next to her on the sofa. Stares straight ahead.*

Sonia *Regards him. Sighs. Stands. Paces the room thinking grievously. After a little while stops by him.*
Leo, Leo.

Edit Huh?

Sonia I want to talk to you about something.

Edit Talk? What about?

Sonia I can't tolerate your suffering anymore. We must put an end to it.

Edit An end to my suffering?
Smiles sadly.
But how?

Sonia   I'll go to Kansas City with my girlfriend. I'll try living there, try to adjust to new circumstances. In any case, I don't care what happens to me. But I want you to live. You must not suffer anymore
  With feeling.
  You're still so young, you must live and be happy.

Edit   I don't know what you mean.

Sonia   I mean that we should separate.
  Shivers. Controls herself.
  And I mean soon before I leave New York.

Edit   Stands *up hastily.*
  You mean we should divorce?

Sonia   *Nods her head.*

Edit   *Laughs hysterically.*
  Ha ha ha ha ha … Very nice of you. Very nice.
  Painfully.
  Aren't you ashamed? We've spent our lives together. You've loved me all these years and you don't even know me. You want me to divorce you and go my merry way?
  Pause.
  You say I should live and be happy. Yes—but could I do that under such circumstances? I'll only be able to live with you Sonia.
  Suppresses a sigh.
  But you must change a little.

Sonia   You mean you want me to get younger.

Edit   I'm not asking you to get younger, that's impossible. And you're not even old. You've just convinced yourself you are. And you've got me believing it, the way you've been acting. That's why we're where we are. But meeting your friend, who is older than you, has pointed out my mistake and the injustice you're putting upon yourself.

Pause.
You must stop mourning your losses. You must try to cheer up and get some life back into you. It will dispel that depressed look in your eyes and maybe also the wrinkles on your face.

Sonia   *Sighs.*

Edit   No more sighs, Sonia, I want to live. You were right when you said it's my birthright.

Sonia   Yes, and I must be the one to help you do that. I think it will do me good to take this trip to Kansas City, to spend some time with my girlfriend and her family for a few weeks. It will be stimulating to travel a little—a change of atmosphere.

Edit   Of course.
Smiling.
But don't divorce me before departing.

Sonia   *Also smiling.*
Oh no, I won't give it another thought.

Edit   God be praised.

Sonia   We must call Ida and let her know we've decided I go with her.

Edit   Yes, that will make her very happy. She was upset earlier thinking you were against it.

Sonia   Maybe you could go pick her up and bring her over here.

Edit   Why get her. Let's go over there together.

Sonia   I don't feel like getting dressed right now, I don't want to go out.

Edit   *Sighs.*

Nu, then I'll go alone. You've got to change, Sonia, change.
Show some mobility; be more flexible; it will change how you
look.

Exits.

Sonia   Change how I look.

Looks in the mirror.

The wrinkles won't smooth themselves out. They're there to
keep my depression captive.

*Thinks it over for a moment. Hastily steps away from the
mirror and walks despairingly around the house. Exits to
bedroom. Returns contemplating a bottle of carbolic acid.*

Ultimately there is no other way out—I must drink this.

*Brings the bottle to her lips. Pulls it back. Looks for
something on the table. Finds a piece of paper. Writes and then
reads what she wrote.*

Dear Leo, my love, the best man in the world, I must free
you. You will not divorce me. But if I'm dead and buried you'll
eventually forget me.

*Quickly drinks the poison. Yells out in pain. Exits to
bedroom. Falls down on the other side of the door. Hacking
cough. Silence.*

EDIT, DAVE, *and* IDA *enter.*

Ida   Oh—what a horrible stench of carbolic.

Dave   Yes—where is it coming from?

Looks around the room.

Where is Sonia? Is she in bed already?

Edit   She can't be; she sent me to get Ida.

Sees the note on the table. Scans it quickly. Yells out.

Ah, ah.

Runs into bedroom. DAVE and IDA follow him.

Seeing SONIA on the floor they all cry out.

*Neighbors—men, women, and children all run in upon
hearing their cries.*

Woman   What's going on—what happened?

Two Men   What happened here?

Dave   Come quickly, quickly, help me.
   The men help DAVE *bring* SONIA *into living room. They lay her on the sofa.*

Dave   *Takes her pulse. Listens to her heart.*

Ida   Can she be saved?

Edit   Is she alive?

Dave   Both my sisters have been punished with death because of crimes against nature.

Bursts out crying.

CURTAIN

GLOSSARY

Bodyankes Anise-flavored pastries; Polish

Brontshe The "she" suffix implies affection, similar to the Yiddish "le"; Polish

Do vidzennya Goodbye (formal); Polish

Dzien dobry Good morning (formal); Polish

Falenica A village near Warsaw, at one time a popular vacation spot

Feh! A common Yiddish exclamation of disgust.

Havdole A short formal prayer/religious ceremony marking the end of the Sabbath. *Pronunciation of the transliteration in the script for the blessing over the wine is in the attached sound file*

J'ai l'honneur de vo saluer It is my honor to say goodbye; French (formal)

Kapote A long formal coat worn by Ultra-Orthodox Jewish men

Khozyayka, pazhalusta, adayte Rivke Burak "Mistress, please give this to Rivke Burak"; Russian

Khupe A canopy beneath which Jewish marriage ceremonies are performed

Kinahora "no evil eye"; a Jewish equivalent of "knock on wood"

Kugel A baked pudding or casserole, most commonly made from potato or egg noodles ("lokshen kugel")

Nu A common Yiddish interjection, equivalent to "well"

Omeyn "Amen"; Hebrew

Reb "Mr.", used as a formal address (with given names only); Yiddish

Shabbos The Jewish Sabbath

"Sheyndele" The "le" suffix at the end of a Yiddish name is a diminutive, implying a close or convivial relationship.

Shiva A week-long mourning period observed following the loss of immediate family members.

Simkhes Celebrations; Yiddish

Skoro li polnotsh nastanyet, skoro'l dozhdusya tyebya Will midnight come soon; will I see you soon

Sukkos A weeklong celebration beginning five days after Yom
   Kippur; commonly translated as "Tabernacles"
Torah The Old Testament; colloquially, all Jewish religious studies
Tsholent A traditional Jewish stew. It is usually simmered overnight
   for twelve hours or more, and eaten for lunch on Shabbos
"Until a hundred and twenty" A common Jewish blessing for a long
   life
Vyaltseva Anastasia Dmitrievna Vyaltseva; a renowned Russian
   mezzo-soprano, specializing in Gypsy art songs; a favorite of the
   popular press, she toured regularly
Yasha Morningstar A folk song
Yom Kippur The most solemn date on the Jewish calendar, in which
   much of the day is spent in synagogue; most Jews, even those
   only mildly observant, will fast for twenty-five hours, neither
   eating nor drinking

BIBLIOGRAPHY

SOURCES OF TRANSLATED PLAYS

Brown, Lena, *Sonya Itelson; oder, a kind, a kind* ms. From the personal collection of Jeffrey Brown.

Lerner, Maria, *Di agune: a drama in fir akten un zeks bilder* (Varshe: yidishe bine, 1908).

Prilutski, Paula, Eyne fun yene: a drama in fir akten fun Paula Prilutski (Paula R.) (Varshe: Nayer farlag, 1914).

WORKS CITED AND CONSULTED

Blankshteyn, Chana. *Fear and Other Stories*. Translated by Anita Norich (Detroit: Wayne State University Press, 2022).

Freeze, ChaeRan. *Jewish Marriage and Divorce in Imperial Russia* (Hanover: Brandeis University Press, 2002).

Fuchs, Rachel G. *Gender and Poverty in Nineteenth-Century Europe* (Cambridge: Cambridge University Press, 2005).

Goldstein, Bluma. *Enforced Marginality: Jewish Narratives on Abandoned Wives* (Berkeley: University California Press, 2007).

Halkin, Hillel. *Vladimir Jabotinsky: A Life* (New Haven: Yale University Press, 2014).

Halpern, Stefanie. "Crossing Over: From the Yiddish Rialto to the American Stage" Ph.D. thesis Jewish Theological Seminary (2017).

Hernandez, Alex Eric. "Prosaic Suffering," *Representations*, No. 138 (Spring 2017), 118–41.

Hess, Jonathan M. *Deborah and Her Sisters: How One Nineteenth-Century Melodrama and a Host of Celebrated Actresses Put Judaism on the World Stage* (Philadelphia, PA: University of Pennsylvania Press, 2018).

Irshai, Ronit. *Fertility and Jewish Law: Feminist Perspectives* (Brandeis University Press: 2012).

Karpilove, Miriam. *Diary of a Lonely Girl, or the Battle against Free Love*. Translated by Jessica Kirzane (Syracuse: Syracuse University Press, 2019).

Klapper, Melissa R. *Ballots, Babies, and Banners of Peace: American Jewish Women's Activism, 1890–1940* (London: New York University Press, 2013).

Klapper, Melissa R. "The Drama of 1916: The American Jewish Community, Birth Control, and Two Yiddish Plays," *The Journal of the Gilded Age and Progressive Era*. Vol. 12, No.4 (October 2013), 502–34.

Levy, Daniela Smolov, "Grand Opera for Yiddish Speakers in Early Twentieth-Century America! Who Knew?!" at https://web.uwm.edu/yiddish-stage/grand-opera-for-yiddish-speakers-in-early-twentieth-century-america-who-knew.

Lichtenstein, Aharon, "Abortion: a Halakhic Perspective," *Tradition: A Journal of Orthodox Thought*. Vol. 25, No. 4 (Summer 1991), 3–12.

Quint, Alyssa, *The Rise of the Modern Yiddish Theater*. (Indiana: Indiana University Press, 2019).

Quint, Alyssa and Seigel, Miryem-Khaye, eds. *Women on the Yiddish Stage*. (Oxford: Legenda Press, 2023).

Seidman, Naomi. *The Marriage Plot (Stanford Studies in Jewish History and Culture)*. Stanford University Press, 2016, 33–4. *Kindle Edition*.

Stanislawski, Michael. *For Whom Do I Toil: Yehudah Leib Gordon and the Crisis of Russian Jewry* (Oxford: Oxford University Press, 1888).

Sperber, Haim. "Agunot, 1851–1914: An Introduction," Annales *de démographie historique, 2018*, No. 2 (136), *Familles juives: Europe Méditerranée*, XIXe–XXe siècles (2018): 107–36.

Turner, Rebecca. "Forgotten *Froyen*: An Analysis of Women Yiddish Playwrights and Their Works from 1877–1938," Honours Bachelor's Master's Thesis McGill University, 2022.

Weiser, Kalman. *Jewish People, Yiddish Nation: Noah Prylucki and the Folkists in Poland*. (Toronto: University of Toronto Press, 2011).

Yarfitz, Mir. "Marriage as Ruse or Migration Route: Jewish Women's Mobility and Sex Trafficking to Argentina, 1890s–1930s," *Women in Judaism: A Multidisciplinary Journal*. Vol. 17, No. 1 (2020).

Zipperstein, Steven J. *The Jews of Odessa: A Cultural History, 1794–1881* (Stanford: Stanford University Press, 1986).

Zylbercweig, Zalmen and Jacob Mestel, *Leksikon fun yidishn teater*, vol. 2, 6 vols. (New York: Elisheva, 1931), 1162–70.